PROVERBS, ECCLESIASTES, AND THE SONG OF SOLOMON

THE IGNATIUS CATHOLIC STUDY BIBLE

REVISED STANDARD VERSION
SECOND CATHOLIC EDITION

PROVERBS, ECCLESIASTES, AND THE SONG OF SOLOMON

With Introduction, Commentary, and Notes

by

Scott Hahn and Curtis Mitch

and

with Study Questions by

Dennis Walters

IGNATIUS PRESS   SAN FRANCISCO

Published with ecclesiastical approval

Original RSV Bible text:
Nihil Obstat: Thomas Hanlon, S.T.L., L.S.S., Ph.L.
Imprimatur: +Peter W. Bartholome, D.D.
Bishop of Saint Cloud, Minnesota
May 11, 1966

Introduction, commentaries and notes:
Nihil obstat: Rev. Msgr. J. Warren Holleran, S.T.D.
Imprimatur: +Most Reverend George Niederauer
Apostolic Administrator, Archdiocese of San Francisco
September 7, 2012

The *nihil obstat* and *imprimatur* are official declarations that a book or pamphlet is free of
doctrinal or moral error. No implication is contained therein that those who have granted the
nihil obstat and *imprimatur* agree with the contents, opinions, or statements expressed.

Second Catholic Edition approved by the
National Council of the Churches of Christ in the USA

Cover art: King Solomon, Romanesque painted ceiling, ca. 1150
Grisons canton, Switzerland (detail)
Gianni Dagli Orti/The Art Archive at Art Resource, NY

Cover design by Riz Boncan Marsella

Published by Ignatius Press in 2013

Printed in the United States of America ∞

CONTENTS

INTRODUCTION TO THE IGNATIUS STUDY BIBLE

You are approaching the "word of God". This is the title Christians most commonly give to the Bible, and the expression is rich in meaning. It is also the title given to the Second Person of the Blessed Trinity, God the Son. For Jesus Christ became flesh for our salvation, and "the name by which he is called is The Word of God" (Rev 19:13; cf. Jn 1:14).

The word of God is Scripture. The Word of God is Jesus. This close association between God's *written* word and his *eternal* Word is intentional and has been the custom of the Church since the first generation. "All Sacred Scripture is but one book, and this one book is Christ, 'because all divine Scripture speaks of Christ, and all divine Scripture is fulfilled in Christ'[1]" (CCC 134). This does not mean that the Scriptures are divine in the same way that Jesus is divine. They are, rather, divinely inspired and, as such, are unique in world literature, just as the Incarnation of the eternal Word is unique in human history.

Yet we can say that the inspired word resembles the incarnate Word in several important ways. Jesus Christ is the Word of God incarnate. In his humanity, he is like us in all things, except for sin. As a work of man, the Bible is like any other book, except without error. Both Christ and Scripture, says the Second Vatican Council, are given "for the sake of our salvation" (*Dei Verbum* 11), and both give us God's definitive revelation of himself. We cannot, therefore, conceive of one without the other: the Bible without Jesus, or Jesus without the Bible. Each is the interpretive key to the other. And because Christ is the subject of all the Scriptures, St. Jerome insists, "Ignorance of the Scriptures is ignorance of Christ"[2] (CCC 133).

When we approach the Bible, then, we approach Jesus, the Word of God; and in order to encounter Jesus, we must approach him in a prayerful study of the inspired word of God, the Sacred Scriptures.

Inspiration and Inerrancy The Catholic Church makes mighty claims for the Bible, and our acceptance of those claims is essential if we are to read the Scriptures and apply them to our lives as the Church intends. So it is not enough merely to nod at words like "inspired", "unique", or "inerrant". We have to understand what the Church means by these terms, and we have to make that understanding our own. After all, what we believe about the Bible will inevitably influence the way we read the Bible. The way we read the Bible, in turn, will determine what we "get out" of its sacred pages.

These principles hold true no matter what we read: a news report, a search warrant, an advertisement, a paycheck, a doctor's prescription, an eviction notice. How (or whether) we read these things depends largely upon our preconceived notions about the reliability and authority of their sources—and the potential they have for affecting our lives. In some cases, to misunderstand a document's authority can lead to dire consequences. In others, it can keep us from enjoying rewards that are rightfully ours. In the case of the Bible, both the rewards and the consequences involved take on an ultimate value.

What does the Church mean, then, when she affirms the words of St. Paul: "All Scripture is inspired by God" (2 Tim 3:16)? Since the term "inspired" in this passage could be translated "God-breathed", it follows that God breathed forth his word in the Scriptures as you and I breathe forth air when we speak. This means that God is the primary author of the Bible. He certainly employed human authors in this task as well, but he did not merely assist them while they wrote or subsequently approve what they had written. God the Holy Spirit is the *principal* author of Scripture, while the human writers are *instrumental* authors. These human authors freely wrote everything, and only those things, that God wanted: the word of God in the very words of God. This miracle of dual authorship extends to the whole of Scripture, and to every one of its parts, so that whatever the human authors affirm, God likewise affirms through their words.

The principle of biblical inerrancy follows logically from this principle of divine authorship. After all, God cannot lie, and he cannot make mistakes. Since the Bible is divinely inspired, it must be without error in everything that its divine and human authors affirm to be true. This means that biblical inerrancy is a mystery even broader in scope than infallibility, which guarantees for us that the Church will always teach the truth concerning faith and morals. Of course the mantle of inerrancy likewise covers faith and morals, but it extends even farther to ensure that all the facts and events of salvation history are accurately presented for us in the Scriptures. Inerrancy is our guarantee that the words and deeds of God found in the Bible are unified and true,

[1] Hugh of St. Victor, *De arca Noe* 2, 8: PL 176, 642: cf. ibid. 2, 9: PL 176, 642–43.
[2] *DV* 25; cf. Phil 3:8 and St. Jerome, *Commentariorum in Isaiam libri xviii*, prol.: PL 24, 17b.

declaring with one voice the wonders of his saving love.

The guarantee of inerrancy does not mean, however, that the Bible is an all-purpose encyclopedia of information covering every field of study. The Bible is not, for example, a textbook in the empirical sciences, and it should not be treated as one. When biblical authors relate facts of the natural order, we can be sure they are speaking in a purely descriptive and "phenomenological" way, according to the way things appeared to their senses.

Biblical Authority   Implicit in these doctrines is God's desire to make himself known to the world and to enter a loving relationship with every man, woman, and child he has created. God gave us the Scriptures not just to inform or motivate us; more than anything he wants to save us. This higher purpose underlies every page of the Bible, indeed every word of it.

In order to reveal himself, God used what theologians call "accommodation". Sometimes the Lord stoops down to communicate by "condescension"—that is, he speaks as humans speak, as if he had the same passions and weakness that we do (for example, God says he was "sorry" that he made man in Genesis 6:6). Other times he communicates by "elevation"—that is, by endowing human words with divine power (for example, through the Prophets). The numerous examples of divine accommodation in the Bible are an expression of God's wise and fatherly ways. For a sensitive father can speak with his children either by condescension, as in baby talk, or by elevation, by bringing a child's understanding up to a more mature level.

God's word is thus saving, fatherly, and personal. Because it speaks directly to us, we must never be indifferent to its content; after all, the word of God is at once the object, cause, and support of our faith. It is, in fact, a test of our faith, since we see in the Scriptures only what faith disposes us to see. If we believe what the Church believes, we will see in Scripture the saving, inerrant, and divinely authored revelation of the Father. If we believe otherwise, we see another book altogether.

This test applies not only to rank-and-file believers but also to the Church's theologians and hierarchy, and even the Magisterium. Vatican II has stressed in recent times that Scripture must be "the very soul of sacred theology" (*Dei Verbum* 24). As Joseph Cardinal Ratzinger, Pope Benedict XVI echoed this powerful teaching with his own, insisting that, "The *normative theologians* are the authors of Holy Scripture" (emphasis added). He reminded us that Scripture and the Church's dogmatic teaching are tied tightly together, to the point of being inseparable: "Dogma is by definition nothing other than an interpretation of Scripture." The defined dogmas of our faith, then, encapsulate the Church's infallible interpretation of Scripture, and theology is a further reflection upon that work.

The Senses of Scripture   Because the Bible has both divine and human authors, we are required to master a different sort of reading than we are used to. First, we must read Scripture according to its *literal* sense, as we read any other human literature. At this initial stage, we strive to discover the meaning of the words and expressions used by the biblical writers as they were understood in their original setting and by their original recipients. This means, among other things, that we do not interpret everything we read "literalistically", as though Scripture never speaks in a figurative or symbolic way (it often does!). Rather, we read it according to the rules that govern its different literary forms of writing, depending on whether we are reading a narrative, a poem, a letter, a parable, or an apocalyptic vision. The Church calls us to read the divine books in this way to ensure that we understand what the human authors were laboring to explain to God's people.

The literal sense, however, is not the only sense of Scripture, since we interpret its sacred pages according to the *spiritual* senses as well. In this way, we search out what the Holy Spirit is trying to tell us, beyond even what the human authors have consciously asserted. Whereas the literal sense of Scripture describes a historical reality—a fact, precept, or event—the spiritual senses disclose deeper mysteries revealed through the historical realities. What the soul is to the body, the spiritual senses are to the literal. You can distinguish them; but if you try to separate them, death immediately follows. St. Paul was the first to insist upon this and warn of its consequences: "God ... has qualified us to be ministers of a new covenant, not in a written code but in the Spirit; for the written code kills, but the Spirit gives life" (2 Cor 3:5–6).

Catholic tradition recognizes three spiritual senses that stand upon the foundation of the literal sense of Scripture (see CCC 115). (1) The first is the *allegorical* sense, which unveils the spiritual and prophetic meaning of biblical history. Allegorical interpretations thus reveal how persons, events, and institutions of Scripture can point beyond themselves toward greater mysteries yet to come (OT) or display the fruits of mysteries already revealed (NT). Christians have often read the Old Testament in this way to discover how the mystery of Christ in the New Covenant was once hidden in the Old and how the full significance of the Old Covenant was finally made manifest in the New. Allegorical significance is likewise latent in the New Testament, especially in the life and deeds of Jesus recorded in the Gospels. Because Christ is the Head of the Church and the source of her spiritual life, what was accomplished in Christ the Head during his earthly life prefigures what he continually produces in his members through grace. The allegorical sense builds up the virtue of faith. (**2**) The second is the *tropological* or *moral* sense, which reveals how the actions of God's people in the Old Testament and the life of Jesus in the New Testament prompt us to form virtuous habits in our own lives. It therefore draws from Scripture warnings against sin and vice as well as inspirations to pursue holiness and purity. The moral sense is intended to build up the virtue of charity. (**3**) The third is the *anagogical* sense, which points upward to heavenly glory. It shows us how countless events in the Bible prefigure our final union with God in eternity and how things that are "seen" on earth are figures of things "unseen" in heaven. Because the anagogical sense leads us to contemplate our destiny, it is meant to build up the virtue of hope. Together with the literal sense, then, these spiritual senses draw out the fullness of what God wants to give us through his Word and as such comprise what ancient tradition has called the "full sense" of Sacred Scripture.

All of this means that the deeds and events of the Bible are charged with meaning beyond what is immediately apparent to the reader. In essence, that meaning is Jesus Christ and the salvation he died to give us. This is especially true of the books of the New Testament, which proclaim Jesus explicitly; but it is also true of the Old Testament, which speaks of Jesus in more hidden and symbolic ways. The human authors of the Old Testament told us as much as they were able, but they could not clearly discern the shape of all future events standing at such a distance. It is the Bible's divine Author, the Holy Spirit, who could and did foretell the saving work of Christ, from the first page of the Book of Genesis onward.

The New Testament did not, therefore, abolish the Old. Rather, the New fulfilled the Old, and in doing so, it lifted the veil that kept hidden the face of the Lord's bride. Once the veil is removed, we suddenly see the world of the Old Covenant charged with grandeur. Water, fire, clouds, gardens, trees, hills, doves, lambs—all of these things are memorable details in the history and poetry of Israel. But now, seen in the light of Jesus Christ, they are much more. For the Christian with eyes to see, water symbolizes the saving power of Baptism; fire, the Holy Spirit; the spotless lamb, Christ crucified; Jerusalem, the city of heavenly glory.

The spiritual reading of Scripture is nothing new. Indeed, the very first Christians read the Bible this way. St. Paul describes Adam as a "type" that prefigured Jesus Christ (Rom 5:14). A "type" is a real person, place, thing, or event in the Old Testament that foreshadows something greater in the New. From this term we get the word "typology", referring to the study of how the Old Testament prefigures Christ (CCC 128–30). Elsewhere St. Paul draws deeper meanings out of the story of Abraham's sons, declaring, "This is an allegory" (Gal 4:24). He is not suggesting that these events of the distant past never really happened; he is saying that the events both happened *and* signified something more glorious yet to come.

The New Testament later describes the Tabernacle of ancient Israel as "a copy and shadow of the heavenly sanctuary" (Heb 8:5) and the Mosaic Law as a "shadow of the good things to come" (Heb 10:1). St. Peter, in turn, notes that Noah and his family were "saved through water" in a way that "corresponds" to sacramental Baptism, which "now saves you" (1 Pet 3:20–21). It is interesting to note that the expression translated as "corresponds" in this verse is a Greek term that denotes the fulfillment or counterpart of an ancient "type".

We need not look to the apostles, however, to justify a spiritual reading of the Bible. After all, Jesus himself read the Old Testament this way. He referred to Jonah (Mt 12:39), Solomon (Mt 12:42), the Temple (Jn 2:19), and the brazen serpent (Jn 3:14) as "signs" that pointed forward to him. We see in Luke's Gospel, as Christ comforted the disciples on the road to Emmaus, that "beginning with Moses and all the prophets, he interpreted to them in all the Scriptures the things concerning himself" (Lk 24:27). It was precisely this extensive spiritual interpretation of the Old Testament that made such an impact on these once-discouraged travelers, causing their hearts to "burn" within them (Lk 24:32).

Criteria for Biblical Interpretation We, too, must learn to discern the "full sense" of Scripture as it includes both the literal and spiritual senses together. Still, this does not mean we should "read into" the Bible meanings that are not really there. Spiritual exegesis is not an unrestrained flight of the imagination. Rather, it is a sacred science that proceeds according to certain principles and stands accountable to sacred tradition, the Magisterium, and the wider community of biblical interpreters (both living and deceased).

In searching out the full sense of a text, we should always avoid the extreme tendency to "over-spiritualize" in a way that minimizes or denies the Bible's literal truth. St. Thomas Aquinas was well aware of this danger and asserted that "all other senses of Sacred Scripture are based on the literal" (*STh* I, 1, 10, *ad* 1, quoted in CCC 116). On the other hand, we should never confine the meaning of a text to the literal, intended sense of its human author, as if the divine Author did not intend the passage to be read in the light of Christ's coming.

Fortunately the Church has given us guidelines in our study of Scripture. The unique character and divine authorship of the Bible call us to read it "in the Spirit" (*Dei Verbum* 12). Vatican II outlines this teaching in a practical way by directing us to read the Scriptures according to three specific criteria:

1. We must "[b]e especially attentive 'to the content and unity of the whole Scripture'" (CCC 112).

2. We must "[r]ead the Scripture within 'the living Tradition of the whole Church'" (CCC 113).

3. We must "[b]e attentive to the analogy of faith" (CCC 114; cf. Rom 12:6).

These criteria protect us from many of the dangers that ensnare readers of the Bible, from the newest inquirer to the most prestigious scholar. Reading Scripture out of context is one such pitfall, and probably the one most difficult to avoid. A memorable cartoon from the 1950s shows a young man poring over the pages of the Bible. He says to his sister: "Don't bother me now; I'm trying to find a Scripture verse to back up one of my preconceived notions." No doubt a biblical text pried from its context can be twisted to say something very different from what its author actually intended.

The Church's criteria guide us here by defining what constitutes the authentic "context" of a given biblical passage. The first criterion directs us to the literary context of every verse, including not only the words and paragraphs that surround it, but also the entire corpus of the biblical author's writings and, indeed, the span of the entire Bible. The *complete* literary context of any Scripture verse includes every text from Genesis to Revelation—because the Bible is a unified book, not just a library of different books. When the Church canonized the Book of Revelation, for example, she recognized it to be incomprehensible apart from the wider context of the entire Bible.

The second criterion places the Bible firmly within the context of a community that treasures a "living tradition". That community is the People of God down through the ages. Christians lived out their faith for well over a millennium before the printing press was invented. For centuries, few believers owned copies of the Gospels, and few people could read anyway. Yet they absorbed the gospel—through the sermons of their bishops and clergy, through prayer and meditation, through Christian art, through liturgical celebrations, and through oral tradition. These were expressions of the one "living tradition", a culture of living faith that stretches from ancient Israel to the contemporary Church. For the early Christians, the gospel could not be understood apart from that tradition. So it is with us. Reverence for the Church's tradition is what protects us from any sort of chronological or cultural provincialism, such as scholarly fads that arise and carry away a generation of interpreters before being dismissed by the next generation.

The third criterion places scriptural texts within the framework of faith. If we believe that the Scriptures are divinely inspired, we must also believe them to be internally coherent and consistent with all the doctrines that Christians believe. Remember, the Church's dogmas (such as the Real Presence, the papacy, the Immaculate Conception) are not something *added* to Scripture; rather, they are the Church's infallible interpretation *of* Scripture.

Using This Study Guide This volume is designed to lead the reader through Scripture according to the Church's guidelines—faithful to the canon, to the tradition, and to the creeds. The Church's interpretive principles have thus shaped the component parts of this book, and they are designed to make the reader's study as effective and rewarding as possible.

Introductions: We have introduced the biblical book with an essay covering issues such as authorship, date of composition, purpose, and leading themes. This background information will assist readers to approach and understand the text on its own terms.

Annotations: The basic notes at the bottom of every page help the user to read the Scriptures with understanding. They by no means exhaust the meaning of the sacred text but provide background material to help the reader make sense of what he reads. Often these notes make explicit what the sacred writers assumed or held to be implicit. They also provide a great deal of historical, cultural, geographical, and theological information pertinent to the inspired narratives—information that can help the reader bridge the distance between the biblical world and his own.

Cross-References: Between the biblical text at the top of each page and the annotations at the bottom, numerous references are listed to point readers to other scriptural passages related to the one being studied. This follow-up is an essential part of any serious study. It is also an excellent way to discover how the content of Scripture "hangs together" in a providential unity. Along with biblical cross-references, the annotations refer to select paragraphs from the *Catechism of the Catholic Church*. These are not doctrinal "proof texts" but are designed to help the reader interpret the Bible in accordance with the mind of the Church. The *Catechism* references listed either handle the biblical text directly or treat a broader doctrinal theme that sheds significant light on that text.

Topical Essays, *Word Studies*, *Charts*: These features bring readers to a deeper understanding of select details. The *topical essays* take up major themes and explain them more thoroughly and theologically than the annotations, often relating them to the doctrines of the Church. Occasionally the annotations are supplemented by *word studies* that put readers in touch with the ancient languages of Scripture. These should help readers to understand better and appreciate the inspired terminology that runs throughout the sacred books. Also included are various *charts* that summarize biblical information "at a glance".

Icon Annotations: Three distinctive icons are interspersed throughout the annotations, each one corresponding to one of the Church's three criteria for biblical interpretation. Bullets indicate the passage or passages to which these icons apply.

Notes marked by the book icon relate to the "content and unity" of Scripture, showing how particular passages of the Old Testament illuminate the mysteries of the New. Much of the information in these notes explains the original context of the citations and indicates how and why this has a direct bearing on Christ or the Church. Through these notes, the reader can develop a sensitivity to the beauty and unity of God's saving plan as it stretches across both Testaments.

Notes marked by the dove icon examine particular passages in light of the Church's "living tradition". Because the Holy Spirit both guides the Magisterium and inspires the spiritual senses of Scripture, these annotations supply information along both of these lines. On the one hand, they refer to the Church's doctrinal teaching as presented by various popes, creeds, and ecumenical councils; on the other, they draw from (and paraphrase) the spiritual interpretations of various Fathers, Doctors, and saints.

Notes marked by the keys icon pertain to the "analogy of faith". Here we spell out how the mysteries of our faith "unlock" and explain one another. This type of comparison between Christian beliefs displays the coherence and unity of defined dogmas, which are the Church's infallible interpretations of Scripture.

Putting It All in Perspective   Perhaps the most important context of all we have saved for last: the interior life of the individual reader. What we get out of the Bible will largely depend on how we approach the Bible. Unless we are living a sustained and disciplined life of prayer, we will never have the reverence, the profound humility, or the grace we need to see the Scriptures for what they really are.

You are approaching the "word of God". But for thousands of years, since before he knit you in your mother's womb, the Word of God has been approaching you.

One Final Note. The volume you hold in your hands is only a small part of a much larger work still in production. Study helps similar to those printed in this booklet are being prepared for *all* the books of the Bible and will appear gradually as they are finished. Our ultimate goal is to publish a single, one-volume Study Bible that will include the entire text of Scripture, along with all the annotations, charts, cross-references, maps, and other features found in the following pages. Individual booklets will be published in the meantime, with the hope that God's people can begin to benefit from this labor before its full completion.

We have included a long list of Study Questions in the back to make this format as useful as possible, not only for individual study, but for group settings and discussions as well. The questions are designed to help readers both "understand" the Bible and "apply" it to their lives. We pray that God will make use of our efforts and yours to help renew the face of the earth! «

INTRODUCTION TO PROVERBS

Author and Date The Book of Proverbs is an anthology of wisdom sayings having different authors and dates of origin. As indicated in the book's opening line, the main contributor and inspiration for the work was King Solomon, who lived and reigned in the tenth century B.C. His name is attached to three collections of sayings in the book, one that extends from 1:1—9:18, another that stretches from 10:1—22:16, and a third that covers 25:1—29:27. There is some uncertainty whether the first collection of sayings is actually ascribed to Solomon or whether his name is used in 1:1 simply as a heading for the book. Either way, attributions to Solomon are hardly surprising, given his reputation in the Bible as a man of towering intellect and exceptional insight (e.g., 1 Kings 4:29–34; 10:23–24; Sir 47:14–17; Mt 12:42). Since there is no convincing reason to deny that Solomon's fame rests on the substance of historical fact, and since there is nothing in the collections ascribed to him that is incompatible with historical circumstances in the tenth century, it is reasonable to accept the Solomonic origin of the nearly twenty-seven (or at least eighteen) chapters credited to him.

Other contributors to the Book of Proverbs include an individual named Agur (30:1–33), of whom nothing else is known, and a king named Lemuel (31:1–31), whose identity is likewise obscure. Another important section, entitled "the words of the wise", is a collection of didactic lore of undetermined origin (22:17—24:34). Lacking reference to persons or events otherwise known to history, these non-Solomonic portions of the book are more or less undatable, except to say that archaic features abound in them and that nothing mentioned in these texts demands a date later than the seventh century B.C. Finally, brief reference is made to "the men of Hezekiah" in 25:1. These are scribes said to have copied out the third collection of Solomon's proverbs, and some scholars identify them as the final editors who gave the Book of Proverbs its present, canonical shape. If nothing else, the notation at 25:1 indicates that the completed edition of Proverbs could not have appeared before Hezekiah's reign (ca. 715 to 686 B.C.), regardless of the original date of the material assembled at that time. Coupled with the observation that nothing in the book is indisputably postexilic, and allowing for some finishing work after Hezekiah's time, it seems likely that the Book of Proverbs reached its final form before 600 B.C., although a somewhat later date cannot be strictly ruled out.

Title The Hebrew original is generally known by the first two words of the book, *mishle shelomoh*, "The Proverbs of Solomon". This heading is attached to the first seven verses, which constitute a preamble to the book, identifying its genre, its primary contributor, its intended readership, and its main purpose. The Greek Septuagint gives the same heading as the Hebrew version, *Paroimiai Salōmōntos*, "Proverbs of Solomon", and the Latin Vulgate titles the work, *Liber Proverbiorum*, "Book of Proverbs".

Structure The broad outline of the Book of Proverbs is fairly straightforward. It begins with a short prologue (1:1–7) followed by extended poetic speeches known as the Wisdom Discourses (1:8—9:18). The rest of the book is dominated by tightly worded maxims that are typically no longer than two or three lines apiece. These are grouped together into various collections labeled Solomon's Proverbs (10:1—22:16), the Words of the Wise (22:17—24:34), Solomon's Proverbs (25:1—29:27), the Words of Agur (30:1–33), the Words of Lemuel (31:1–9), and a concluding poem on the virtues of a courageous wife (31:10–31). For the most part, these sections consist of short snippets of wisdom that function as self-contained observations and admonitions. Occasionally it is possible to detect a theme or common expression that unites a cluster of sayings, but this is more the exception than the rule. The majority of sayings in Proverbs resemble pearls strung together on a necklace: each has a message that is beautiful and valuable in its own right, yet each is more or less independent of those that precede and follow.

Literary Features Proverbs displays a range of poetic techniques and devices common to the Semitic world of the Bible. The first to appear are *didactic speeches*, most of which are moral exhortations from a father to a son (e.g., 1:8–19; 2:1–22; 3:1–12) and three of which feature Wisdom, personified as a woman, offering her counsel to all who will listen (1:20–33; 8:1–36; 9:1–6). Thereafter one most often encounters proverbs expressed in parallel lines or couplets. Frequently the parallelism is *synonymous*, which means the second line restates the idea expressed in the first line in a slightly different way (e.g., 11:25; 16:18; 19:5). Other times it is *antithetical*, meaning the second line states something in contrast to the first line or looks at the same situation in reverse (e.g., 10:1; 12:25; 15:17). Examples can likewise be found of *synthetic* or *progressive* parallelism, in which the second line advances the thought of the first line with some additional insight (e.g., 4:1; 18:22; 26:11). Lastly, some use is made of *numerical proverbs*, in which the second line expresses a number one digit higher than that stated in the first line and the couplet is followed by a list of precisely that many examples (e.g., 6:16–19; 30:15–16, 18–19, 21–31). Other conventions employed in the book include *proverbs of comparison*, where one thing is pronounced "better than" another (e.g., 19:1; 22:1; 28:6), and one *acrostic poem*, a composition divided into twenty-two units that correspond in sequence to the letters of the Hebrew alphabet (31:10–31).

Themes and Characteristics   The Book of Proverbs may be described as a treasury of wisdom for successful living. Though not a moral code in any technical sense, it aims at the formation of character by imparting values and encouraging virtues. Its sayings offer guidance for navigating the twists and turns of everyday life with prudent discernment and praiseworthy conduct. Wisdom of this sort is derived from studied reflection on the natural and human worlds, especially the realm of personal relationships. Strategies for success in Proverbs are based, not on the untried theories of academics, but on the accumulated insights of past generations. Experience is thus revered as one of the great teachers of wisdom, and young and old alike do well to heed the practical knowledge of those who have gone before them.

Most of the biblical proverbs function as situational sayings. Unlike, for instance, the Ten Commandments, which lay down universal laws that admit of no exceptions, sapiential teachings are concerned with choices to be made in particular circumstances. For this reason, sage advice that is applicable to one situation may not be beneficial in another (see note on 26:4–5). This is not to say that wisdom morality is relative or lacking a basis in absolute standards of right and wrong; it is only to say that proverbs are more concerned with applying principles for wise conduct than with formulating legal precepts. So too, proverbs often express generalizations that describe the way things usually are, not the way they always are. Recommendations are thus made on the basis of patterns and tendencies in life and should not be viewed as mathematical formulas guaranteed to yield predictable results. Broad principles that underlie many of the book's sayings include the importance of prudence and a generally thoughtful approach to living (13:16; 14:8; 15:28), the need for moderation and the avoidance of excess (10:19; 25:16; 30:8–9), a concern for social propriety based on doing the right thing at the right time (15:23; 25:20; 27:14), and the advantage of self-control for living a full and profitable life (16:32; 17:27; 19:11; 25:28; 29:11).

The foundation of wisdom instruction is "the fear of the LORD". This is the one motif that punctuates the book from beginning to end (1:7, 29; 2:5; 3:7; 8:13; 9:10; 10:27; 14:2, 26–27; 15:16, 33; 16:6; 19:23; 22:4; 23:17; 24:21; 31:30). Since wisdom ultimately comes from God (2:6), one can hardly be called wise who fails to revere the Lord. Everyone is obliged to discern the lessons of life by use of reason and to conform to the order that God's wisdom has built into creation (3:19–20; 8:22–31). Life is always tending in one of two directions, either accepting or refusing this responsibility, often called "the two ways" (see note on 1:15). (**1**) The righteous follow *the way of wisdom and life*. These listen to the voice of wisdom (1:33) and lead a life of prayer (15:8, 29). They are urged to trust in the Lord (3:5; 16:20) and to be diligent in work (10:4; 12:24), humble in spirit (3:7; 15:33; 29:23), open to correction (6:23; 17:10; 19:25), and committed to truthful and guarded speech (4:24; 10:19; 12:19; 13:3; 21:23). Compassion for the poor (29:7) should make them kind and generous with their resources (11:24–25; 14:31; 19:17; 22:9; 22:16; 31:20). Parents have a duty to lead their children along these paths by wise instruction and loving discipline (13:24; 19:18; 23:13–14; 29:15, 17). Young men, to whom much of the counsel of the book is directed, are put on guard against the dangers of peer pressure (1:10–16), bad company (13:20), and especially the enticements of sexually promiscuous women (2:16–19; 5:3–20; 6:23–35; 7:4–27; 23:26–28). Instead, they are to value the blessings of a good and prudent wife (12:4; 18:22; 19:14; 31:10–31). All of this amounts to following "the paths of uprightness" (2:13; 4:11). (**2**) The senseless, by contrast, follow *the way of foolishness and death*. Lacking sound discretion, they are given to pride (8:13; 16:5, 18; 21:4), laziness (6:9–11; 10:5; 20:4; 21:25; 26:14), drunkenness (20:1; 23:29–35), and all manner of perverse and deceitful speech (2:12; 6:12; 10:18, 32; 12:22; 20:19; 26:28). They tend to be merciless (21:10), contentious (20:3; 26:21), and quick-tempered (14:17, 29; 15:18). Fools have no qualms about perverting justice (17:15, 23) and conducting crooked business deals (11:1; 20:10, 23). What is worse, they despise correction from others that would lead them toward wisdom (9:7–8; 10:17; 12:1; 13:1). The way of folly is ultimately "the way of evil" (2:12), and the one who follows it "dies for lack of discipline" (5:23).

Christian Perspective   The teaching of the New Testament gives witness in various ways to the impact of the Book of Proverbs. Most importantly, its doctrine of Jesus Christ is indebted to the personification of divine Wisdom, especially where Wisdom is described as a preexistent companion with God (8:22–29) and a mediator through whom God fashioned the world (8:30–31). These ideas are evoked, not only by the assertion that Christ is the embodiment of "wisdom" (1 Cor 1:30), but also by the revelation that Christ the Word was "in the beginning with God" (Jn 1:2) and that "all things were created through him" (Col 1:16; Heb 1:2). Beyond this, the NT's reliance on Proverbs can be seen in various quotations and allusions to the book, which imply that its practical wisdom remains pastorally relevant to the Christian faithful. At least one NT reference follows the Hebrew wording of the book, where it is said that love covers a multitude of sins and offenses (10:12; Jas 5:20; 1 Pet 4:8). Most other references follow the Greek Septuagint translation of Proverbs, which invites us to see the Lord's discipline as an act of fatherly love (3:11–12; Heb 12:5–6), which tells us that God opposes the proud but favors the humble (3:34; Jas 4:6; 1 Pet 5:5), which warns of the severity of God's judgment (11:31; 1 Pet 4:18), which forbids getting drunk with wine (23:31; Eph 5:18), and which advises showing kindness to enemies rather than seeking personal revenge (25:21–22; Rom 12:20). Finally, an echo from Proverbs can be heard in the teaching that wisdom comes as a gift from God (2:6; Jas 1:5), just as the memorable image of a dog returning to its vomit can be applied to backsliders in the faith (26:11; 2 Pet 2:22).

OUTLINE OF PROVERBS

1. **Proverbs of Solomon: First Collection (1:1—9:18)**
   A. Prologue (1:1–7)
   B. Wisdom Discourses (1:8—9:18)

2. **Proverbs of Solomon: Second Collection (10:1—22:16)**

3. **Words of the Wise (22:17—24:34)**

4. **Proverbs of Solomon: Third Collection (25:1—29:27)**

5. **Words of Agur (30:1–33)**

6. **Words of Lemuel (31:1–9)**

7. **Poem on the Courageous Wife (31:10–31)**

THE BOOK OF
THE PROVERBS

The Call of Wisdom

1 The proverbs of Solomon, son of David, king of Israel:

2That men may know wisdom and instruction,
   understand words of insight,
3receive instruction in wise dealing,
   righteousness, justice, and equity;
4that prudence may be given to the simple,
   knowledge and discretion to the
      youth—
5the wise man also may hear and increase in
   learning,
and the man of understanding acquire
   skill,
6to understand a proverb and a figure,
   the words of the wise and their riddles.

7The fear of the Lord is the beginning of
   knowledge;
   fools despise wisdom and instruction.

8Hear, my son, your father's instruction,
   and reject not your mother's teaching;
9for they are a fair garland for your head,
   and pendants for your neck.

1:1–7 The prologue or preamble of the book. It identifies the genre of the work (1:1), its main contributor (1:1), its intended purpose (1:2–6), its target audience (1:4–5), and its foundational conviction (1:7).

1:1 Solomon: The legendary wise man of the Bible who inspired the wisdom tradition of the OT. He was the tenth **son of David** (1 Chron 3:1–5) and ruled as **king of Israel** from ca. 970 to 930 b.c. (1 Kings 1–11). Many regard this opening line as a title or superscription for the entire Book of Proverbs. It is also possible that Solomon's name is meant to identify him as the author of the first collection of teachings in chaps. 1–9. Other sections of the book attributed to Solomon are found in 10:1—22:16 and 25:1—29:27.

1:4–5 The book addresses **the youth**, who need formation in the skills of responsible living, as well as **the wise**, who can still advance on the path of moral and social virtue. For the biblical meaning of wisdom, see word study: *Wisdom* at 1 Kings 3:28.

1:7 fear of the Lord: The essential virtue of wisdom and the master theme of the book from beginning (1:7) to end (31:30). Far from being a wholly secular and nontheological work, Proverbs teaches that pursuing wisdom is a spiritual quest that requires as our first responsibility a pious reverence for God (9:10), including a recognition of his sovereignty over human life and conduct (24:21). In practical terms, fear of the Lord means living humbly and uprightly (14:2; 15:33; 23:17) and turning away from evil (3:7; 8:13; 16:6). It leads one toward life (14:27; 19:23) and offers blessings of longevity and prosperity (3:16; 10:27; 22:4). The principle enunciated in this verse is paralleled in Job 28:28; Ps 111:10; Sir 1:27 (CCC 1831, 2095–97). • Sin has its beginning in a lack of wisdom, just as one who is virtuous and fears God is the wisest of all. If fearing God means having wisdom,
and the sinner has no such fear, then he possesses no wisdom and is the most foolish of all (St. John Chrysostom, *Homilies on John* 41). Servile fear, which corrects the error of sins, is the first divine fear. Perfect love casts out this fear. Holy fear, which comes later, is supplemented by love rather than replaced by it. It is the fear of a good son who is afraid to offend his loving father in the least (St. Bede, *Commentary on Proverbs* 1, 1).

1:8–19 The first of several discourses in chaps. 1–9 delivered by a father to his son.

1:8 my son: The home was the primary setting of moral and religious formation in biblical Israel (Deut 4:9–10; 11:19). Hence the mother's role as a teacher is mentioned alongside the father's role (6:20; 30:17; 31:1). It is possible that an institutional system of public education operated in preexilic Israel, perhaps in connection with the Davidic monarchy, but there is no direct evidence for Jewish schools until the second century

---

Word Study

Proverb (Prov 1:6)

Mashal (Heb.): A broad term that encompasses a variety of literary forms. It may be related to one of two verbs, one meaning "to rule" and the other meaning "to be like". Either way, the word basically denotes an utterance, whether a popular saying (1 Sam 10:12), a parable or allegory (Ezek 17:2), or a prophetic discourse (Num 23:7). Sometimes it has the negative connotation of a taunt (Is 14:4) or a byword that one speaks mockingly or derisively about an object of scorn (Ps 44:14). Most commonly, a *mashal* denotes an instructional saying that is poetic in form, concise in length, and memorable in content. These tend to be observations based on experience that offer advice on how to live successfully. Proverbs were central to the cultivation of wisdom throughout the ancient Near East. In the Bible, Solomon is remembered as the father and founder of the wisdom tradition. He is said to have uttered three thousand proverbs (1 Kings 4:32) and is credited with several collections of sayings in the Book of Proverbs (see Prov 1:1; 10:1; 25:1).

The proverb or saying (*mashal*) was a typical form of expression in a society that depended to a large extent on oral tradition. Each saying expressed some important truth in pithy and memorable form. The proverbs contained in this book were, of course, regarded as divinely inspired teaching and had a correspondingly weighty authority. The book contains a number of collections of proverbs, two of which are ascribed to Solomon (10:1–22:16 and 25:1–29:27), but it is not likely that all the proverbs in these collections are in fact attributable to Solomon. It is probable that 10:1–22:16 forms the original nucleus of the book.

The general subject of the proverbs is the art of right living. Some points are dealt with in detail, for example, wisdom and folly, justice and injustice, and so on. They are not simply maxims of natural wisdom but presuppose a background of revealed religion and inculcate its principles. Religion is in fact regarded as the basis of all morality. The book was finally edited and put together after the Exile.

¹⁰My son, if sinners entice you,
  do not consent.
¹¹If they say, "Come with us, let us lie in wait for
    blood,
    let us wantonly ambush the innocent;
¹²like Sheol let us swallow them alive
    and whole, like those who go down to the Pit;
¹³we shall find all precious goods,
    we shall fill our houses with spoil;
¹⁴throw in your lot among us,
    we will all have one purse"—
¹⁵my son, do not walk in the way with them,
    hold back your foot from their paths;
¹⁶for their feet run to evil,
    and they make haste to shed blood.
¹⁷For in vain is a net spread
    in the sight of any bird;
¹⁸but these men lie in wait for their own blood,
    they set an ambush for their own lives.
¹⁹Such are the ways of all who get gain by violence;
    it takes away the life of its possessors.
²⁰Wisdom cries aloud in the street;
    in the markets she raises her voice;
²¹on the top of the walls^a she cries out;
    at the entrance of the city gates she speaks:
²²"How long, O simple ones, will you love being
    simple?
  How long will scoffers delight in their scoffing
    and fools hate knowledge?
²³Give heed^b to my reproof;
  behold, I will pour out my thoughts^c to you;
    I will make my words known to you.

²⁴Because I have called and you refused to listen,
    have stretched out my hand and no one has
      heeded,
²⁵and you have ignored all my counsel
    and would have none of my reproof,
²⁶I also will laugh at your calamity;
    I will mock when panic strikes you,
²⁷when panic strikes you like a storm,
    and your calamity comes like a whirlwind,
    when distress and anguish come upon you.
²⁸Then they will call upon me, but I will not
      answer;
    they will seek me diligently but will not find
      me.
²⁹Because they hated knowledge
    and did not choose the fear of the LORD,
³⁰would have none of my counsel,
    and despised all my reproof,
³¹therefore they shall eat the fruit of their way
    and be sated with their own devices.
³²For the simple are killed by their turning away,
    and the complacence of fools destroys
      them;
³³but he who listens to me will dwell secure
    and will be at ease, without dread of evil."

The Treasure of Wisdom

2 My son, if you receive my words
  and treasure up my commandments with you,
²making your ear attentive to wisdom
    and inclining your heart to understanding;
³yes, if you cry out for insight
    and raise your voice for understanding,

1:20, 21: 8:1–3.

B.C. (Sir 51:23). The wisdom literature from Egypt and Meso-potamia also presents fathers instructing their sons in proper behavior (CCC 2221–29).

1:10 sinners: Habitual evildoers, not persons guilty of an occasional transgression.

1:11 Come with us: Temptations to sin often confront young people as peer pressure. **wait for blood:** A warning against violence motivated by greed (1:13).

1:12 Sheol: The netherworld of the dead, a realm of utter darkness and gloom thought to be located deep in the earth. See word study: *Sheol* at Num 16:30.

1:15 the way: One of the overarching metaphors used in Proverbs (2:8; 3:6; 4:11; 5:5–6, etc.). Evoking the image of a road or footpath, the way stands for the direction of one's life as characterized by one's actions and decisions, which are themselves represented by stepping, walking, or running (e.g., 1:16; 2:7; 4:12). Essentially there are only two roads of travel: the way of wisdom, which leads to righteousness and life, and the way of folly, which tends toward wickedness and death. For the wisdom doctrine of "the two ways", see note on Ps 1.

1:16 run to evil ... blood: A similar saying appears in Is 59:7.

1:17 in vain: A son who heeds his father's warning can avoid the snares of the wicked like a bird evades capture when he sees the hunter laying his trap.

1:20–33 The first of three discourses in chaps. 1–9 delivered by Woman Wisdom (also 8:1–36 and 9:1–6). Like a prophetess, she calls out in public places urging all to receive her sensible instruction. Those who refuse her call are charting a course toward calamity (1:26) and distress (1:27), for they will come to their senses too late (1:28).

1:22 simple ones: People who are immature in behavior, inexperienced in decision making, and generally impious (1:29).

1:23 my reproof: Fools stubbornly refuse to learn from their mistakes. Wisdom's correction is meant to expose the glamour of sin as a deception that brings undesirable consequences as discipline from the Lord (Wis 11:16). Ultimately, the aim of God's reproof is our repentance (3:11–12; Heb 12:5–11).

1:33 at ease: Wisdom bestows peace of mind and soul upon those who embrace her counsel.

2:1–22 A discourse on the benefits of wisdom, which is nothing less than a knowledge of God (2:5). Once possessed, it will give young men the moral sense to avoid the perversities of lawless men (2:12–15) and the seduction of loose women (2:16–19). Several themes in this chapter are developed further in subsequent chapters.

2:1 My son: Wisdom is instilled in a young man by his father. See note on 1:8. **treasure up:** Remembering a father's commandments will serve as a safeguard against foolish behavior (cf. Ps 119:11).

2:2 your heart: In biblical thinking, the heart encompasses all the faculties of the inner person, including mind and memory. See word study: *Heart* at Deut 30:6.

---

^aHeb uncertain.
^bHeb *Turn.*
^cHeb *spirit.*

⁴if you seek it like silver
  and search for it as for hidden treasures;
⁵then you will understand the fear of the Lord
  and find the knowledge of God.
⁶For the Lord gives wisdom;
  from his mouth come knowledge and
    understanding;
⁷he stores up sound wisdom for the upright;
  he is a shield to those who walk in
    integrity,
⁸guarding the paths of justice
  and preserving the way of his saints.
⁹Then you will understand righteousness and
    justice
  and equity, every good path;
¹⁰for wisdom will come into your heart,
  and knowledge will be pleasant to your soul;
¹¹discretion will watch over you;
  understanding will guard you;
¹²delivering you from the way of evil,
  from men of perverted speech,
¹³who forsake the paths of uprightness
  to walk in the ways of darkness,
¹⁴who rejoice in doing evil
  and delight in the perverseness of evil;
¹⁵men whose paths are crooked,
  and who are devious in their ways.

¹⁶You will be saved from the loose[d] woman,
  from the adventuress[e] with her smooth words,

¹⁷who forsakes the companion of her youth
  and forgets the covenant of her God;
¹⁸for her house sinks down to death,
  and her paths to the shades;
¹⁹none who go to her come back
  nor do they regain the paths of life.

²⁰So you will walk in the way of good men
  and keep to the paths of the righteous.
²¹For the upright will inhabit the land,
  and men of integrity will remain in it;
²²but the wicked will be cut off from the land,
  and the treacherous will be rooted out of it.

Exhortation to Be Wise and to Honor God

3 My son, do not forget my teaching,
  but let your heart keep my commandments;
²for length of days and years of life
  and abundant welfare will they give you.
³Let not loyalty and faithfulness forsake you;
  bind them about your neck,
  write them on the tablet of your heart.
⁴So you will find favor and good repute[f]
  in the sight of God and man.

⁵Trust in the Lord with all your heart,
  and do not rely on your own insight.
⁶In all your ways acknowledge him,
  and he will make straight your paths.
⁷Be not wise in your own eyes;
  fear the Lord, and turn away from evil.

3:4: Rom 12:17; Rom 12:17. **3:7:** Rom 12:16; Rom 12:16.

2:4 hidden treasures: The search for wisdom is compared to mining for precious metals also in Job 28:1–19.

2:5 fear of the Lord: The indispensable virtue of the wise. See note on 1:7.

2:6 the Lord gives wisdom: Wisdom is a divine gift given to those who ask for it (2:3–5; Sir 1:1; Jas 1:5). Thus, in addition to study, reflection, and learning from one's elders, prayer is an essential activity of the wise man (15:8, 29; Sir 51:13–17). Solomon is living proof that God gives understanding to the one who asks for it (1 Kings 3:5–12) (CCC 1831).

2:12 perverted speech: Includes lying (6:17), giving false witness (12:17), and urging others to commit sin (1:11; 7:5) (CCC 2476–87).

2:15 crooked: In contrast to the straight paths of righteous living (3:6).

2:16 the loose woman: Literally, "the strange woman". Some think the description refers to her nationality as a non-Israelite, but more likely it indicates that she belongs to another man. In any case, she is a married woman who seduces young men into sexual sin. In doing so, she betrays her husband's trust and violates the marriage covenant they made before God (2:17). Avoiding the adulteress is crucial since a commitment to chastity will become all the more difficult if the lustful passions are indulged (2:19). At another level, this female seductress seems to exemplify Woman Folly with her invitations to forsake the wisdom of moral virtue. See notes on 9:1–18 and 9:13.

2:17 the covenant: Marriage was considered a covenant in ancient Israel (Ezek 16:8; Mal 2:14). Adultery is a viola-tion of the matrimonial covenant with one's spouse as well as Israel's national covenant with the Lord (Ex 20:14; CCC 2380–81).

2:18 the shades: The spirits of the dead inhabiting the netherworld below (Job 26:5).

2:21 the land: The Lord gives the righteous of Israel secure possession of the Promised Land (Ps 37:29), but he uproots the wicked from their ancestral lands (2:22; Deut 28:63).

3:1–35 The chapter has four main units: the book's third father-to-son teaching (3:1-12), a poem on the value of wisdom (3:13–18), a short reflection on wisdom and creation (3:19–20), and a fourth father-to-son teaching (3:21–35). Each section proposes incentives to commit oneself to God and embrace the life of wisdom.

3:2 welfare: The Hebrew term is *shalom*, meaning "peace" and "well-being". A long life full of peace and prosperity is the promised reward for obedience.

3:3 loyalty and faithfulness: Often translated "stead-fast love and faithfulness", this familiar word pair typically describes God's unwavering commitment to his people (Ex 34:6; Ps 86:15; 108:4; 115:1, etc.). Here a father urges his son to direct both his actions (**your neck**) and his inward inten-tions (**your heart**) according to this standard of fidelity to the Lord.

3:5 your own insight: Wisdom urges one to recognize the limits of human understanding. Since only God is infinitely knowledgeable about man's life and circumstances, it is a form of pride to live solely on the basis of human insight. The bib-lical notion of wisdom includes humility, faith, and a living relationship with the Lord.

3:7 fear ... turn away: The spiritual and moral compo-nents of wisdom. This description is given of righteous Job (Job 1:1, 8).

---

[d]Heb *strange*.
[e]Heb *foreign woman*.
[f]Cn: Heb *understanding*.

⁸It will be healing to your flesh[g]
and refreshment[h] to your bones.

⁹Honor the LORD with your substance
and with the first fruits of all your produce;
¹⁰then your barns will be filled with plenty,
and your vats will be bursting with wine.

¹¹My son, do not despise the LORD's discipline
or be weary of his reproof,
¹²for the LORD reproves him whom he loves,
as a father the son in whom he delights.

¹³Happy is the man who finds wisdom,
and the man who gets understanding,
¹⁴for the gain from it is better than gain from silver
and its profit better than gold.
¹⁵She is more precious than jewels,
and nothing you desire can compare with her.
¹⁶Long life is in her right hand;
in her left hand are riches and honor.
¹⁷Her ways are ways of pleasantness,
and all her paths are peace.
¹⁸She is a tree of life to those who lay hold of her;
those who hold her fast are called happy.

¹⁹The LORD by wisdom founded the earth;
by understanding he established the heavens;
²⁰by his knowledge the deeps broke forth,
and the clouds drop down the dew.

²¹My son, keep sound wisdom and discretion;
let them not escape from your sight,[i]

²²and they will be life for your soul
and adornment for your neck.
²³Then you will walk on your way securely
and your foot will not stumble.
²⁴If you sit down,[j] you will not be afraid;
when you lie down, your sleep will be sweet.
²⁵Do not be afraid of sudden panic,
or of the ruin[k] of the wicked, when it comes;
²⁶for the LORD will be your confidence
and will keep your foot from being caught.
²⁷Do not withhold good from those to whom it[l]
is due,
when it is in your power to do it.
²⁸Do not say to your neighbor, "Go, and come
again,
tomorrow I will give it"—when you have it
with you.
²⁹Do not plan evil against your neighbor
who dwells trustingly beside you.
³⁰Do not contend with a man for no reason,
when he has done you no harm.
³¹Do not envy a man of violence
and do not choose any of his ways;
³²for the perverse man is an abomination to the
LORD,
but the upright are in his confidence.
³³The LORD's curse is on the house of the wicked,
but he blesses the abode of the righteous.
³⁴Toward the scorners he is scornful,
but to the humble he shows favor.
³⁵The wise will inherit honor,
but fools get[m] disgrace.

3:11, 12: Heb 12:5, 6.

3:9-10 An exhortation to pay tithes. In biblical times, this meant giving 10 percent of one's annual harvest to the sanctuary in order to support the ministry of its priests and Levites (Num 18:8-32). Tithing is not only an expression of thanks to the Lord for his gifts; it comes with a promise that abundant blessings will pour down upon the giver in return (Mal 3:10-12).

3:11-12 Divine discipline is a form of fatherly training. Though it is often experienced in the sufferings and disappointments of life, it is a sign of the Father's love that he intervenes to correct the misbehavior of his children and to lead them to spiritual maturity. • The Book of Hebrews quotes these verses to encourage Christians facing the trials of persecution (Heb 12:5-6). The aim of such painful ordeals is to make us sharers in God's holiness (Heb 12:10).

3:13 Happy is the man: Or, "Blessed is the man", a common expression in the Bible's wisdom literature (8:34; 28:14; 29:18). For its meaning, see word study: *Blessed* at Ps 1:1.

3:14 better than gold: The value of wisdom exceeds even the most esteemed treasures of the world (8:10, 19; 16:16). The same is elsewhere said of the Lord's commandments (Ps 19:10; 119:72, 127).

3:18 tree of life: Mentioned also in 11:30; 13:12; 15:4. • Evoking memories of the tree of life from Gen 2:9, Proverbs depicts wisdom as a source of divine blessing and happiness. In effect, those who find wisdom receive a taste of the undisturbed peace and contentment that once reigned in the primordial paradise of Eden. • The Eucharist, called supersubstantial bread, is also called "the tree of life" in Scripture. If one extends his hand and partakes of it, he will live forever. This tree Solomon named "the wisdom of God" (Origen of Alexandria, *On Prayer* 27, 10).

3:19-20 Divine wisdom was the instrument of creation (Ps 104:24). By means of it, the Lord made all things to reflect his glory and intelligence. Wisdom is thus reflected throughout the cosmos in the physical laws of nature as well as in the moral and spiritual laws that lead to human fulfillment. The role of wisdom at creation is more fully described in 8:22-36.

3:20 the deeps: The subterranean ocean thought to reside under the earth (Ps 24:1-2). In the poetic descriptions of Genesis, its waters irrigated Eden (Gen 2:6) and surged up over the dry land at the time of the flood (Gen 7:11).

3:26 keep your foot: Unlike transgressors, who become ensnared in their sinful pursuits (1:18; 7:22-23).

3:33 curse ... blesses: The sanctions of the covenant that the Lord metes out to his people in the form of retributions and rewards (Deut 11:26-28).

3:34 to the humble: The Lord's favor is shown when he answers the prayers of the humble and prospers their way (Sir 35:17). • Twice the NT quotes the Greek LXX version of this passage to discourage pride and

[g]Heb *navel*.
[h]Or *medicine*.
[i]Reversing the order of the clauses.
[j]Gk: Heb *lie down*.
[k]Heb *storm*.
[l]Heb *Do not withhold good from its owners*.
[m]Cn: Heb *exalt*.

A Father's Advice

4 Hear, O sons, a father's instruction,
   and be attentive, that you may gain[n] insight;
[2]for I give you good precepts:
   do not forsake my teaching.
[3]When I was a son with my father,
   tender, the only one in the sight of my mother,
[4]he taught me, and said to me,
   "Let your heart hold fast my words;
   keep my commandments, and live;
[5]do not forget, and do not turn away from the
      words of my mouth.
   Get wisdom; get insight.[o]
[6]Do not forsake her, and she will keep you;
   love her, and she will guard you.
[7]The beginning of wisdom is this: Get wisdom,
   and whatever you get, get insight.
[8]Prize her highly,[p] and she will exalt you;
   she will honor you if you embrace her.
[9]She will place on your head a fair garland;
   she will bestow on you a beautiful crown."

[10]Hear, my son, and accept my words,
   that the years of your life may be many.
[11]I have taught you the way of wisdom;
   I have led you in the paths of uprightness.
[12]When you walk, your step will not be hampered;
   and if you run, you will not stumble.
[13]Keep hold of instruction, do not let go;
   guard her, for she is your life.
[14]Do not enter the path of the wicked,
   and do not walk in the way of evil men.
[15]Avoid it; do not go on it;
   turn away from it and pass on.

[16]For they cannot sleep unless they have done
      wrong;
   they are robbed of sleep unless they have
      made someone stumble.
[17]For they eat the bread of wickedness
   and drink the wine of violence.
[18]But the path of the righteous is like the light of
      dawn,
   which shines brighter and brighter until full
      day.
[19]The way of the wicked is like deep darkness;
   they do not know over what they stumble.

[20]My son, be attentive to my words;
   incline your ear to my sayings.
[21]Let them not escape from your sight;
   keep them within your heart.
[22]For they are life to him who finds them,
   and healing to all his flesh.
[23]Keep your heart with all vigilance;
   for from it flow the springs of life.
[24]Put away from you crooked speech,
   and put devious talk far from you.
[25]Let your eyes look directly forward,
   and your gaze be straight before you.
[26]Take heed to[q] the path of your feet,
   then all your ways will be sure.
[27]Do not swerve to the right or to the left;
   turn your foot away from evil.

Warning against Loose Women

5 My son, be attentive to my wisdom,
   incline your ear to my understanding;
[2]that you may keep discretion,
   and your lips may guard knowledge.

3:34 (Gk): Jas 4:6; 1 Pet 5:5.   **4:26 (Gk):** Heb 12:13; Heb 12:13.

---

encourage humility among believers (Jas 4:6; 1 Pet 5:5; CCC 2559, 2628). • Pride is evil because no excuse can be given for it. The matter is put in this way lest one think that pride is a trifling sin. On the strength of Holy Scripture, we can see that God is stern with the arrogant, so we must shun every sin, especially pride (St. Jerome, *Homilies* 95).

4:1–27 The chapter consists of three poems, each offering a father's wisdom to his sons (4:1–9, 10–19, 20–27). Appeals to follow his teaching and warnings against forsaking it are coupled with promises of a happy and fulfilled life. On this motif in Proverbs, see note on 1:8.

4:3 with my father: Paternal wisdom is like a family heirloom bequeathed to the next generation. **tender:** The same Hebrew term describes Solomon as "inexperienced" in 1 Chron 22:5 and 29:1.

4:6–9 Wisdom is like a devoted bride (Wis 8:2) who faithfully honors her husband. She is comparable also to a Queen Mother who places a crown upon her son (4:9) on his wedding day (Song 3:11). The feminine personification of wisdom occurs several times in the Bible's wisdom literature (1:20–33; Wis 7:24–30).

4:7 The beginning: For similar statements, see 1:7; 9:10; Job 28:28; Ps 111:10.

4:10–19 Contrasts "the way of wisdom" (4:11) with "the way of the wicked" (4:19). See note on 1:15.

4:16 they cannot sleep: Evil men are restless for mischief. They are neither at peace within themselves nor content to live at peace with others.

4:18 the light of dawn: For the righteous, peace of mind increases over time, just as the brightness and heat of the sun gradually intensify during the morning hours leading up to midday.

4:20–27 A father's appeal for complete devotion to his teaching. His words are reinforced in a tangible way by addressing various parts of the body that together represent the whole person (ears, 4:20; heart, 4:21; mouth or tongue, 4:24; eyes, 4:25; feet, 4:26).

4:25 look directly forward: Implies a firm commitment and singleness of purpose.

4:26 Take heed to the path: The Greek LXX version reads "make straight paths for your feet" and is cited in Heb 12:13.

4:27 Do not swerve: A call to walk the straight road of moral righteousness, being careful not to veer off in the direction of sin. Similar language is used in exhortations to observe the Lord's commandments faithfully (Deut 5:32; 28:14; Josh 1:7).

5:1–23 The dangers of adultery are contrasted with the delights of married life. Involvement with a "loose woman" (5:3) ultimately brings social disgrace, financial loss, and painful regret (5:9–12). However, fidelity to one's "wife" (5:18) brings opportunity for lasting happiness and love (5:19). The

---

[n]Heb *know*.
[o]Reversing the order of the lines.
[p]The meaning of the Hebrew is uncertain.
[q]The meaning of the Hebrew word is uncertain.

³For the lips of a loose woman drip honey,
　　and her speech^r is smoother than oil;
⁴but in the end she is bitter as wormwood,
　　sharp as a two-edged sword.
⁵Her feet go down to death;
　　her steps follow the path to^s Sheol;
⁶she does not take heed to^t the path of life;
　　her ways wander, and she does not know it.

⁷And now, O sons, listen to me,
　　and do not depart from the words of my mouth.
⁸Keep your way far from her,
　　and do not go near the door of her house;
⁹lest you give your honor to others
　　and your years to the merciless;
¹⁰lest strangers take their fill of your strength,^u
　　and your labors go to the house of an alien;
¹¹and at the end of your life you groan,
　　when your flesh and body are consumed,
¹²and you say, "How I hated discipline,
　　and my heart despised reproof!
¹³I did not listen to the voice of my teachers
　　or incline my ear to my instructors.
¹⁴I was at the point of utter ruin
　　in the assembled congregation."

¹⁵Drink water from your own cistern,
　　flowing water from your own well.
¹⁶Should your springs be scattered abroad,
　　streams of water in the streets?
¹⁷Let them be for yourself alone,
　　and not for strangers with you.

¹⁸Let your fountain be blessed,
　　and rejoice in the wife of your youth,
¹⁹　　a lovely deer, a graceful doe.
Let her affection fill you at all times with delight,
　　be infatuated always with her love.
²⁰Why should you be infatuated, my son, with a
　　loose woman
　　and embrace the bosom of an adventuress?
²¹For a man's ways are before the eyes of the
　　LORD,
　　and he watches^v all his paths.
²²The iniquities of the wicked ensnare him,
　　and he is caught in the toils of his sin.
²³He dies for lack of discipline,
　　and because of his great folly he is lost.

Practical Admonitions and Warnings

6 My son, if you have become surety for your
　　neighbor,
　　have given your pledge for a stranger;
²if you are snared in the utterance of your lips,^w
　　caught in the words of your mouth;
³then do this, my son, and save yourself,
　　for you have come into your neighbor's power:
　　go, hasten,^x and importune your neighbor.
⁴Give your eyes no sleep
　　and your eyelids no slumber;
⁵save yourself like a gazelle from the hunter,^y
　　like a bird from the hand of the fowler.
⁶Go to the ant, O sluggard;
　　consider her ways, and be wise.
⁷Without having any chief,
　　officer or ruler,

---

chapter combines practical advice with a marked esteem for marital chastity (CCC 2339, 2349).

5:3 lips ... drip honey: Represents the enticing words of the seductress (6:24; 7:5; 22:14).

5:4 wormwood: An exceptionally bitter herb (Lam 3:15; Rev 8:11).

5:5 Sheol: The realm of the dead. See word study: *Sheol* at Num 16:30.

5:8 do not go near: A warning to avoid the near occasions of sexual sin (cf. Gen 39:10).

5:9 the merciless: Probably refers to the avenging husband of the adulteress (6:34–35).

5:15–18 The **well** or **fountain** is a poetic image for one's bride (Song 4:12, 15). She is to be cherished as a source of life, love, and refreshment. Likewise, just as water wells in the arid Near East were often guarded as private property, so a husband must take care to protect his wife from the advances of other men (**strangers**, 5:17). Part of this involves reserving his affections for his wife alone, lest she come to feel unloved and eventually seek intimacy elsewhere. The marital bond is an exclusive bond that makes all romantic and sexual activity by married persons with non-spouses a sin of adultery (Ex 20:14; Deut 5:18) (CCC 2362, 2380–81).

5:19 doe: Graceful creatures that symbolize feminine beauty (Song 2:9; 4:5; 7:3). **her love:** Fanning the flames of marital love can strengthen a couple's relationship and provide a safeguard against temptations to infidelity.

5:21 eyes of the LORD: If the prospect of shame and remorse is not enough to dissuade the young man from an adulterous affair, he should remember that God sees all and will hold him accountable for his actions (15:3; Job 31:1–4; 34:21; Jer 16:17).

6:1–35 Young men are urged to avoid pledges (6:1–5), laziness (6:6–11), troublemakers (6:12–15), and sins abominable to the Lord (6:16–19). After this, the father issues another warning, reminiscent of 5:7–14, on the danger of adultery (6:20–35).

6:1 surety: A pledge of one's life or resources as collateral for someone else in debt (cf. Gen 43:9). The practice is discouraged in Proverbs as an unwise and unnecessary risk (11:15; 17:18; 20:16; 22:26–27). **your pledge:** Literally, "your hands". Pledges of surety were probably ratified with a type of handshake.

6:3 importune your neighbor: The father advises pleading with a creditor (or debtor) to back out of a surety arrangement.

6:6 the ant: One of nature's most diligent creatures from which man can observe the wisdom of foresight and industriousness (30:25). If a tiny insect can gather and store food for the winter (6:8) without the prodding of a superior (6:7), then the young man can surely drag himself out of bed to earn a living and secure his well-being for the days ahead. Otherwise, hunger and hardship will spring upon the idle man unawares (24:33–34). • Wise Solomon praises the laborer by rebuking the sluggard, contrasting him with the tiniest of insects. We should fear lest this fault be

---

^rHeb *palate.*
^sHeb *lay hold of.*
^tThe meaning of the Hebrew word is uncertain.
^uOr *wealth.*
^vThe meaning of the Hebrew word is uncertain.
^wCn Compare Gk Syr: Heb *the words of your mouth.*
^xOr *humble yourself.*
^yCn: Heb *hand.*

[8]she prepares her food in summer,
and gathers her sustenance in harvest.
[9]How long will you lie there, O sluggard?
When will you arise from your sleep?
[10]A little sleep, a little slumber,
a little folding of the hands to rest,
[11]and poverty will come upon you like a vagabond,
and want like an armed man.

[12]A worthless person, a wicked man,
goes about with crooked speech,
[13]winks with his eyes, scrapes[z] with his feet,
points with his finger,
[14]with perverted heart devises evil,
continually sowing discord;
[15]therefore calamity will come upon him suddenly;
in a moment he will be broken beyond healing.

[16]There are six things which the LORD hates,
seven which are an abomination to him:
[17]haughty eyes, a lying tongue,
and hands that shed innocent blood,
[18]a heart that devises wicked plans,
feet that make haste to run to evil,
[19]a false witness who breathes out lies,
and a man who sows discord among brothers.

[20]My son, keep your father's commandment,
and forsake not your mother's teaching.
[21]Bind them upon your heart always;
tie them about your neck.
[22]When you walk, they[a] will lead you;
when you lie down, they[a] will watch over you;
and when you awake, they[a] will talk with you.
[23]For the commandment is a lamp and the teaching
a light,

and the reproofs of discipline are the way of
life,
[24]to preserve you from the evil woman,
from the smooth tongue of the adventuress.
[25]Do not desire her beauty in your heart,
and do not let her capture you with her
eyelashes;
[26]for a harlot may be hired for a loaf of bread,[b]
but an adulteress[c] stalks a man's very life.
[27]Can a man carry fire in his bosom
and his clothes not be burned?
[28]Or can one walk upon hot coals
and his feet not be scorched?
[29]So is he who goes in to his neighbor's wife;
none who touches her will go unpunished.
[30]Men do not despise[d] a thief if he steals
to satisfy his appetite when he is hungry.
[31]And if he is caught, he will pay sevenfold;
he will give all the goods of his house.
[32]He who commits adultery has no sense;
he who does it destroys himself.
[33]Wounds and dishonor will he get,
and his disgrace will not be wiped away.
[34]For jealousy makes a man furious,
and he will not spare when he takes
revenge.
[35]He will accept no compensation,
nor be appeased though you multiply gifts.

False Attractions of Adultery

7 My son, keep my words
and treasure up my commandments with
you;
[2]keep my commandments and live,
keep my teachings as the apple of your eye;
[3]bind them on your fingers,
write them on the tablet of your heart.

---

found in us, for he who gave us the ability to work requires labor in proportion to our capacity (St. Basil, *Long Rules* 37).

6:10 folding of the hands: An image of the sluggard crossing his arms in preparation for a nap (24:33).

6:12 worthless person: A liar and troublemaker whose mischief sows "discord" between other people (6:14). Assured that such devious persons are headed for ruin, the youth is cautioned against imitating or keeping company with them (6:15).

6:13 winks: Suggests the person is up to no good (10:10).

6:16–19 One of several numerical proverbs in which objects of praise, censure, or similarity are itemized in a list (30:15–16, 18–19, 21–23, 29–31). This one catalogues seven abominations in the sight of God: arrogance, lying, violence, premeditating evil, eagerness for mischief, perjury, and causing family strife. Most of these sins are associated with specific parts of the body (**eyes, tongue, hands, heart, feet**).

6:21 Bind them: Similar exhortations are given in 3:3 and 7:3.

6:23 a lamp: An image for moral guidance, which is light for the path of living. The word of God is described in this way in Ps 119:105.

6:24–35 Again the young man is warned against the wiles of the adulterous woman (5:3–14). He is put on guard against her seductive speech (6:24), her captivating beauty (6:25), and her flirtatious gestures (6:25). The price of giving in to lustful attraction is nothing less than his "life" (6:26) (CCC 2351).

6:27 fire: An apt image for sexual passion (cf. 1 Cor 7:9).

6:30 thief: Adultery and thievery were closely associated in the biblical world, where a man's bride was considered his personal property (cf. Ex 20:17). However, one can make amends for stealing (6:31), but no compensation can fully undo the harm caused by marital infidelity (6:35).

6:33 Wounds: Inflicted on the adulterer when the enraged husband of the adulteress assaults him with physical blows (6:34).

7:1–27 A final warning against sexual involvement with another man's wife (also 2:16–19; 5:3–14, 20–23; 6:23–35). This time the father recounts an experience of witnessing a young man taken in by the seductions of an adulteress (7:6–23). Hereafter in Proverbs the dangers of harlots and promiscuous women are mentioned only briefly (22:14; 23:27–28; 29:3).

7:2 the apple: The center or pupil of the eye, which is instinctively guarded from harm.

7:3 fingers ... heart: Perhaps a way of saying that a father's wisdom should influence a son's outward actions as well as his inward intentions.

---

[z]Or *taps*.
[a]Heb *it*.
[b]Cn Compare Gk Syr Vg Tg: Heb *for because of a harlot to a piece of bread*.
[c]Heb *a man's wife*.
[d]Or *Do not men despise. . . ?*

⁴Say to wisdom, "You are my sister,"
    and call insight your intimate friend;
⁵to preserve you from the loose woman,
    from the adventuress with her smooth words.

⁶For at the window of my house
    I have looked out through my lattice,
⁷and I have seen among the simple,
    I have perceived among the youths,
    a young man without sense,
⁸passing along the street near her corner,
    taking the road to her house
⁹in the twilight, in the evening,
    at the time of night and darkness.

¹⁰And behold, a woman meets him,
    dressed as a harlot, wily of heart.ᵉ
¹¹She is loud and wayward,
    her feet do not stay at home;
¹²now in the street, now in the market,
    and at every corner she lies in wait.
¹³She seizes him and kisses him,
    and with impudent face she says to him:
¹⁴"I had to offer sacrifices,
    and today I have paid my vows;
¹⁵so now I have come out to meet you,
    to seek you eagerly, and I have found you.
¹⁶I have decked my couch with coverings,
    colored spreads of Egyptian linen;
¹⁷I have perfumed my bed with myrrh,
    aloes, and cinnamon.
¹⁸Come, let us take our fill of love till morning;
    let us delight ourselves with love.
¹⁹For my husband is not at home;
    he has gone on a long journey;
²⁰he took a bag of money with him;
    at full moon he will come home."

²¹With much seductive speech she persuades him;
    with her smooth talk she compels him.
²²All at once he follows her,
    as an ox goes to the slaughter,
    or as a stag is caught fastᶠ
²³   till an arrow pierces its entrails;
    as a bird rushes into a snare;
    he does not know that it will cost him his
      life.

²⁴And now, O sons, listen to me,
    and be attentive to the words of my mouth.
²⁵Let not your heart turn aside to her ways,
    do not stray into her paths;
²⁶for many a victim has she laid low;
    yes, all her slain are a mighty host.
²⁷Her house is the way to Sheol,
    going down to the chambers of death.

Eternity of Wisdom

8 Does not wisdom call,
    does not understanding raise her voice?
²On the heights beside the way,
    in the paths she takes her stand;
³beside the gates in front of the town,
    at the entrance of the portals she cries aloud:
⁴"To you, O men, I call,
    and my cry is to the sons of men.
⁵O simple ones, learn prudence;
    O foolish men, pay attention.
⁶Hear, for I will speak noble things,
    and from my lips will come what is right;
⁷for my mouth will utter truth;
    wickedness is an abomination to my lips.
⁸All the words of my mouth are righteous;
    there is nothing twisted or crooked in them.
⁹They are all straight to him who understands
    and right to those who find knowledge.

8:1–3: 1:20, 21.

7:4 my sister: An epithet sometimes used of one's bride (Song 4:9; 5:1). Sons are urged to make wisdom—not the loose woman (7:5)—their most intimate companion in life. See note on 4:6–9 and word study: *My Sister* at Song 4:9.

7:8 the road to her house: The young man is not an unwitting victim of seduction; he has gone looking for trouble.

7:9 night: Ironically, the adulterous affair is witnessed despite the cover of darkness.

7:10 as a harlot: It is unknown what made the dress of a prostitute distinctive, though it may have been a type of facial veil (cf. Gen 38:15). **wily of heart:** The Greek LXX renders this: "which makes the hearts of young men flutter".

7:13 seizes ... kisses him: The woman makes aggressive advances to secure the young man's consent.

7:14 offer sacrifices: The precise meaning of the statement is unclear. Perhaps she intends to dispel notions that she is irreligious, appealing to the pious scruples of her lover. Or, too, this may be an invitation for the young man to share a sacrificial meal with her, thus getting him behind closed doors (cf. Lev 7:11–15). Either way, she makes an appearance of godliness in order to accomplish her ungodly plan.

7:17 perfumed my bed: The woman has created a romantic atmosphere in preparation for a night of lovemaking (7:18). **Myrrh ... cinnamon:** Beautiful-smelling spices (Song 4:14).

7:22 as an ox: The young man is so captivated by the woman that he surrenders to his lower instincts like an irrational beast.

7:26 many a victim: The woman has embraced many lovers. She is like a warrioress who has slain an army of men seduced by her wiles.

7:27 Sheol: The netherworld of the dead. See word study: *Sheol* at Num 16:30.

8:1–36 The second discourse of Woman Wisdom, who portrays herself as a teacher of truth (8:7), a counselor of kings (8:15–16), and a guide to prosperity in life (8:18). Not a hidden or esoteric wisdom, her summons goes forth in public places (8:2–3), urging one and all to learn the virtues of moral understanding (8:12) and to despise all that is evil and arrogant (8:13). In addition to her gifts, mention is made also of Wisdom's origin with God (8:22–31). The first Wisdom speech appeared in 1:20–33, and her third address follows in 9:1–6. • In the Church's tradition, the wisdom speeches of Proverbs are sometimes read in relation to the Blessed Virgin Mary (CCC 721).

8:5 simple ones: Immature and foolish persons. See note on 1:22.

ᵉThe meaning of the Hebrew is uncertain.
ᶠCn Compare Gk: Heb uncertain.

¹⁰Take my instruction instead of silver,
  and knowledge rather than choice gold;
¹¹for wisdom is better than jewels,
  and all that you may desire cannot compare
    with her.
¹²I, wisdom, dwell in prudence,ᵍ
  and I find knowledge and discretion.
¹³The fear of the LORD is hatred of evil.
  Pride and arrogance and the way of evil
    and perverted speech I hate.
¹⁴I have counsel and sound wisdom,
  I have insight, I have strength.
¹⁵By me kings reign,
  and rulers decree what is just;
¹⁶by me princes rule,
  and nobles governʰ the earth.
¹⁷I love those who love me,
  and those who seek me diligently find me.
¹⁸Riches and honor are with me,
  enduring wealth and prosperity.
¹⁹My fruit is better than gold, even fine gold,
  and my yield than choice silver.
²⁰I walk in the way of righteousness,
  in the paths of justice,

²¹endowing with wealth those who love me,
  and filling their treasuries.

²²The LORD created me at the beginning of his
    work,ⁱ
  the first of his acts of old.
²³Ages ago I was set up,
  at the first, before the beginning of the earth.
²⁴When there were no depths I was brought forth,
  when there were no springs abounding with
    water.
²⁵Before the mountains had been shaped,
  before the hills, I was brought forth;
²⁶before he had made the earth with its fields,ʲ
  or the first of the dust ʲ of the world.
²⁷When he established the heavens, I was there,
  when he drew a circle on the face of the deep,
²⁸when he made firm the skies above,
  when he established ʲ the fountains of the deep,
²⁹when he assigned to the sea its limit,
  so that the waters might not transgress his
    command,
  when he marked out the foundations of the
    earth,

8:11 better than jewels: Scripture esteems the virtues of wisdom more than precious metals and gemstones (3:14–15; 8:19).

8:12 prudence: Or, "cleverness".

8:12–14 Six of the attributes listed in these verses (**wisdom** and **knowledge**, 8:12; **fear of the LORD**, 8:13; **counsel, insight** [or understanding], and **strength** [or might], 8:14) are attributed to the Spirit of the Lord and his Messiah in Is 11:2–3 (CCC 1831).

8:15 By me kings reign: A truth exemplified in King Solomon, who received extraordinary wisdom from God to rule over Israel (1 Kings 3:9–28; Sir 47:13–17).

8:17 find me: As a man searches and finds a wife (18:22; 31:10; Song 3:1–4).

8:18 wealth and prosperity: Another truth illustrated in the life of King Solomon, whose shrewd economic policies generated enormous wealth for his growing empire (1 Kings 10:6–29; Sir 47:18). Later, however, Solomon abandoned wisdom for folly and experienced the Lord's chastisement (1 Kings 11:1–25; Sir 47:19–20).

8:22–31 The preexistence of Wisdom is revealed. Before the world and history came into being, Wisdom was present with God and yet distinct from God, even begotten by him (see note on 8:22). More than simply a passive witness to the creation event, Wisdom assumed the role of a master craftsman according to whose plan heaven and earth were put in order (3:19; 8:30). Similar descriptions of Wisdom can be found in Ps 104:24; Wis 7:22; 9:9; Sir 1:4, 9; 24:9 (CCC 288). • The personification of Wisdom in the OT prepares for the revelation of the Trinity in the NT. In particular, this theme reaches its full development when Jesus is revealed as the eternal Son of God. Not only is Christ the incarnation of God's wisdom (1 Cor 1:24), but he was present with God before the foundation of the world (Jn 1:1; 17:5) as the divine mediator through whom all things were made (Jn 1:3; Col 1:15–17; Heb 1:2). • The Lord possessed Wisdom at the beginning of his ways because he possessed the Son, with whom he ordered all things when creation was born. Christ

was begotten of the Father before any beginning could be conceived or spoken of (St. Bede, *Commentary on Proverbs* 1, 8).

8:22–23 God's Wisdom is said to originate **at the beginning** of creation (8:22) as well as **before the beginning** of creation (8:23). This is not a contradiction if we understand that divine Wisdom is an uncreated perfection in the mind of God as well as something exemplified in the created entities that God has made. Wisdom in the former sense is eternal; wisdom in the latter sense is as old as the cosmos.

8:22 created me: Or, "begot me", an alternative translation suggested by the description of Wisdom being "brought forth" (8:24–25), imagery elsewhere associated with begetting and childbirth (Deut 32:18; Is 45:10; 66:7; Jer 4:31). **at the beginning of his work, the first of his acts of old:** The Greek LXX reads: "as the beginning of his ways, for his works". • The Greek wording is echoed in Rev 3:14, where Christ is identified as "the beginning of God's creation". • The passage is a prophecy of the Incarnation, meaning the Lord Jesus was created of the Virgin for the purpose of redeeming the works of the Father. Thus, the flesh of Christ is for the sake of created things, yet his divinity existed before them (St. Ambrose, *On the Christian Faith* 3, 7).

8:23 the first: The Hebrew term suggests that Wisdom is both prior to creation in existence and superior to creation in excellence.

8:24 no depths: I.e., when there was no subterranean ocean, called "the deep", which was thought to reside underground as the source of water flowing up from below in the form of springs (8:27; Gen 7:11; Job 38:16).

8:25 I was brought forth: The Greek LXX reads: "he begets me". • This refers to our Savior, the true Wisdom. But whatever is assigned a cause ("The LORD created me", 8:22) we understand of his humanity, and whatever is absolute and without origin ("he begets me", 8:25) we reckon of his divinity (St. Gregory Nazianzen, *Theological Orations* 4, 2).

8:27 a circle: Probably the horizon. In the poetic imagery of Genesis, the dome of the sky, called the firmament, is pictured as an inverted bowl placed down upon the world. Its perimeter forms the encircling skyline (Gen 1:6–8; Job 26:10).

8:29 the sea its limit: The seas and oceans, thought to represent the unruly forces of chaos, are kept under control by

---

ᵍHeb obscure.
ʰGk: Heb *all the governors of.*
ⁱHeb *way.*
ʲThe meaning of the Hebrew is uncertain.

30 then I was beside him, like a master workman;[1]
and I was daily his[m] delight,
    rejoicing before him always,
[31]rejoicing in his inhabited world
    and delighting in the sons of men.

[32]And now, my sons, listen to me:
    happy are those who keep my ways.
[33]Hear instruction and be wise,
    and do not neglect it.
[34]Happy is the man who listens to me,
    watching daily at my gates,
    waiting beside my doors.
[35]For he who finds me finds life
    and obtains favor from the LORD;
[36]but he who misses me injures himself;
    all who hate me love death."

The Feast of Wisdom; and General Maxims

9 Wisdom has built her house,
    she has set up[n] her seven pillars.
[2]She has slaughtered her beasts, she has mixed
        her wine,
    she has also set her table.
[3]She has sent out her maids to call
    from the highest places in the town,
[4]"Whoever is simple, let him turn in here!"
    To him who is without sense she says,
[5]"Come, eat of my bread
    and drink of the wine I have mixed.

[6]Leave simpleness,[o] and live,
    and walk in the way of insight."

[7]He who corrects a scoffer gets himself abuse,
    and he who reproves a wicked man incurs
        injury.
[8]Do not reprove a scoffer, or he will hate you;
    reprove a wise man, and he will love you.
[9]Give instruction[p] to a wise man, and he will be
        still wiser;
    teach a righteous man and he will increase in
        learning.
[10]The fear of the LORD is the beginning of wisdom,
    and the knowledge of the Holy One is insight.
[11]For by me your days will be multiplied,
    and years will be added to your life.
[12]If you are wise, you are wise for yourself;
    if you scoff, you alone will bear it.

[13]A foolish woman is noisy;
    she is wanton[q] and knows no shame.[r]
[14]She sits at the door of her house,
    she takes a seat on the high places of the town,
[15]calling to those who pass by,
    who are going straight on their way,
[16]"Whoever is simple, let him turn in here!"
    And to him who is without sense she says,
[17]"Stolen water is sweet,
    and bread eaten in secret is pleasant."

---

the power of God's word. The belief that God set strict boundaries for the world's water reservoirs appears several times in the Bible (Gen 1:9; Job 38:8–11; Ps 104:6–9).

8:30 master workman: Wisdom is likewise personified as "the fashioner of all things" in Wis 7:22.

8:31 rejoicing: A similar description is given of the angels' response to creation in Job 38:7.

8:32 happy: Or, "blessed". See word study: *Blessed* at Ps 1:1.

9:1–18 Chapter 9 begins with the third discourse of Woman Wisdom (9:1–6) and ends with a description of her counterpart, Woman Folly (9:13–18). The contrast between them is brought out by a series of parallels: both issue a summons from the "highest places" (9:3, 14) and invite those who are "simple" (9:4, 16) into their "home" (9:1, 14) for a banquet of "bread" and drink (9:5, 17). But whereas wisdom's guests "live" (9:6), the guests of the foolish woman join the company of "the dead" (9:18). The two banquets represent the "two ways" that lie before us: wisdom and folly, virtue and vice, godly and ungodly living. See note on 1:15.

9:1 her house: Not an actual schoolhouse, but a metaphor for the Book of Proverbs itself (or the following chapters). Another possibility is that the house with seven columns is a reference to the world built in seven days (Gen 1:1–2:4) on pillars (1 Sam 2:8) with the help of Wisdom, God's "master workman" (8:30). • The Wisdom of God, which is the Word coeternal with the Father, built as a house for himself a human body in the womb of the Virgin, and he set his table with bread and wine, the table at which stands the priesthood of the line of Melchizedek (St. Augustine, *City of God* 17, 20).

9:2 mixed her wine: Enhancing its taste with spices (Song 8:2). • Through Solomon, the Spirit reveals a type of the Lord's sacrifice, mention being made of the slain victim, the bread and wine, the altar, and the apostles. By saying the wine is mixed, he proclaims with a prophetic voice that the Lord's chalice is mixed with water and wine (St. Cyprian, *Letters* 63, 5).

9:4 simple: Those who are morally immature and inexperienced in wise decision making.

9:5 bread ... wine: Divine instruction is the food and drink that Wisdom serves to the guests who answer her call (Sir 15:3; 24:19–21; Is 55:1–2). Concretely, her banquet consists of the proverbs and maxims of the book, which give disciples a taste of divine insight into the ways of moral excellence and human flourishing.

9:7 scoffer: An arrogant person who is set in his evil ways and who mocks the idea of upright and responsible living (1:22; 13:1; 15:12).

9:9 still wiser: Instruction in wisdom benefits not only the young and inexperienced (1:4) but also the mature and learned (1:5; 21:11).

9:10 fear of the LORD: Recalling the maxim in 1:7, this thematic statement stands at the beginning and end of the first section of Proverbs. See note on 1:7. **the Holy One:** A title for Yahweh occurring only here and at 30:3.

9:11 years: For the blessing of prolonged life, see 3:2, 16; 10:27; 19:23; Deut 5:16.

9:13 noisy: Recalls the adulteress in 7:11. The promiscuous woman, here personified as Woman Folly, is openly and audibly flirtatious in attracting the attention of young men.

9:17 Stolen water: Perhaps an image related to 5:15, where a man's water is his wife. In this case, the sin of adultery is in view. **Sweet ... pleasant:** The seductress lures the foolish

---

[1]Another reading is *little child.*
[m]Gk: Heb lacks *his.*
[n]Gk Syr Tg: Heb *hewn.*
[o]Gk Syr Vg Tg: Heb *simple ones.*
[p]Heb lacks *instruction.*
[q]Cn Compare Syr Vg: The meaning of the Hebrew is uncertain.
[r]Gk Syr: The meaning of the Hebrew is uncertain.

¹⁸But he does not know that the dead^s are there,
that her guests are in the depths of Sheol.

Wise Sayings of Solomon

10

The proverbs of Solomon.

A wise son makes a glad father,
but a foolish son is a sorrow to his mother.
²Treasures gained by wickedness do not profit,
but righteousness delivers from death.

³The Lord does not let the righteous go hungry,
but he thwarts the craving of the wicked.
⁴A slack hand causes poverty,
but the hand of the diligent makes rich.
⁵A son who gathers in summer is prudent,
but a son who sleeps in harvest brings shame.
⁶Blessings are on the head of the righteous,
but the mouth of the wicked conceals
violence.

---

man with the prospect of illicit pleasures experienced behind closed doors.

9:18 Sheol: The realm of the dead. See note on 1:12.

10:1—22:16 The second main collection of wisdom instructions in Proverbs. It consists of 375 sayings, matching the numerical value of the Hebrew name for Solomon, with whom they are said to originate. Though it is difficult to find unifying themes that account for the present arrangement of the sayings, it is clear that several clusters of proverbs in this section are grouped together on the basis of a common vocabulary (called "catchwords"). In general, the Solomonic proverbs range over a wide variety of topics in which wisdom is expressed as observations about life or exhortations to virtuous conduct; they likewise imply that wisdom and righteous-

ness are closely aligned, as are wickedness and foolishness. Another collection of Solomon's proverbs appears in 25:1—29:27. See introduction: *Author and Date*.

10:1 A wise son: Related sayings appear at 13:1 and 15:20.

10:2 do not profit: Ill-gotten wealth is not only a fleeting prize but a moral liability in the eyes of God. Soon enough, death will rob the crooked man of his valuables (11:4; 21:6). **delivers from death:** Also stated in 11:4. What is here the benefit of **righteousness** is also the benefit of charity expressed through almsgiving (Tob 4:10).

10:4 slack: The lazy and unmotivated person is headed for hardship and want (6:6-11; 12:24; 19:15; CCC 1866). **diligent:** The industrious person is justly rewarded for his discipline and work ethic (12:11, 24, 27; 13:4; 14:23).

10:5 in summer: When crops are harvested and stored for the coming winter months.

^sHeb *shades*.

Wisdom Literature in the Bible

The wisdom literature forms a distinct collection of writings in the Old Testament, quite different from the legal, historical, and prophetic books. The collection includes Proverbs, Ecclesiastes, Song of Solomon, Wisdom, Sirach, and Job. Expressed in didactic poetry, these books advocate a practical wisdom that is universal in application rather than unique to the concerns of Israel. The latest sapiential writings, Wisdom and Sirach, do give attention to the history and religious heritage of the covenant people, but these features are almost entirely lacking in the earlier books. For the most part, biblical wisdom addresses itself to all aspects of life and is communicated in terms that are familiar to all.

One reason for this is *historical*. Archeology has revealed that the cultivation of wisdom was commonplace throughout the ancient Near East, so the Israelites were by no means the only ones to pursue an ordered life and to disseminate principles for wise living in maxims that were easy to remember. Wisdom writings and teachings were abundant both in Israel and among its neighbors. And these were expressed in a common language because they were based on the common needs and experiences of people everywhere. The use of nontechnical speech, along with advice on a broad spectrum of personal and social conduct, helped to facilitate the sharing of wisdom through cross-cultural dialogue among peoples from Egypt to Palestine to Arabia to Mesopotamia.

Another reason may be labeled *evangelical*. Though often underappreciated, the figure of Solomon stands out in the Bible as one who is remembered both for his "wisdom" and for his instruction of "Gentiles". Not only did he receive extraordinary wisdom from God to govern the internal affairs of Israel (1 Kings 3:3-14), but this wisdom gained him international acclaim among foreign sages throughout the Middle East (1 Kings 4:29-31). Caravans of monarchs and dignitaries from distant lands converged on Jerusalem to learn the wisdom of Solomon (1 Kings 4:34). Most famous was the Queen of Sheba, who came to test the king's mind with difficult questions, only to find that his understanding surpassed the already glowing reports that had reached her (1 Kings 10:1-7). Moreover, her encounter with Solomon's divine wisdom became an occasion to glorify the God of Israel: "Blessed be the Lord your God", she exclaimed to the king, "who has delighted in you and set you on the throne of Israel!" (1 Kings 10:9).

These considerations suggest a connection between wisdom and the Gentiles that helps to account for Solomon's inspiration of the wisdom tradition in Israel. In particular, the original purpose of wisdom is illuminated by his actions. Solomon composed thousands of proverbs and songs (1 Kings 4:32), not only for the benefit of Israel (1 Kings 3:28), but to enlighten the nations beyond Israel (1 Kings 10:23-24). With the possible exception of the Song of Solomon, the wisdom books are suited to the instruction of non-Israelites in the rudiments of responsible living, beginning with "the fear of the Lord" (Prov 1:7; Job 28:28; Eccles 12:13; Sir 1:27). Gentiles, through contact with the inspired teaching of Solomon and the sages who carried on his legacy, could thus be drawn closer to Yahweh and made ready to accept the truth of his revelation. This, too, helps to explain why the wisdom books speak a down-to-earth, easily understood, experiential language to which people of all backgrounds can relate.

⁷The memory of the righteous is a blessing,
  but the name of the wicked will rot.
⁸The wise of heart will heed commandments,
  but a prating fool will come to ruin.
⁹He who walks in integrity walks securely,
  but he who perverts his ways will be found
  out.
¹⁰He who winks the eye causes trouble,
  but he who boldly reproves makes peace.ᵗ
¹¹The mouth of the righteous is a fountain of life,
  but the mouth of the wicked conceals violence.
¹²Hatred stirs up strife,
  but love covers all offenses.
¹³On the lips of him who has understanding
  wisdom is found,
  but a rod is for the back of him who lacks
  sense.
¹⁴Wise men lay up knowledge,
  but the babbling of a fool brings ruin near.
¹⁵A rich man's wealth is his strong city;
  the poverty of the poor is their ruin.
¹⁶The wage of the righteous leads to life,
  the gain of the wicked to sin.
¹⁷He who heeds instruction is on the path to life,
  but he who rejects reproof goes astray.
¹⁸He who conceals hatred has lying lips,
  and he who utters slander is a fool.
¹⁹When words are many, transgression is not
  lacking,
  but he who restrains his lips is prudent.
²⁰The tongue of the righteous is choice silver;
  the mind of the wicked is of little worth.

²¹The lips of the righteous feed many,
  but fools die for lack of sense.
²²The blessing of the LORD makes rich,
  and he adds no sorrow with it.ᵘ
²³It is like sport to a fool to do wrong,
  but wise conduct is pleasure to a man of
  understanding.
²⁴What the wicked dreads will come upon him,
  but the desire of the righteous will be granted.
²⁵When the tempest passes, the wicked is no more,
  but the righteous is established for ever.
²⁶Like vinegar to the teeth, and smoke to the eyes,
  so is the sluggard to those who send him.
²⁷The fear of the LORD prolongs life,
  but the years of the wicked will be short.
²⁸The hope of the righteous ends in gladness,
  but the expectation of the wicked comes to
  nothing.
²⁹The LORD is a stronghold to him whose way is
  upright,
  but destruction to evildoers.
³⁰The righteous will never be removed,
  but the wicked will not dwell in the land.
³¹The mouth of the righteous brings forth wisdom,
  but the perverse tongue will be cut off.
³²The lips of the righteous know what is acceptable,
  but the mouth of the wicked, what is perverse.

11 A false balance is an abomination to the
  LORD,
  but a just weight is his delight.
²When pride comes, then comes disgrace;
  but with the humble is wisdom.

10:12: Jas 5:20; 1 Pet 4:8.

10:7 memory: A good name (i.e., reputation) was valued as something that lives on after the death of the righteous person (3:4; 22:1; Eccles 7:1).

10:8 prating fool: The overly talkative person who is quick to chatter but slow to stop and listen (10:19).

10:10 winks the eye: Suggests the person is up to no good (6:13).

10:12 love covers all offenses: A spirit of charity and mercy can absorb the blows of personal injury without harboring sentiments of bitterness or revenge (17:9). The notion of "covering" sins and offenses is an OT idiom for forgiveness (Neh 4:5; Ps 32:1). • A paraphrase of this verse appears in Jas 5:20, where love is expressed by correcting an erring disciple, and again in 1 Pet 4:8, where love that is merciful and overlooks grievances is recommended to strengthen personal relationships.

10:13 a rod: Associated with the pain and unpleasantness of correction (13:24; 14:3; 23:13; 26:3).

10:17 heeds instruction: The wise are teachable, open to correction (9:8), and eager to gain understanding (10:14; 12:1).

10:18–21 A cluster of sayings on prudent and impious speech.

10:18 lying lips: The sin of one who pretends to be friendly by the way he speaks, though his heart is filled with hatred (Ps 5:9; CCC 2482–86). **utters slander:** The sin of one who openly expresses his contempt of another (CCC 2477).

10:19 When words are many: A warning against intemperate speech, especially the babbling and excessive speech of the fool (10:8; Sir 20:8). The wise man, by contrast, keeps his tongue in check and is guarded in his use of words (11:12; 13:3; 21:23; Jas 1:19; 3:2). Being prudent, he knows how to say the right thing at the right time (Sir 20:1–7).

10:22 the LORD makes rich: Human efforts and investments must have God's blessing in order to prosper (Ps 127:1–2). Wealth attained with the Lord's help is not attended by a nagging sense of guilt or remorse.

10:23 pleasure: Doing what is right brings satisfaction as its reward (21:15).

10:24 desire ... will be granted: Provided the righteous "take delight in the LORD" (Ps 37:4).

10:27 fear of the LORD: The first and most essential virtue of the wise person (1:7; 9:10). **prolongs life:** For this blessing, see also 3:2, 16; 9:11; 19:23.

10:30 the land: Canaan. See note on 2:21.

10:32 what is acceptable: What wins the favor of God and others (3:4; 1 Sam 2:26; Lk 2:52).

11:1 A false balance: A scale rigged for cheating. Normally this meant that sellers secretly exchanged or incorrectly marked their counterweights in order to cheat the buyer. Scripture demands justice in the marketplace (Lev 19:35–36; Deut 25:13–16) and condemns dishonest business practices such as this (Amos 8:4–6; Mic 6:10–12) (CCC 2409). **an abomination:** See also 20:10.

11:2 pride ... disgrace: Sooner or later the Lord always humbles the proud with his judgment, whether it be individuals or nations (16:18; Is 10:12; 14:13–15; Mt 23:12). **humble:** Humility is another virtue of the wise (22:4; 29:23).

ᵗGk: Heb *but a prating fool will come to ruin.*
ᵘOr *and toil adds nothing to it.*

³The integrity of the upright guides them,
  but the crookedness of the treacherous
    destroys them.
⁴Riches do not profit in the day of wrath,
  but righteousness delivers from death.
⁵The righteousness of the blameless keeps his way
    straight,
  but the wicked falls by his own
    wickedness.
⁶The righteousness of the upright delivers them,
  but the treacherous are taken captive by their
    lust.
⁷When the wicked dies, his hope perishes,
  and the expectation of the godless comes to
    nothing.
⁸The righteous is delivered from trouble,
  and the wicked gets into it instead.
⁹With his mouth the godless man would destroy
    his neighbor,
  but by knowledge the righteous are delivered.
¹⁰When it goes well with the righteous, the city
    rejoices;
  and when the wicked perish there are shouts
    of gladness.
¹¹By the blessing of the upright a city is exalted,
  but it is overthrown by the mouth of the
    wicked.
¹²He who belittles his neighbor lacks sense,
  but a man of understanding remains
    silent.
¹³He who goes about as a talebearer reveals secrets,
  but he who is trustworthy in spirit keeps a
    thing hidden.
¹⁴Where there is no guidance, a people falls;
  but in an abundance of counselors there is
    safety.

¹⁵He who gives surety for a stranger will smart
    for it,
  but he who hates suretyship is secure.
¹⁶A gracious woman gets honor,
  and violent men get riches.
¹⁷A man who is kind benefits himself,
  but a cruel man hurts himself.
¹⁸A wicked man earns deceptive wages,
  but one who sows righteousness gets a sure
    reward.
¹⁹He who is steadfast in righteousness will live,
  but he who pursues evil will die.
²⁰Men of perverse mind are an abomination to the
    LORD,
  but those of blameless ways are his
    delight.
²¹Be assured, an evil man will not go unpunished,
  but those who are righteous will be delivered.
²²Like a gold ring in a swine's snout
  is a beautiful woman without discretion.
²³The desire of the righteous ends only in good;
  the expectation of the wicked in wrath.
²⁴One man gives freely, yet grows all the richer;
  another withholds what he should give, and
    only suffers want.
²⁵A liberal man will be enriched,
  and one who waters will himself be watered.
²⁶The people curse him who holds back grain,
  but a blessing is on the head of him who sells
    it.
²⁷He who diligently seeks good seeks favor,
  but evil comes to him who searches for it.
²⁸He who trusts in his riches will wither,ᵛ
  but the righteous will flourish like a green leaf.
²⁹He who troubles his household will inherit wind,
  and the fool will be servant to the wise.

11:3 crookedness: To follow a crooked path is to live a sinful life that deviates from the straight path of God's moral standards. See note on 1:15.

11:4 the day of wrath: A day of divine judgment (cf. Is 10:3; Zeph 1:18; Rom 2:5). It is the day when death or calamity strips the wealthy of their earthly treasures (cf. Lk 12:16–21). **delivers from death:** See note on 10:2.

11:12 remains silent: The wise one is prudent in speech, holding his tongue rather than gossiping or slandering his neighbor (10:19; 13:3; 21:23).

11:14 counselors: The sages of Israel had a high regard for wise counsel (12:15; 15:22; 20:18; 24:6).

11:15 surety: Roughly equivalent to an ancient form of collateral. See note on 6:1.

11:16 honor: A lasting blessing (10:7; 31:28). **riches:** A fleeting prize (11:4; 21:6).

11:20 blameless: Not sinless, but firmly committed to living by the Law of God (Ps 119:1; Lk 1:6). One who is blameless fears the Lord, speaks the truth, and turns away from evil (Ps 15:2; 19:13; Job 1:1).

11:22 a gold ring: In biblical antiquity women's jewelry often included a nose ring (Gen 24:47; Ezek 16:12). The point here is that feminine beauty is vain unless the woman fears the Lord and refuses to dishonor herself in the presence

of men (31:30) (CCC 2521–22). • One who reads and memorizes Scripture but who fails to depart from sins of the flesh is like a ring in the snout of a pig. There is no profit if he gives himself to the loveliness of Scripture yet remains stuck in thoughts and deeds covered with mud (St. John Cassian, *Conferences* 14).

11:24 gives freely ... richer: It is a paradox that God rewards our generosity with a greater abundance of his blessings (22:9). Paul expounds on this truth in 2 Cor 9:6–12. The miser, by contrast, wins neither friends nor the favor of God for his stinginess (21:13). Readers should note that proverbs typically deal in generalizations and should not be treated like formulas that, if followed, guarantee the desired result, be it health, wealth, or a long life. Besides that, the "riches" that God bestows upon the faithful are often spiritual rather than material (cf. Lk 16:9, 11; Rom 2:4).

11:25 A liberal man: A person who is generous with his resources.

11:26 holds back grain: In a greedy attempt to drive up the market price (CCC 2409).

11:28 trusts in his riches: Balances out various statements in Proverbs that describe material prosperity as a reward for wise living (8:18; 11:25). God may choose to bless the righteous with wealth, but their trust should always remain in the Lord (3:5; Ps 52:8) rather than in riches (Ps 62:10). This is the wisdom that is more valuable than gold and silver (3:14; 8:10, 19). **like a green leaf:** Resembles the simile in Ps 1:3.

ᵛCn: Heb *fall.*

³⁰The fruit of the righteous is a tree of life,
　　but lawlessness^w takes away lives.
³¹If the righteous is repaid on earth,
　　how much more the wicked and the sinner!

12 Whoever loves discipline loves knowledge,
　　but he who hates reproof is stupid.
²A good man obtains favor from the LORD,
　　but a man of evil devices he condemns.
³A man is not established by wickedness,
　　but the root of the righteous will never be
　　　moved.
⁴A good wife is the crown of her husband,
　　but she who brings shame is like rottenness in
　　　his bones.
⁵The thoughts of the righteous are just;
　　the counsels of the wicked are treacherous.
⁶The words of the wicked lie in wait for blood,
　　but the mouth of the upright delivers men.
⁷The wicked are overthrown and are no more,
　　but the house of the righteous will stand.
⁸A man is commended according to his good sense,
　　but one of perverse mind is despised.
⁹Better is a man of humble standing who works
　　for himself
　　than one who plays the great man but lacks
　　　bread.
¹⁰A righteous man has regard for the life of his
　　beast,
　　but the mercy of the wicked is cruel.
¹¹He who tills his land will have plenty of bread,
　　but he who follows worthless pursuits has no
　　　sense.

¹²The strong tower of the wicked comes to ruin,
　　but the root of the righteous stands firm.^x
¹³An evil man is ensnared by the transgression of
　　his lips,
　　but the righteous escapes from trouble.
¹⁴From the fruit of his words a man is satisfied
　　with good,
　　and the work of a man's hand comes back to
　　　him.
¹⁵The way of a fool is right in his own eyes,
　　but a wise man listens to advice.
¹⁶The vexation of a fool is known at once,
　　but the prudent man ignores an insult.
¹⁷He who speaks the truth gives honest evidence,
　　but a false witness utters deceit.
¹⁸There is one whose rash words are like sword
　　thrusts,
　　but the tongue of the wise brings healing.
¹⁹Truthful lips endure for ever,
　　but a lying tongue is but for a moment.
²⁰Deceit is in the heart of those who devise evil,
　　but those who plan good have joy.
²¹No ill befalls the righteous,
　　but the wicked are filled with trouble.
²²Lying lips are an abomination to the LORD,
　　but those who act faithfully are his delight.
²³A prudent man conceals his knowledge,
　　but fools^y proclaim their folly.
²⁴The hand of the diligent will rule,
　　while the slothful will be put to forced labor.
²⁵Anxiety in a man's heart weighs him down,
　　but a good word makes him glad.

11:31 (Gk): 1 Pet 4:18.

11:30 a tree of life: Symbolizes how the righteous man is a source of life for others. His honesty, loyalty, generosity, and sanctity have an uplifting influence that inspires others and makes their lives better. Hence, when the Lord prospers the way of his servants, "the city rejoices" (11:10). • The tree of life is Christ, who has brought forth the fruits of knowledge and virtue. Those who eat from it will receive eternal life and enjoy the tree of life in paradise with Adam and all the righteous (St. Hippolytus, *On Proverbs* fragment).

11:31 repaid: Disciplined by the Lord for his wrongdoing (3:11–12). The proverb reads differently in the Greek LXX, which states: "If the righteous man is barely saved, where will the ungodly man and sinner appear?" • Peter quotes the Greek version of this passage with reference to God's judgment in 1 Pet 4:18.

12:1 discipline: Either divine correction (3:11–12) or verbal correction by one with the courage to admonish another for his misdeeds (Gal 6:1; Jas 5:19–20). Unlike the wise, who accept correction for their own good (9:8–9), the foolish take offense when others reproach them (9:7).

12:3 the root: Evokes the image of a sturdy tree (11:30), whose roots provide an immovable foundation for its life and growth (10:30; Ps 1:3).

12:4 A good wife: The joy and honor of her husband (Sir 26:1). The virtues of a praiseworthy wife are elaborated in 31:10–31.

12:7 house of the righteous: The lesson of the proverb is similarly illustrated by Jesus in the parable of the Builders (Mt 7:24–27; Lk 6:47–49).

12:9 plays the great man: I.e., pretends to be a wealthy and important person (13:7).

12:10 his beast: The wise man is humane in his treatment of animals (Deut 25:4). Unlike the wicked, who show little compassion or gentleness toward living creatures, the righteous do not exercise their God-given dominion over the beasts in a cruel or tyrannical way (Gen 1:28) (CCC 2416–18).

12:11 He who tills: A similar proverb appears in 28:19.

12:15 listens to advice: On the importance of wise counsel, see 11:14, 15:22, and 24:6.

12:16 ignores an insult: The wise man possesses the inner strength to control both his temper and his tongue when provoked (29:11).

12:19 for ever: Honesty earns lasting respect. **for a moment:** Dishonesty, whatever its short-term benefits, is eventually exposed and punished.

12:20 plan good: Or, better, "advise peace". The NT likewise esteems those who promote peace between people (Mt 5:9; Rom 12:18; Heb 12:14).

12:22 Lying lips: Also declared abominable to the Lord in 6:16–17 (CCC 2482–86).

12:23 conceals his knowledge: Prudence recognizes that silence is sometimes better than speech (21:23; Sir 20:5–7). Imprudence displays itself when someone tries to impress others with his intelligence and/or learning and comes off looking like a know-it-all who talks too much. See note on 10:19.

---

^wCn Compare Gk Syr: Heb *a wise man.*
^xCn: The Hebrew of verse 12 is obscure.
^yHeb *the heart of fools.*

26A righteous man turns away from evil,**z**
  but the way of the wicked leads them astray.
27A slothful man will not catch his prey,**a**
  but the diligent man will get precious wealth.**b**
28In the path of righteousness is life,
  but the way of error leads to death.**c**

13 A wise son hears his father's instruction,
  but a scoffer does not listen to rebuke.
2From the fruit of his mouth a good man eats good,
  but the desire of the treacherous is for violence.
3He who guards his mouth preserves his life;
  he who opens wide his lips comes to ruin.
4The soul of the sluggard craves, and gets nothing,
  while the soul of the diligent is richly supplied.
5A righteous man hates falsehood,
  but a wicked man acts shamefully and
  disgracefully.
6Righteousness guards him whose way is upright,
  but sin overthrows the wicked.
7One man pretends to be rich, yet has nothing;
  another pretends to be poor, yet has great
  wealth.
8The ransom of a man's life is his wealth,
  but a poor man has no means of redemption.**d**
9The light of the righteous rejoices,
  but the lamp of the wicked will be put out.
10By insolence the heedless make strife,
  but with those who take advice is wisdom.
11Wealth hastily gotten**e** will dwindle,
  but he who gathers little by little will increase it.
12Hope deferred makes the heart sick,
  but a desire fulfilled is a tree of life.

13He who despises the word brings destruction on
  himself,
  but he who respects the commandment will be
  rewarded.
14The teaching of the wise is a fountain of life,
  that one may avoid the snares of death.
15Good sense wins favor,
  but the way of the faithless is their ruin.**f**
16In everything a prudent man acts with
  knowledge,
  but a fool flaunts his folly.
17A bad messenger plunges men into trouble,
  but a faithful envoy brings healing.
18Poverty and disgrace come to him who ignores
  instruction,
  but he who heeds reproof is honored.
19A desire fulfilled is sweet to the soul;
  but to turn away from evil is an abomination
  to fools.
20He who walks with wise men becomes wise,
  but the companion of fools will suffer harm.
21Misfortune pursues sinners,
  but prosperity rewards the righteous.
22A good man leaves an inheritance to his
  children's children,
  but the sinner's wealth is laid up for the
  righteous.
23The fallow ground of the poor yields much food,
  but it is swept away through injustice.
24He who spares the rod hates his son,
  but he who loves him is diligent to discipline
  him.

12:27 catch his prey: Or, "roast his game". The proverb appears to rebuke one who is too lazy to hunt for food, just as other proverbs frown upon one who is too lazy to tend and harvest his fields (6:6–11; 10:4–5; 12:11).

13:1 scoffer: One who mocks the idea of upright and responsible living (1:22; 9:7; 15:12).

13:2 eats good: Enjoys peace and happiness. **violence:** Wicked persons have no qualms about the ruthless use of force to get what they desire (1:11; 4:17).

13:3 guards his mouth: Either by keeping silent or by using careful and thoughtful speech when appropriate (11:12; 17:27–28; 21:23; Sir 20:1–7). **opens wide his lips:** Indicates one who speaks rashly, thoughtlessly, and excessively (10:19; 12:18; 18:7).

13:5 hates falsehood: I.e., because he lives by the standards of God, who hates "a lying tongue" (6:17).

13:7 pretends: An act of foolishness that only deceives others and causes them to form a false judgment about the person (12:9; CCC 2477).

13:8 no means of redemption: The poor have no money or valuables to pay off an enemy in exchange for their life. In this respect, at least, poverty is an advantage over possessing great wealth, since the less fortunate are less likely to become targets for individuals seeking ransom money.

13:9 light: A symbol of life (4:18).

13:10 the heedless: Those who are too proud and self-confident to learn from the wise counsel of others (12:15; 15:12).

13:11 hastily gotten: Literally, "from vanity". Presumably this refers to acquiring money in dishonorable ways. **little by little:** One of the benefits of diligence and industry is financial abundance for one's family (12:11, 27; 13:22).

13:12 a tree of life: A source of deep satisfaction. See note on 3:18.

13:13 word ... commandment: Terms earlier associated with the teachings of wisdom passed on by parents to their children (e.g., 2:1; 3:1; 4:4; 7:1–2).

13:15 wins favor: From both God and neighbor (3:4; 8:35).

13:17 A bad messenger: An unreliable courier who misrepresents the sender to his intended recipients.

13:20 walks with: A proverb about the importance of keeping good company and avoiding the companionship of fools. The saying implies that one becomes like those who surround him, for good or ill.

13:22 inheritance: The wise are careful to set aside wealth for the benefit of their children and grandchildren (2 Cor 12:14). **sinner's wealth:** A similar sentiment is expressed in Job 27:16–17.

13:23 injustice: Oppression by the powerful and influential appears to be in view.

13:24 spares the rod: I.e., fails to correct sinful and childish behavior. Neglect of a child's moral formation is a grave disservice that robs young people of the virtues necessary to live in God's favor and to conduct themselves honorably at home and in society (29:17). Elsewhere in Proverbs, the rod

---

zCn: The meaning of the Hebrew is uncertain.
aCn Compare Gk Syr: The meaning of the Hebrew is uncertain.
bCn: The meaning of the Hebrew is uncertain.
cCn: The meaning of the Hebrew is uncertain.
dCn: Heb *does not hear rebuke*.
eGk Vg: Heb *from vanity*.
fCn Compare Gk Syr Vg Tg: Heb *is enduring*.

²⁵The righteous has enough to satisfy his appetite,
  but the belly of the wicked suffers want.

14 Wisdom*ᵍ* builds her house,
  but folly with her own hands tears it down.

²He who walks in uprightness fears the LORD,
  but he who is devious in his ways despises
    him.

³The talk of a fool is a rod for his back,*ʰ*
  but the lips of the wise will preserve them.

⁴Where there are no oxen, there is no*ⁱ* grain;
  but abundant crops come by the strength of
    the ox.

⁵A faithful witness does not lie,
  but a false witness breathes out lies.

⁶A scoffer seeks wisdom in vain,
  but knowledge is easy for a man of
    understanding.

⁷Leave the presence of a fool,
  for there you do not meet words of knowledge.

⁸The wisdom of a prudent man is to discern his way,
  but the folly of fools is deceiving.

⁹God scorns the wicked,*ʲ*
  but the upright enjoy his favor.

¹⁰The heart knows its own bitterness,
  and no stranger shares its joy.

¹¹The house of the wicked will be destroyed,
  but the tent of the upright will flourish.

¹²There is a way which seems right to a man,
  but its end is the way to death.*ᵏ*

¹³Even in laughter the heart is sad,
  and the end of joy is grief.

¹⁴A perverse man will be filled with the fruit of his
    ways,
  and a good man with the fruit of his deeds.*ˡ*

¹⁵The simple believes everything,
  but the prudent looks where he is going.

¹⁶A wise man is cautious and turns away from
    evil,
  but a fool throws off restraint and is careless.

¹⁷A man of quick temper acts foolishly,
  but a man of discretion is patient.*ᵐ*

¹⁸The simple acquire folly,
  but the prudent are crowned with knowledge.

¹⁹The evil bow down before the good,
  the wicked at the gates of the righteous.

²⁰The poor is disliked even by his neighbor,
  but the rich has many friends.

²¹He who despises his neighbor is a sinner,
  but happy is he who is kind to the poor.

²²Do they not err that devise evil?
  Those who devise good meet loyalty and
    faithfulness.

²³In all toil there is profit,
  but mere talk tends only to want.

²⁴The crown of the wise is their wisdom,*ⁿ*
  but folly is the garland*ᵒ* of fools.

²⁵A truthful witness saves lives,
  but one who utters lies is a betrayer.

²⁶In the fear of the LORD one has strong confidence,
  and his children will have a refuge.

²⁷The fear of the LORD is a fountain of life,
  that one may avoid the snares of death.

---

of discipline is said to cleanse the heart of evil (20:30), to rid a child's life of foolishness (22:15), to impart wisdom (29:15), and to save a child from death (23:13–14). Ultimately, parents who lovingly discipline their children imitate the fatherly ways of God, who reproves his people in order to train them in righteousness (3:11–12; Deut 8:5; Heb 12:5–11) (CCC 2221–24).

14:1 Wisdom: The Hebrew is "Wisdom of women", and the Greek LXX reads "Wise women". The saying appears to praise wives and mothers who manage their households well, that is, in a way that **builds** up and strengthens the family. For the virtues of home management, see 31:10–31.

14:2 fears the LORD: Faith and morality form a unity in the vision of Proverbs. See note on 1:7.

14:3 rod for his back: Careless speech has a way of coming back to smite the foolish man, making him suffer for his reckless use of words (10:13; 26:3).

14:4 oxen: Animals without which farmlands would produce little food. Perhaps this observation is a reminder to treat one's livestock humanely, since beasts of burden are indispensable for life in an agricultural society (12:10; CCC 2416–18).

14:6 in vain: Because the one who scoffs at responsible living neither fears God (1:7) nor regards the counsel and correction of others (9:7–8; 13:1; 15:12).

14:11 house ... destroyed: Similar to the proverb in 12:7.

14:12 a way which seems right: Points to the fact that fallen human beings often have a faulty perception of reality. Because sin darkens and impairs the intellect, people have a frightening capacity for erroneous judgment and self-deception (Is 5:20; Rom 1:20–22; Eph 4:17–19). This proverb appears again in 16:25.

14:13 end of joy: An observational proverb, pointing out that happiness in this life is never permanent or undiluted.

14:15 believes everything: The simpleton is gullible and therefore susceptible to foolish behavior because he lacks the virtue of prudence, which counsels against carelessness and throwing off moral restraints (see 14:16; CCC 1806).

✠ **14:17 quick temper:** Persons who are easily angered are prone to commit sins of passion (29:22). The wise man controls his emotions in order to avoid the transgressions that typically follow when tempers flare up (14:29; 15:18; 19:19; Jas 1:19–20). • If you become angry, conquer your wrath with reason. Be angry that you have become so easily roused, and you will not sin. One who is angry with himself ceases to be angry with another (St. Ambrose, *Duties of the Clergy* 1, 21).

14:21 a sinner: Because the Lord commands us to love our neighbor (Lev 19:18). **kind to the poor:** Concern for persons in need means sharing food with them (22:9) and defending their rights (31:9). These and similar acts of kindness bring honor to God (14:31) (CCC 2443–49).

14:23 toil ... mere talk: Hard work is contrasted with unproductive chatter.

14:26 children: God's blessings are enjoyed by entire families when parents revere the Lord and teach their sons and daughters to do likewise (Deut 6:1–7).

14:27 fountain of life: Similar to the proverb in 13:14.

ᵍHeb *Wisdom of women.*
ʰCn: Heb *a rod of pride.*
ⁱHeb *a manger of.*
ʲCn: Heb *obscure.*
ᵏHeb *ways of death.*
ˡCn: Heb *from upon him.*
ᵐGk: Heb *is hated.*
ⁿCn Compare Gk: Heb *riches.*
ᵒCn: Heb *folly.*

²⁸In a multitude of people is the glory of a king,
  but without people a prince is ruined.
²⁹He who is slow to anger has great understanding,
  but he who has a hasty temper exalts folly.
³⁰A tranquil mind gives life to the flesh,
  but passion makes the bones rot.
³¹He who oppresses a poor man insults his Maker,
  but he who is kind to the needy honors him.
³²The wicked is overthrown through his evil-doing,
  but the righteous finds refuge through his
    integrity.ᵖ
³³Wisdom abides in the mind of a man of
    understanding,
  but it is not�q known in the heart of fools.
³⁴Righteousness exalts a nation,
  but sin is a reproach to any people.
³⁵A servant who deals wisely has the king's favor,
  but his wrath falls on one who acts shamefully.

15 A soft answer turns away wrath,
  but a harsh word stirs up anger.
²The tongue of the wise dispenses knowledge,ʳ
  but the mouths of fools pour out folly.
³The eyes of the Lord are in every place,
  keeping watch on the evil and the good.
⁴A gentle tongue is a tree of life,
  but perverseness in it breaks the spirit.
⁵A fool despises his father's instruction,
  but he who heeds admonition is prudent.

⁶In the house of the righteous there is much treasure,
  but trouble befalls the income of the wicked.
⁷The lips of the wise spread knowledge;
  not so the minds of fools.
⁸The sacrifice of the wicked is an abomination to
    the Lord,
  but the prayer of the upright is his delight.
⁹The way of the wicked is an abomination to the
    Lord,
  but he loves him who pursues righteousness.
¹⁰There is severe discipline for him who forsakes
    the way;
  he who hates reproof will die.
¹¹Sheol and Abad′don lie open before the Lord,
  how much more the hearts of men!
¹²A scoffer does not like to be reproved;
  he will not go to the wise.
¹³A glad heart makes a cheerful countenance,
  but by sorrow of heart the spirit is broken.
¹⁴The mind of him who has understanding seeks
    knowledge,
  but the mouths of fools feed on folly.
¹⁵All the days of the afflicted are evil,
  but a cheerful heart has a continual feast.
¹⁶Better is a little with the fear of the Lord
  than great treasure and trouble with it.
¹⁷Better is a dinner of herbs where love is
  than a fatted ox and hatred with it.

14:31 insults his Maker: Because every person, rich and poor alike, is made in the image of God (22:2; Gen 1:26). The Lord will hold perpetrators of injustice accountable for their shameful treatment of the needy (17:5; Mt 25:41–45).

14:33 heart: The Bible often associates mental activity with the heart, which denotes the hidden interior of the person, where the faculties of intellect and will were said to operate and human emotions were said to originate. See word study: *Heart* at Deut 30:6.

14:34 exalts a nation: The welfare of entire nations depends upon their commitment to live and to legislate according to the standards of God. The nation of Israel stands as the premier example of this in the Bible. When it adheres to the Lord's ways, it prospers under the blessings of the covenant (Deut 28:1-14); but when it abandons the Lord and allows sin to reign in society and its institutions, it suffers the curses of the covenant, manifest in such things as poverty, sickness, famine, and conflict on a broad scale (Deut 28:15-68).

15:1 soft answer: An observational proverb that advocates controlling one's temper and tongue. For similar sayings on this theme, see 10:19; 12:16; 13:3; 14:29; 15:18; 21:23.

15:3 in every place: Affirms the omniscience of God, meaning that all human actions are seen and known by the Lord (5:21; Job 34:21), even the hidden thoughts and intentions of a person's heart (15:11; 1 Sam 16:7; Ps 139:1; Heb 4:12–13).

15:4 a tree of life: A source of refreshment and encouragement for others. See note on 3:18. **perverseness:** Here this refers to sins of speech that injure the reputation of others. This includes slander, rash comments, and bearing false witness against the innocent (10:18; 11:9; 12:18; CCC 2476-78).

15:6 In the house: Behind this statement is the ancient theory of retribution, the belief that God's just recompense for saints and sinners is meted out in this life as prosperity (**treasure**) and adversity (**trouble**). Additional revelation, beginning in the OT and coming to fullness in the NT, will show that divine rewards and punishments are also given after death (Wis 3:1–4; Dan 12:2; Mt 25:46). Moreover, the prospect of "treasure" for the righteous is not restricted to material wealth but can also denote spiritual blessings (Mt 6:19–21; 2 Cor 8:9).

15:8 sacrifice of the wicked: Unacceptable to the Lord, who expects our worship to be joined to a contrite heart and a commitment to live by his laws. Scripture insists that the liturgical and ethical aspects of life must be in harmony; otherwise, the Lord is not honored by our praise and adoration (1 Sam 15:22; Ps 50:23; 51:16–17; Is 1:11–17; Amos 5:21–24). **prayer of the upright:** The wise man is also a prayerful man. See note on 2:6.

15:9 pursues righteousness: Strives to observe the Lord's commandments (Deut 6:25; Lk 1:6). • Jesus affirms the essential message of this proverb in the fourth Beatitude (Mt 5:6).

15:10 severe discipline: Administered by God (3:11–12). **the way:** The path of upright living. See note on 1:15.

15:11 Sheol and Abaddon: Two Hebrew terms associated with the netherworld of the dead, the latter meaning "destruction" (27:20; Job 28:22). Even the realm of deceased souls, thought to be hidden deep in the earth, is visible to the penetrating eyes of the Lord (Job 26:6). How much more, the proverb reasons, are the secrets of **men** known by the Lord. See note on 15:3.

15:15 a cheerful heart: One that rises above difficult circumstances and finds joy in the Lord such as Israel experienced during its religious feasts (Lev 23:40; 2 Chron 30:21, 26).

15:16 a little: Having modest means and possessions. Blessedness lies, not in great wealth, but in a living relationship with God. For similar sayings, see 16:7, 17:1, and Ps 37:16.

ᵖGk Syr: Heb *in his death.*
qGk Syr: Heb *lacks not.*
ʳCn: Heb *makes knowledge good.*

¹⁸A hot-tempered man stirs up strife,
but he who is slow to anger quiets contention.
¹⁹The way of a sluggard is overgrown with
thorns,
but the path of the upright is a level highway.
²⁰A wise son makes a glad father,
but a foolish man despises his mother.
²¹Folly is a joy to him who has no sense,
but a man of understanding walks aright.
²²Without counsel plans go wrong,
but with many advisers they succeed.
²³To make an apt answer is a joy to a man,
and a word in season, how good it is!
²⁴The wise man's path leads upward to life,
that he may avoid Sheol beneath.
²⁵The LORD tears down the house of the proud,
but maintains the widow's boundaries.
²⁶The thoughts of the wicked are an abomination
to the LORD,
the words of the pure are pleasing to him.ˢ
²⁷He who is greedy for unjust gain makes trouble
for his household,
but he who hates bribes will live.
²⁸The mind of the righteous ponders how to
answer,
but the mouth of the wicked pours out evil
things.
²⁹The LORD is far from the wicked,
but he hears the prayer of the righteous.

³⁰The light of the eyes rejoices the heart,
and good news refreshesᵗ the bones.
³¹He whose ear heeds wholesome admonition
will abide among the wise.
³²He who ignores instruction despises himself,
but he who heeds admonition gains
understanding.
³³The fear of the LORD is instruction in wisdom,
and humility goes before honor.

Solomon's Proverbs on Life and Conduct

16 The plans of the mind belong to man,
but the answer of the tongue is from the
LORD.
²All the ways of a man are pure in his own eyes,
but the LORD weighs the spirit.
³Commit your work to the LORD,
and your plans will be established.
⁴The LORD has made everything for its purpose,
even the wicked for the day of trouble.
⁵Every one who is arrogant is an abomination to
the LORD;
be assured, he will not go unpunished.
⁶By loyalty and faithfulness iniquity is atoned for,
and by the fear of the LORD a man avoids evil.
⁷When a man's ways please the LORD,
he makes even his enemies to be at peace with
him.
⁸Better is a little with righteousness
than great revenues with injustice.

15:19 overgrown: A sign of laziness—in this case, the refusal to put forth the effort to live honorably and wisely (24:30–31). **level highway:** The result of personal diligence and a commitment to clear away obstacles that stand in the way of following wisdom (CCC 2427–28).

15:20 A wise son: A variation of the proverb at 10:1.

15:22 counsel: On the importance of wise advice, see 11:14; 12:15; 24:6.

15:23 a word in season: A thoughtful and well-timed comment (25:11).

15:24 upward to life: One of the blessings of wise conduct is prolonged life (3:16; 9:11). Death is thereby delayed, and one avoids for a time the netherworld of **Sheol**. Once belief in an afterlife had clearly formed in the theology of Israel, thanks to additional revelation, sayings such as this suggested the idea that wisdom leads to eternal life in heaven.

15:25 widow's: The Lord's concern for widows is frequently stated in the Bible (Ex 22:22; Deut 10:18; Ps 68:5; 146:9; Sir 35:14; Jas 1:27; etc.). **boundaries:** Stone landmarks used to identify property lines. Moving them was tantamount to stealing another's land (22:28; 23:10; Deut 19:14; CCC 2403).

15:27 He who is greedy: A reference to corrupt judges who accept bribe money.

15:29 prayer of the righteous: Their intercession is powerful in gaining a favorable response from the Lord (Jas 5:16).

15:30 light of the eyes: The bright and exuberant look of one who delivers good news.

15:33 fear of the LORD: The first step toward living wisely. See note on 1:7. **humility goes before honor:** A humble estimation of self is an essential virtue of wisdom (3:34; 18:12)

and leads eventually to one's exaltation (Mt 23:12; 1 Pet 5:6). The opposite truth is stated in the proverb, "Pride goes ... before a fall" (16:18).

16:1 plans ... answer: Though somewhat obscure, the proverb seems to refer to the mystery that things do not always go as people plan, for sometimes God wills or permits an occurrence that overrides human intentions.

16:2 in his own eyes: For this idea, see note on 14:12.

16:3 will be established: The Lord can prosper our work when we dedicate it to him and ask for his help (3:6; Ps 90:17; 127:1).

16:4 day of trouble: A day of divine judgment when hardship or death befalls the wicked man and the justice of God is made manifest in history (11:4; Rom 3:5–6).

✝ **16:6 loyalty and faithfulness:** Tangible acts of kindness and mercy toward others performed as acts of repentance (CCC 1434, 1438). One who practices charity draws near to God and becomes more like him, whose loyal and faithful commitment to his people is frequently mentioned in the Bible (Ex 34:6; Ps 86:15; 108:4; 115:1). For the Hebrew term rendered "loyalty", see word study: *Steadfast Love* at Ex 34:6. **iniquity is atoned for:** Not that good works can absolve the eternal guilt of our sins, which only God can do, but they can lessen or eliminate the debt of temporal suffering that sin also imposes on our lives. Atonement in this sense is the effort of the penitent to make up for his wrongdoing by exercising the love he withheld when committing sin. See Tob 12:9; Sir 3:14, 30; and note on Dan 4:27. • The Lord, indicating how we can be pure, also says that alms must be given. He who is merciful advises that mercy be shown to others; and since he seeks the salvation of those he redeemed at a great cost, he teaches that persons polluted after the grace of baptism can once again be cleansed (St. Cyprian, *Works and Almsgiving* 2).

16:8 Better is a little: Similar to the proverbs in 15:16–17.

ˢCn Compare Gk: Heb *pleasant words are pure.*
ᵗHeb *makes fat.*

⁹A man's mind plans his way,
  but the Lord directs his steps.
¹⁰Inspired decisions are on the lips of a king;
  his mouth does not sin in judgment.
¹¹A just balance and scales are the Lord's;
  all the weights in the bag are his work.
¹²It is an abomination to kings to do evil,
  for the throne is established by righteousness.
¹³Righteous lips are the delight of a king,
  and he loves him who speaks what is right.
¹⁴A king's wrath is a messenger of death,
  and a wise man will appease it.
¹⁵In the light of a king's face there is life,
  and his favor is like the clouds that bring the
  spring rain.
¹⁶To get wisdom is betterᵘ than gold;
  to get understanding is to be chosen rather
  than silver.
¹⁷The highway of the upright turns aside from
  evil;
  he who guards his way preserves his life.
¹⁸Pride goes before destruction,
  and a haughty spirit before a fall.
¹⁹It is better to be of a lowly spirit with the poor
  than to divide the spoil with the proud.
²⁰He who gives heed to the word will prosper,
  and happy is he who trusts in the Lord.
²¹The wise of heart is called a man of discernment,
  and pleasant speech increases persuasiveness.

²²Wisdom is a fountain of life to him who has it,
  but folly is the chastisement of fools.
²³The mind of the wise makes his speech judicious,
  and adds persuasiveness to his lips.
²⁴Pleasant words are like a honeycomb,
  sweetness to the soul and health to the body.
²⁵There is a way which seems right to a man,
  but its end is the way to death.ᵛ
²⁶A worker's appetite works for him;
  his mouth urges him on.
²⁷A worthless man plots evil,
  and his speech is like a scorching fire.
²⁸A perverse man spreads strife,
  and a whisperer separates close friends.
²⁹A man of violence entices his neighbor
  and leads him in a way that is not good.
³⁰He who winks his eyes plansʷ perverse things,
  he who compresses his lips brings evil to
  pass.
³¹A hoary head is a crown of glory;
  it is gained in a righteous life.
³²He who is slow to anger is better than the
  mighty,
  and he who rules his spirit than he who takes
  a city.
³³The lot is cast into the lap,
  but the decision is wholly from the Lord.

17 Better is a dry morsel with quiet
  than a house full of feasting with strife.

16:9 plans ... directs: Scripture affirms human free will (Deut 30:11–14; Sir 15:15) as well as divine sovereignty over the world (Ps 37:23; 135:6; Rom 9:19–23). How the two operate together in the choices and plans and experiences of life is a theological mystery that lies beyond the grasp of human understanding.

16:10–15 A cluster of proverbs dealing with kings. Implied in these sayings is the notion that kings in Israel had a unique relationship with God as his representatives on earth.

16:10 Inspired decisions: The king, by virtue of his anointing, was helped by the Lord in rendering justice to his people. This is most clearly illustrated in the life of Solomon (1 Kings 3:16–28).

16:11 A just balance: Used for honest business dealings. See note on 11:1. **weights in the bag:** Merchants used stones of different sizes to weigh out goods in the marketplace (Mic 6:11).

16:15 light of a king's face: A shining countenance is poetic imagery for the benevolence of a superior shown toward a person of lesser rank (Num 6:25–26). **spring rain:** Anticipates a harvest of blessings to come (Ps 72:6; Hos 6:3).

16:16 better than gold: The value of wisdom exceeds even the most esteemed treasures of the world (3:13–14; 8:10, 19).

16:18 Pride ... before a fall: The person who is arrogant, overconfident, or inflated with self-importance is destined for humiliation (11:12; Mt 23:12), for "God opposes the proud" (1 Pet 5:5). On the other hand, Proverbs teaches that "humility goes before honor" (15:33; 18:12).

16:20 happy: For the meaning of this, see word study: *Blessed* at Ps 1:1. **trusts in the Lord:** Along with a reverent

fear of the Lord (1:7; 9:10), personal adherence to the Lord is fundamental to a life of authentic wisdom (3:5–6; Ps 34:8; 84:12).

16:21 pleasant speech: The wise choose their words carefully so as to speak persuasively (16:23) and encouragingly to others (16:24).

16:22 a fountain of life: A source of prudent discernment that leads to a prosperous life.

16:25 There is a way: The same proverb appears in 14:12.

16:27 like a scorching fire: Slanderous and inflammatory speech provokes anger in others (15:1) and causes evil to spread (Jas 3:6). It is particularly destructive to personal relationships (16:28).

16:30 He who winks: A perpetrator of mischief (6:12–13; 10:10).

16:31 hoary head: White hair not only represents the wisdom of years (20:29), but it can be a sign of a life prolonged by wise living (3:16; 10:27).

16:32 slow to anger: The wise know how to control their temper and exercise the virtue of meekness (14:29; 15:18; 19:11; Jas 1:19). • Taking cities is a lesser victory than controlling anger because these places are outside of us. The greater victory is achieved by patience, for then a person conquers and subdues himself, enabling him to bear with others in humility (St. Gregory the Great, *Homilies on the Gospels* 35).

16:33 lot: Perhaps an allusion to one of the sacred lots, called Urim and Thummim, which were kept in the breast-piece of the high priest (Lev 8:8). Marked sticks or stones that were cast like dice, lots were used to discern the Lord's will for Israel in specific situations (Num 27:21; 1 Sam 28:6). Other types of lots could be cast in non-cultic situations (Neh 11:1; Ps 22:18).

17:1 Better: For similar "better than" proverbs, see 15:16–17 and 16:8.

ᵘGk Syr Vg Tg: Heb *how much better.*
ᵛHeb *ways of death.*
ʷGk Syr Vg Tg: Heb *to plan.*

²A slave who deals wisely will rule over a son who
    acts shamefully,
    and will share the inheritance as one of the
        brothers.
³The crucible is for silver, and the furnace is for
    gold,
    and the LORD tries hearts.
⁴An evildoer listens to wicked lips;
    and a liar gives heed to a mischievous tongue.
⁵He who mocks the poor insults his Maker;
    he who is glad at calamity will not go
        unpunished.
⁶Grandchildren are the crown of the aged,
    and the glory of sons is their fathers.
⁷Fine speech is not becoming to a fool;
    still less is false speech to a prince.
⁸A bribe is like a magic stone in the eyes of him
    who gives it;
    wherever he turns he prospers.
⁹He who forgives an offense seeks love,
    but he who repeats a matter alienates a friend.
¹⁰A rebuke goes deeper into a man of understanding
    than a hundred blows into a fool.
¹¹An evil man seeks only rebellion,
    and a cruel messenger will be sent against
        him.
¹²Let a man meet a she-bear robbed of her cubs,
    rather than a fool in his folly.
¹³If a man returns evil for good,
    evil will not depart from his house.
¹⁴The beginning of strife is like letting out water;
    so quit before the quarrel breaks out.

¹⁵He who justifies the wicked and he who
        condemns the righteous
    are both alike an abomination to the LORD.
¹⁶Why should a fool have a price in his hand to buy
    wisdom,
    when he has no mind?
¹⁷A friend loves at all times,
    and a brother is born for adversity.
¹⁸A man without sense gives a pledge,
    and becomes surety in the presence of his
        neighbor.
¹⁹He who loves transgression loves strife;
    he who makes his door high seeks destruction.
²⁰A man of crooked mind does not prosper,
    and one with a perverse tongue falls into
        calamity.
²¹A stupid son is a grief to a father;
    and the father of a fool has no joy.
²²A cheerful heart is a good medicine,
    but a downcast spirit dries up the bones.
²³A wicked man accepts a bribe from the bosom
    to pervert the ways of justice.
²⁴A man of understanding sets his face toward
    wisdom,
    but the eyes of a fool are on the ends of the earth.
²⁵A foolish son is a grief to his father
    and bitterness to her who bore him.
²⁶To impose a fine on a righteous man is not good;
    to flog noble men is wrong.
²⁷He who restrains his words has knowledge,
    and he who has a cool spirit is a man of
        understanding.

17:2 deals wisely: Wisdom is valued wherever it is found, irrespective of social classes and conventions. Only rarely would a household **slave** receive a share of a family's **inheritance** (Gen 15:3), as this was normally divided among the surviving sons (Deut 21:15–17).

17:3 the LORD tries hearts: I.e., he tests the genuineness of our faith in the fires of adversity (Sir 2:4–5; Jas 1:2–4; 1 Pet 1:6–7). Comparing this to the smelting of metals also suggests that suffering can purify our hearts of selfishness and misplaced priorities. Elsewhere in Proverbs we learn that God sees into the hiddenness of the heart (15:11) and even weighs the heart in order to determine its goodness (21:2; 24:12).

17:5 insults his Maker: Callous disdain for the needy is an offense against God, whose image is borne by every person he has made (Gen 1:27), whether rich or poor (22:2). This proverb is similar to the one in 14:31, only here the sin is defined, not as oppression, but as rejoicing in another's misfortune. By contrast, kindness to the poor is honored by the Lord (19:17) (CCC 2443–49).

17:8 magic stone: A bribe is like a charm that wins the favor of crooked men (17:23) and gains temporary advantages for its user.

17:9 forgives an offense: Literally, "covers a transgression", a Hebrew idiom for forgiveness (10:12; Neh 4:5; Ps 32:1). The point of the saying is that friendship is strengthened by mercy but undermined by detraction, i.e., the sin of publicizing the faults of another (CCC 2477).

17:10 rebuke: The wise take heed of correction (9:9; 10:17; 12:15), whereas fools take offense at admonishment from others (9:7–8; 13:1; 15:12).

17:12 rather than a fool: Facing the wrath of a protective mother bear is comparable to the danger of following or befriending a fool. Hence one is urged to avoid the company of the unwise (14:7).

17:14 quit before the quarrel: Readers are advised to be peacemakers (Mt 5:9). If one is locked in disagreement with another, he should try to ease the tension before it erupts into a full-scale conflict. Controlling one's temper is also an integral part of living wisely (14:29; 15:18; 17:27).

17:15 justifies the wicked: A warning against perverting legal justice. This occurs when judges knowingly acquit the guilty of their crimes and sentence the innocent to punishment (cf. Deut 25:1; Is 5:22–23).

17:16 a price: As though wisdom could be purchased with money.

17:17 born for adversity: A true friend is like a family member who stays by one's side in good times and in bad (18:24).

17:18 becomes surety: For the meaning of this, see note on 6:1.

17:19 makes his door high: A visual image of pride that comes before ruin (16:18; 18:12).

17:21 grief to a father: As well as sorrow and bitterness to a mother (10:1; 17:25).

17:24 ends of the earth: Implies that the fool is scattered in his pursuits and lacks focus on what is most important. In effect, his attention strays in all directions except toward wisdom.

17:26 fine ... flog: Two examples of judicial injustice (17:15).

17:27 restrains his words: Guarded speech is recommended as a virtue of wisdom (11:12; 21:23). **cool spirit:** One who is patient and slow to anger (14:29; 15:18; 16:32; 19:11).

²⁸Even a fool who keeps silent is considered wise;
　　when he closes his lips, he is deemed
　　intelligent.

18 He who is estranged[x] seeks pretexts[y]
　　to break out against all sound judgment.
²A fool takes no pleasure in understanding,
　　but only in expressing his opinion.
³When wickedness comes, contempt comes also;
　　and with dishonor comes disgrace.
⁴The words of a man's mouth are deep waters;
　　the fountain of wisdom is a gushing stream.
⁵It is not good to be partial to a wicked man,
　　or to deprive a righteous man of justice.
⁶A fool's lips bring strife,
　　and his mouth invites a flogging.
⁷A fool's mouth is his ruin,
　　and his lips are a snare to himself.
⁸The words of a whisperer are like delicious
　　morsels;
　　they go down into the inner parts of the body.
⁹He who is slack in his work
　　is a brother to him who destroys.
¹⁰The name of the Lord is a strong tower;
　　the righteous man runs into it and is safe.
¹¹A rich man's wealth is his strong city,
　　and like a high wall protecting him.[z]
¹²Before destruction a man's heart is haughty,
　　but humility goes before honor.
¹³If one gives answer before he hears,
　　it is his folly and shame.

¹⁴A man's spirit will endure sickness;
　　but a broken spirit who can bear?
¹⁵An intelligent mind acquires knowledge,
　　and the ear of the wise seeks knowledge.
¹⁶A man's gift makes room for him
　　and brings him before great men.
¹⁷He who states his case first seems right,
　　until the other comes and examines him.
¹⁸The lot puts an end to disputes
　　and decides between powerful contenders.
¹⁹A brother helped is like a strong city,[a]
　　but quarreling is like the bars of a castle.
²⁰From the fruit of his mouth a man is satisfied;
　　he is satisfied by the yield of his lips.
²¹Death and life are in the power of the tongue,
　　and those who love it will eat its fruits.
²²He who finds a wife finds a good thing,
　　and obtains favor from the Lord.
²³The poor use entreaties,
　　but the rich answer roughly.
²⁴There are[b] friends who pretend to be friends,[c]
　　but there is a friend who sticks closer than a
　　brother.

19 Better is a poor man who walks in his
　　integrity
　　than a man who is perverse in speech, and is
　　a fool.
²It is not good for a man to be without knowledge,
　　and he who makes haste with his feet misses
　　his way.

18:1 estranged: The meaning of the proverb is obscure. At a minimum, it observes that a person who alienates himself from others tends to be quarrelsome.

18:2 no pleasure: Unlike the wise person, who delights in gaining wisdom for life (18:15).

18:4 deep waters: Symbolic of profound insight (20:5). **fountain of wisdom:** Wise words are a source of refreshment and edification to those who listen (10:11; 13:14; 16:22).

18:5 not good: A warning to judges against showing favoritism from the bench (17:15). Justice must be rendered impartially to all without distinction (Lev 19:15; Deut 16:19–20).

18:6 a flogging: Either a lashing imposed by a court (19:29; Deut 25:2) or the undesirable consequences that follow in the wake of foolish speech (10:13; 18:7).

18:8 whisperer: One who spreads rumors and gossip. This activity is dangerous because others, being fallen human beings, tend to eat up unsavory reports like tasty desserts.

18:9 slack: For similar warnings against laziness, see 6:6–11; 10:4; 12:27; 19:15.

18:10–11 A contrast is implied in the juxtaposition of these two verses. The Lord is a fortress of protection for those who call upon his **name** in prayer and worship (Ps 18:2; 91:14; 144:1–2). Wealth, however, provides only a temporary and unstable **wall** of defense for those who are blessed with much. The value of riches is thus subordinated to a relationship with God (cf. Ps 52:6–7).

18:12 haughty ... humility: Combines sayings from 15:33 and 16:18.

18:13 before he hears: It is the mark of a fool to blurt out his opinions (18:2) before taking the time to listen (Sir 11:8). Instead, one should be "quick to hear" and "slow to speak" (Jas 1:19).

18:14 a broken spirit: A depressed and discouraged spirit, tempting the person to despair of brighter days in the future (cf. 15:13; 17:22).

18:15 mind: Literally, "heart", which is the locus of mental activity in the Hebrew conception of man. See word study: *Heart* at Deut 30:6.

18:16 man's gift: Possibly a bribe (17:8).

18:17 until the other: A practical observation about the importance of listening to both sides of a story.

18:18 lot: Casting lots was an equitable way of settling a matter under dispute. For its use in discerning God's will, see note on 16:33.

18:20 fruit of his mouth: Wise and gracious speech seems to be in view.

18:21 power of the tongue: A topic of reflection also in Sir 37:18–23 and Jas 3:1–12.

18:22 finds a wife: The goodness of marriage is affirmed as a gift from God. A husband is called to cherish his bride (5:18–19) and to recognize the Lord's blessing in a good and prudent wife (12:4; 19:14; 31:10). On a theological level, the value of "finding a wife" is comparable to the benefit of "finding wisdom" as one's companion for life; in both cases, **one obtains favor from the Lord** (8:35) (CCC 1603–5).

19:1 walks in his integrity: Lives an upright and honest life. The point of the saying is that even poverty is better than dishonesty (see 19:22).

19:2 he who makes haste: One who acts impulsively without reflecting on the wisdom of his actions (21:5; 29:20).

---

[x]Heb *separated.*
[y]Gk Vg: Heb *desire.*
[z]Or *in his imagination.*
[a]Gk Syr Vg Tg: The meaning of the Hebrew is uncertain.
[b]Syr Tg: Heb Syr Tg: Heb *A man of.*
[c]Cn Compare Syr Vg Tg: Heb Cn Compare Syr Vg Tg: Heb *to be broken.*

³When a man's folly brings his way to ruin,
  his heart rages against the LORD.
⁴Wealth brings many new friends,
  but a poor man is deserted by his friend.
⁵A false witness will not go unpunished,
  and he who utters lies will not escape.
⁶Many seek the favor of a generous man,
  and every one is a friend to a man who gives
  gifts.
⁷All a poor man's brothers hate him;
  how much more do his friends go far from
  him!
  He pursues them with words, but does not
  have them.ᵈ
⁸He who gets wisdom loves himself;
  he who keeps understanding will prosper.
⁹A false witness will not go unpunished,
  and he who utters lies will perish.
¹⁰It is not fitting for a fool to live in luxury,
  much less for a slave to rule over princes.
¹¹Good sense makes a man slow to anger,
  and it is his glory to overlook an offense.
¹²A king's wrath is like the growling of a lion,
  but his favor is like dew upon the grass.
¹³A foolish son is ruin to his father,
  and a wife's quarreling is a continual dripping
  of rain.
¹⁴House and wealth are inherited from fathers,
  but a prudent wife is from the LORD.
¹⁵Slothfulness casts into a deep sleep,
  and an idle person will suffer hunger.

¹⁶He who keeps the commandment keeps his life;
  he who despises the wordᵉ will die.
¹⁷He who is kind to the poor lends to the LORD,
  and he will repay him for his deed.
¹⁸Discipline your son while there is hope;
  do not set your heart on his destruction.
¹⁹A man of great wrath will pay the penalty;
  for if you deliver him, you will only have to do
  it again.ᶠ
²⁰Listen to advice and accept instruction,
  that you may gain wisdom for the future.
²¹Many are the plans in the mind of a man,
  but it is the purpose of the LORD that will be
  established.
²²What is desired in a man is loyalty,
  and a poor man is better than a liar.
²³The fear of the LORD leads to life;
  and he who has it rests satisfied;
  he will not be visited by harm.
²⁴The sluggard buries his hand in the dish,
  and will not even bring it back to his mouth.
²⁵Strike a scoffer, and the simple will learn
  prudence;
  reprove a man of understanding, and he will
  gain knowledge.
²⁶He who does violence to his father and chases
  away his mother
  is a son who causes shame and brings
  reproach.
²⁷Cease, my son, to hear instruction
  only to stray from the words of knowledge.

19:3 against the LORD: The fool is quick to blame God for his troubles. He should rather accept responsibility for his actions than suppose that the Lord is the cause of his folly (Sir 15:11–12).

19:4 poor ... deserted: An observation that poverty is a burden twice over, for its victims are not only penniless but often friendless (19:7). Wisdom counsels us to help the poor in their affliction (14:21, 31; 19:17; 22:9; 31:20) (CCC 2443–49).

19:5 a false witness: A proverb repeated nearly verbatim in 19:9. **not go unpunished:** Giving false testimony is a violation of divine law (Ex 20:16). Dishonesty such as this may go undetected by others, but the Lord, who sees all, will eventually bring the liar and perjurer to face his judgment (CCC 2476). See note on 15:3.

19:9 A false witness: Nearly identical to 19:5.

19:10 not fitting: Wisdom entails knowing one's place in the social order and not acting presumptuously. For similar sayings, see 30:21–22 and Eccles 10:5–7.

19:11 slow to anger: The wise make an effort to control their temper (14:29; 15:18; 16:32; Jas 1:19).

19:13 ruin ... rain: An observation that undisciplined children and a contentious spouse quickly erode happiness in the home.

19:14 a prudent wife: A portrait of her virtues is painted in 31:10–31. To be married to a wise and honorable woman is a sign of the Lord's favor (18:22).

19:15 sleep: A favorite activity of the lazy and unmotivated person (6:9–11; 20:13).

19:16 the commandment: Probably a reference, not to the Decalogue or other precepts of the Torah, but to the wis-

dom teachings enshrined in Proverbs. At least this is how earlier passages in the book use this language (2:1; 3:1; 7:1–2; etc.).

19:17 kind to the poor: By various acts of compassion and practical assistance, typically called almsgiving (Tob 4:7; Sir 17:22). The Lord promises to reward our works of mercy, sometimes with temporal blessings (Sir 29:12), but ultimately with his mercy (Tob 12:9; Sir 3:30) and the inheritance of eternal life (Mt 25:34–40; Lk 12:33). Concern for the rights and needs of the poor is expressed several times in Proverbs (14:31; 17:5; 21:13; 22:9) (CCC 1434, 2443–49). • Love for the poor is precious in the sight of God. He who transcends all and loves mercy will accept your bounty. Lend to him without fear, and you will receive back what you have given with interest (St. Cyril of Alexandria, *Commentary on Luke* 103).

19:18 Discipline: On parental correction, see note on 13:24. **his destruction:** Self-inflicted harm is the result of failing to train a child in proper behavior.

19:21 purpose of the LORD: The mystery of divine Providence is a real but inscrutable factor in making life choices. All of our plans should be made with an openness to God's will (CCC 303). See notes on 16:1 and 16:9.

19:23 fear of the LORD: One of the major themes in Proverbs. See note on 1:7.

19:24 buries his hand: An instance of comic exaggeration used to poke fun at laziness (26:15). It is based on the ancient custom of participants at a meal eating or dipping from a common bowl. The sluggard, being too lazy even to feed himself, is bound to "suffer hunger" (19:15).

19:26 causes shame: Wisdom teachers envisioned harsh judgments in store for rebellious children (20:20; 30:17). The Mosaic Law treated serious disrespect for parents as a capital crime (Ex 21:17; Deut 21:18–21).

ᵈHeb uncertain.
ᵉCn Compare 13:13: Heb *his ways.*
ᶠHeb obscure.

²⁸A worthless witness mocks at justice,
and the mouth of the wicked devours iniquity.
²⁹Condemnation is ready for scoffers,
and flogging for the backs of fools.

20 Wine is a mocker, strong drink a brawler;
and whoever is led astray by it is not wise.
²The dread wrath of a king is like the growling of
a lion;
he who provokes him to anger forfeits his
life.
³It is an honor for a man to keep aloof from strife;
but every fool will be quarreling.
⁴The sluggard does not plow in the autumn;
he will seek at harvest and have nothing.
⁵The purpose in a man's mind is like deep water,
but a man of understanding will draw it out.
⁶Many a man proclaims his own loyalty,
but a faithful man who can find?
⁷A righteous man who walks in his integrity—
blessed are his sons after him!
⁸A king who sits on the throne of judgment
winnows all evil with his eyes.
⁹Who can say, "I have made my heart clean;
I am pure from my sin"?
¹⁰Diverse weights and diverse measures
are both alike an abomination to the LORD.
¹¹Even a child makes himself known by his acts,
whether what he does is pure and right.
¹²The hearing ear and the seeing eye,
the LORD has made them both.

¹³Love not sleep, lest you come to poverty;
open your eyes, and you will have plenty of
bread.
¹⁴"It is bad, it is bad," says the buyer;
but when he goes away, then he boasts.
¹⁵There is gold, and abundance of costly stones;
but the lips of knowledge are a precious jewel.
¹⁶Take a man's garment when he has given surety
for a stranger,
and hold him in pledge when he gives surety
for foreigners.
¹⁷Bread gained by deceit is sweet to a man,
but afterward his mouth will be full of gravel.
¹⁸Plans are established by counsel;
by wise guidance wage war.
¹⁹He who goes about gossiping reveals secrets;
therefore do not associate with one who speaks
foolishly.
²⁰If one curses his father or his mother,
his lamp will be put out in utter darkness.
²¹An inheritance gotten hastily in the beginning
will in the end not be blessed.
²²Do not say, "I will repay evil";
wait for the LORD, and he will help you.
²³Diverse weights are an abomination to the LORD,
and false scales are not good.
²⁴A man's steps are ordered by the LORD;
how then can man understand his way?
²⁵It is a snare for a man to say rashly, "It is holy,"
and to reflect only after making his vows.

19:29 scoffers: Those who are set in their evil ways and mockingly refuse the counsels of wisdom (9:7; 13:1; 15:12).

20:1 strong drink: Excessive consumption of alcohol leads to all manner of foolish behavior (23:29–35; Sir 9:9; 31:29–30). Often the drunkard ends up in poverty (21:17; 23:21) (CCC 2290). See note on Eph 5:18.

20:2 wrath of a king: Recalls the first line of 19:12.

20:4 sluggard: The one who is too lazy to work his fields (cf. 10:5). **autumn:** In Palestine, crops were sown after the rains of October and November moistened the soil.

20:8 winnows: Winnowing was a procedure used by farmers to separate grain kernels from the husks of chaff that enclosed them. This was done with a fork-like shovel on a threshing floor (Mt 3:12). Here it serves as a metaphor for a king's ability to sift out perpetrators of **evil** from among his subjects. The idea is illustrated in the life of Solomon, who asked God for the wisdom to distinguish the guilty from the innocent (1 Kings 3:9) in legal cases brought before him (1 Kings 3:16–28).

20:9 Who can say: The question is rhetorical, implying that no one can purify himself from guilt incurred by wrongdoing. Only God has the power to take away sins (Ps 103:12; Jn 1:29) and to cleanse the heart of all unrighteousness (Ps 51:2, 10; 1 Jn 1:9).

20:10 weights: Stones used as counterweights on a scale. See note on 11:1. **measures:** The Hebrew refers to an *ephah*, a dry measure roughly equivalent to two-thirds of a bushel. Sellers could cheat the buyer by dealing out grain in baskets that were smaller in volume than the standard size (CCC 2409).

20:13 sleep: The unmotivated sluggard prefers napping to the hard work of growing and harvesting food (6:9–11).

20:14 It is bad: The words of one who bargains with a merchant by downplaying the worth of his product in order to buy it at a lower price.

20:15 knowledge: More valuable than precious metals and gemstones (3:13–15).

20:16 surety: In this case a piece of clothing used as a pledge or collateral against someone else's debt (cf. Ex 22:26). See note on 6:1.

20:17 full of gravel: A graphic depiction of remorse and regret (cf. Job 20:12–14).

20:18 counsel: Kings typically consulted royal advisors when making decisions about political and military policy (2 Sam 16:23; 1 Kings 12:6–11).

20:20 curses his father: A capital crime in ancient Israel (Ex 21:17). **Lamp ... put out:** An image of one's life or well-being being snuffed out by some calamity (13:9).

20:21 gotten hastily: Implies that something irregular or even dishonorable was involved in the acquisition of the inheritance (cf. 13:11). An example may be seen in the opening verses of the parable of the Prodigal Son (Lk 15:11–16).

20:22 I will repay: Exacting personal revenge is forbidden. Instead, one should entrust his (non-criminal) grievances to the justice of the Lord (24:29; Sir 28:1). This is also the explicit teaching of the NT (Mt 5:38–41; Rom 12:17–19; 1 Pet 3:9) (CCC 2262).

20:23 Diverse weights: Restates the point made in 20:10. **false scales:** Used to cheat buyers in the marketplace. See note on 11:1.

20:24 ordered by the LORD: God's Providence is a mystery that touches our everyday lives and actions. See note on 16:9.

20:25 vows: Money or other valuables could be dedicated to the Lord's sanctuary with a vow. Because items set apart for religious service became **holy**, it was better not to vow an offering in the first place than to change one's mind and withhold it after the pledge had already been made (Deut 23:21–23; Eccles 5:4–5).

²⁶A wise king winnows the wicked,
and drives the wheel over them.
²⁷The spirit of man is the lamp of the LORD,
searching all his innermost parts.
²⁸Loyalty and faithfulness preserve the king
and his throne is upheld by righteousness.ᵍ
²⁹The glory of young men is their strength,
but the beauty of old men is their gray hair.
³⁰Blows that wound cleanse away evil;
strokes make clean the innermost parts.

21 The king's heart is a stream of water in the hand of the LORD;
he turns it wherever he will.
²Every way of a man is right in his own eyes,
but the LORD weighs the heart.
³To do righteousness and justice
is more acceptable to the LORD than sacrifice.
⁴Haughty eyes and a proud heart,
the lamp of the wicked, are sin.
⁵The plans of the diligent lead surely to abundance,
but every one who is hasty comes only to want.
⁶The getting of treasures by a lying tongue
is a fleeting vapor and a snare of death.

⁷The violence of the wicked will sweep them away,
because they refuse to do what is just.
⁸The way of the guilty is crooked,
but the conduct of the pure is right.
⁹It is better to live in a corner of the housetop
than in a house shared with a contentious woman.
¹⁰The soul of the wicked desires evil;
his neighbor finds no mercy in his eyes.
¹¹When a scoffer is punished, the simple becomes wise;
when a wise man is instructed, he gains knowledge.
¹²The righteous observes the house of the wicked;
the wicked are cast down to ruin.
¹³He who closes his ear to the cry of the poor
will himself cry out and not be heard.
¹⁴A gift in secret averts anger;
and a bribe in the bosom, strong wrath.
¹⁵When justice is done, it is a joy to the righteous,
but dismay to evildoers.
¹⁶A man who wanders from the way of understanding
will rest in the assembly of the dead.

20:26 winnows: Refers to the king's ability to distinguish the righteous from the wicked, as in 20:8. **drives the wheel:** Alludes to a threshing process that separates wheat kernels from their husks, called chaff (Is 28:27–28).

20:27 spirit of man: The breath of life that comes from God (Gen 2:7) gives man a capacity for interior reflection and knowledge (Job 32:8).

20:28 loyalty and faithfulness: Characterize a worthy king's commitment to the welfare of his people. See note on 3:3.

20:30 cleanse away evil: The moral benefit of corporal discipline, which helps to train the will in right behavior by turning it away from sin. This principle is applicable both to the discipline administered by parents (13:24) and to the discipline of the Lord, who corrects his wayward children through various difficulties and disappointments in life (3:11–12). Proverbs envisions discipline that is physical and that serves as a deterrent for wrongful behavior, but it does not authorize actions that are abusive or injurious to children. The term "wounding" is used with rhetorical license and should not be taken literally.

21:1 stream of water: Symbolizes the will of the king, which is directed by the Lord, much as the farmer determines the course of an irrigation canal. Even the political life of nations and their rulers is governed by the mystery of divine Providence (Wis 6:1–11; Rom 13:1–7; CCC 269, 303).

21:2 in his own eyes: For this idea, see note on 14:12. **weighs the heart:** Regardless of human perception, which is often faulty, God's evaluation of good and evil actions is in perfect accord with reality. See notes on 14:12 and 24:12.

21:3 more acceptable: Devotion to the Lord in love and obedience is valued higher than sacrificial offerings (1 Sam 15:22; Jud 16:16; Hos 6:6; Mk 12:33). The liturgical actions of the wicked are unacceptable (15:8; 21:27) because the sincerity of their worship is contradicted by the sinfulness of their works (cf. Is 1:11–17; Amos 5:22–24; Mal 1:10–14).

21:4 the lamp: Or, possibly, "the tilled ground", an image of one's deeds and endeavors in life.

21:6 a fleeting vapor: Or, "vanity". Wealth amassed by deceit is worthless; instead of securing one's future, it leads to a faster ruin (10:2).

21:7 violence: In the words of Jesus, "all who take the sword will perish by the sword" (Mt 26:52). **sweep them away:** Like fish that are caught and hauled ashore in a fisherman's net (cf. Hab 1:15).

21:8 The way: A person's manner of life. See note on 1:15.

21:9 It is better: A duplicate of the saying in 25:24. **contentious woman:** The proverb bemoans the burden of living with a quarrelsome wife (21:19; 27:15; Sir 25:16). In contrast to the disagreeable wife, a good and prudent wife is one of the Lord's most treasured gifts to a man (18:22; 19:14; 31:10–31).

21:11 scoffer: A definition is given in 21:24. **simple:** Uninstructed in wisdom. See note on 1:22.

21:12 The righteous: Or, better, "the Righteous One", referring to God.

21:13 the cry of the poor: Concern for those in need is expressed several times in Proverbs (14:31; 17:5; 19:17; 22:9). Here, giving help to the poor and underprivileged is a condition for receiving similar treatment in return. The merciless can expect no mercy from the Lord in their own time of need (Mt 5:7; 6:14–15) (CCC 2443–49). • Poverty is crueler than a beast of prey. You must aid its victims and give ear to their cry. Give that you may receive, and hear that you may be heard. Almsgiving and charity crown us with the glory of God and bring us to the undying happiness that Christ gives to those who love him (St. Cyril of Alexandria, *Commentary on Luke* 103).

21:14 A gift ... a bribe: An observational proverb about the effectiveness of bribery. Its implicit purpose is to caution against the practice. That accepting bribes is a perversion of justice is stated explicitly in 17:23.

21:16 the dead: Literally, "the shades", a name for the spirits of the dead thought to reside in the netherworld of Sheol (2:18; Job 26:5; Is 26:14). The proverb seems to envision an early or terrible death for the person who strays from wisdom.

ᵍGk: Heb *loyalty*.

¹⁷He who loves pleasure will be a poor man;
   he who loves wine and oil will not be rich.
¹⁸The wicked is a ransom for the righteous,
   and the faithless for the upright.
¹⁹It is better to live in a desert land
   than with a contentious and fretful woman.
²⁰Precious treasure remainsʰ in a wise man's
      dwelling,
   but a foolish man devours it.
²¹He who pursues righteousness and kindness
   will find lifeⁱ and honor.
²²A wise man scales the city of the mighty
   and brings down the stronghold in which they
      trust.
²³He who keeps his mouth and his tongue
   keeps himself out of trouble.
²⁴"Scoffer" is the name of the proud, haughty man
   who acts with arrogant pride.
²⁵The desire of the sluggard kills him
   for his hands refuse to labor.
²⁶All day long the wicked covets,ʲ
   but the righteous gives and does not hold
      back.
²⁷The sacrifice of the wicked is an abomination;
   how much more when he brings it with evil
      intent.
²⁸A false witness will perish,
   but the word of a man who hears will
      endure.
²⁹A wicked man puts on a bold face,
   but an upright man considersᵏ his ways.

³⁰No wisdom, no understanding, no counsel,
   can avail against the LORD.
³¹The horse is made ready for the day of battle,
   but the victory belongs to the LORD.

22 A good name is to be chosen rather than
      great riches,
   and favor is better than silver or gold.
²The rich and the poor meet together;
   the LORD is the maker of them all.
³A prudent man sees danger and hides himself;
   but the simple go on, and suffer for it.
⁴The reward for humility and fear of the LORD
   is riches and honor and life.
⁵Thorns and snares are in the way of the perverse;
   he who guards himself will keep far from
      them.
⁶Train up a child in the way he should go,
   and when he is old he will not depart from it.
⁷The rich rules over the poor,
   and the borrower is the slave of the lender.
⁸He who sows injustice will reap calamity,
   and the rod of his fury will fail.
⁹He who has a bountiful eye will be blessed,
   for he shares his bread with the poor.
¹⁰Drive out a scoffer, and strife will go out,
   and quarreling and abuse will cease.
¹¹He who loves purity of heart,
   and whose speech is gracious, will have the
      king as his friend.
¹²The eyes of the LORD keep watch over knowledge,
   but he overthrows the words of the faithless.

22:8 (Gk): 1 Cor 9:7.

21:17 loves pleasure: By implication, the person lacks discipline and a strong work ethic.

21:18 ransom for the righteous: The application of this saying is uncertain. A possible illustration is the Exodus event, in which the first-born of Egypt perish in order to secure the redemption of Israel, the first-born of the Lord (Ex 4:22; 12:29–30; Deut 7:8).

21:19 contentious ... woman: Repeats the sentiment in 21:9.

21:20 devours it: The fool squanders his wealth rather than saving it wisely.

21:22 the stronghold: Represents the intellectual arguments and defenses that godless men raise in opposition to the Lord. Armed with a knowledge of truth, those who are wise can expose godless skepticism as unfounded and undermine confidence in worldly ways of thinking. The lesson in general terms is that wisdom prevails over power (24:5; Eccles 9:16).

21:23 keeps his mouth: Careful use of speech is one of the premier virtues of wisdom (10:19; 13:3; 16:23).

21:26 does not hold back: The wise are known for their selfless generosity. Sometimes the Lord rewards them by entrusting them with greater financial resources (11:24–25).

21:28 a man who hears: A thoughtful and honest man.

21:29 bold face: A sign of willful stubbornness.

21:30 No wisdom ... avail: A reminder that human wisdom, being limited in scope and depth of perception, cannot

compare to the infinite understanding of God (Is 55:9). Humility and trust in the Lord are the appropriate response to this fact (3:5–6; 16:3, 20).

21:31 the victory: The proverb acknowledges the primacy of God's grace in the life of his people. Whatever success comes from their efforts, it is thanks to the Lord and the help that he provides (cf. Ps 44:1–8; Phil 4:13).

22:1 good name: The value of an honorable reputation is highly esteemed in the Bible's wisdom literature (3:4; Eccles 7:1; Sir 41:12–13).

22:2 rich ... poor: All persons, regardless of their economic situation, are of equal dignity before the Creator (14:31; 29:13; Job 31:13–15).

22:4 humility: The antithesis of pride and an integral part of wisdom (11:2; 15:33; 29:23). **fear of the LORD:** The principal virtue of the wise. See note on 1:7. **riches:** Not to be preferred to wisdom (8:10–11), but sometimes a reward for living wisely (10:22; 11:24).

22:6 Train up a child: Parental instruction and discipline help to impart life lessons to children that can stay with them into adulthood. On this topic in Proverbs, see 13:24; 22:15; 23:13–14; 29:15, 17.

22:7 the borrower is the slave: An observational proverb that warns against incurring debt irresponsibly and unnecessarily. In the biblical world, one could literally become a slave to his creditor until the balance of what he owed was paid off (cf. Lev 25:47).

22:8 rod of his fury: His power to exploit others.

22:9 bountiful eye: Literally, "good eye", referring to the generous spirit of someone who gives liberally to others. Opposite this, a person with an "evil eye" is someone who is stingy (23:6) or miserly (28:22).

ʰGk: Heb *and oil.*
ⁱGk: Heb *life and righteousness.*
ʲGk: Heb *all day long he covets covetously.*
ᵏAnother reading is *establishes.*

¹³The sluggard says, "There is a lion outside!
　　I shall be slain in the streets!"
¹⁴The mouth of a loose woman is a deep pit;
　　he with whom the LORD is angry will fall
　　　　into it.
¹⁵Folly is bound up in the heart of a child,
　　but the rod of discipline drives it far from him.
¹⁶He who oppresses the poor to increase his own
　　wealth,
　　or gives to the rich, will only come to want.

Sayings of the Wise

¹⁷Incline your ear, and hear the words of the wise,
　　and apply your mind to my knowledge;
¹⁸for it will be pleasant if you keep them within
　　you,
　　if all of them are ready on your lips.
¹⁹That your trust may be in the LORD,
　　I have made them known to you today, even
　　　　to you.

²⁰Have I not written for you thirty sayings
　　of admonition and knowledge,
²¹to show you what is right and true,
　　that you may give a true answer to those who
　　　　sent you?

²²Do not rob the poor, because he is poor,
　　or crush the afflicted at the gate;

²³for the LORD will plead their cause
　　and despoil of life those who despoil them.
²⁴Make no friendship with a man given to anger,
　　nor go with a wrathful man,
²⁵lest you learn his ways
　　and entangle yourself in a snare.
²⁶Be not one of those who give pledges,
　　who become surety for debts.
²⁷If you have nothing with which to pay,
　　why should your bed be taken from under
　　　　you?
²⁸Remove not the ancient landmark
　　which your fathers have set.
²⁹Do you see a man skilful in his work?
　　he will stand before kings;
　　he will not stand before obscure men.

Precepts and Warnings

23 When you sit down to eat with a ruler,
　　observe carefully what[1] is before you;
²and put a knife to your throat
　　if you are a man given to appetite.
³Do not desire his delicacies,
　　for they are deceptive food.
⁴Do not toil to acquire wealth;
　　be wise enough to desist.
⁵When your eyes light upon it, it is gone;
　　for suddenly it takes to itself wings,
　　flying like an eagle toward heaven.

22:13 a lion outside!: The lazy person's excuse for not working is so wildly exaggerated as to be laughable (26:13).

22:14 mouth of a loose woman: Ensnares young men with enticing words of seduction (5:3; 6:24; 7:5).

22:15 rod of discipline: Helps to dissuade foolish and immature behavior. See note on 13:24.

22:17—24:34 Two collections of sayings introduced by the headings at 22:17 and 24:23. Many scholars detect parallels between this section of Proverbs and an ancient Egyptian work called the *Instruction of Amenemope*. This work, predating the Israelite monarchy and arranged into 30 chapters, is an ensemble of fatherly maxims on how to live a successful life. As many as 20 passages in 22:17—23:11 may be inspired by sayings that appear in this Egyptian composition. Since the cultivation of wisdom was an international pursuit in the biblical world, it is no surprise that Israel should appropriate insights from other Near Eastern cultures in this way. See essay: *Wisdom Literature in the Bible* at Prov 10.

22:19 trust ... in the LORD: Acquiring wisdom helps to foster a personal relationship with God built on faith and prayerful reliance (3:5).

22:22 the gate: The main entrance into a walled town served as a public forum where legal cases and business transactions were handled by a council of elders (31:23; Ruth 4:1-6).

22:23 their cause: Yahweh is the Defender of the helpless and impoverished, requiting those who exploit or oppress them (17:5; Ps 140:12; Is 3:13-15).

22:24 a wrathful man: A person of short temper such as described in 14:16-17 and 29:22.

22:26 surety for debts: On this practice, see note on 6:1.

22:28 the ancient landmark: Boundary stones used to mark property lines. Moving them implies the intent to steal another's land (23:10; Deut 19:14; CCC 2403).

23:2 knife to your throat: An image of self-restraint, which is recommended for the one who struggles with overeating. In this case, the virtue of temperance promotes proper table manners, which is all the more important when dining with a person of importance (Sir 31:12-22).

23:4 wealth: A fleeting prize not worth the effort so many expend to acquire it (11:28; 27:24; Eccles 5:10-17).

Word Study

Thirty Sayings (22:20)

Shalishiwm (Heb.): An adverb, normally vocalized *shilshom*, meaning "before" or "in times past" (Gen 31:2; Ex 4:10; Josh 4:18; 2 Sam 5:2). Because its form in the Masoretic Hebrew text is unusual, and it appears at the head of a collection of proverbs that may be related to an Egyptian work, divided into 30 sections, called the *Instruction of Amenemope* (see note on 22:17—24:34), many scholars propose that the word should be emended to read *sheloshim*, meaning "thirty". Merely shortening the stroke of a single consonant would yield this spelling. Also, the Greek Septuagint translates the word "three times", which may indicate that the original term was, in fact, numerical. Nevertheless, despite the arguments in favor of emending the text to read "thirty sayings", there is no agreement among scholars on how to divide the following section of Proverbs into 30 distinct teachings.

---

[1]Or *who*.

[6]Do not eat the bread of a man who is stingy;
  do not desire his delicacies;
[7]for he is like one who is inwardly reckoning.[m]
  "at and drink!"he says to you;
  but his heart is not with you.
[8]You will vomit up the morsels which you have
    eaten,
  and waste your pleasant words.
[9]Do not speak in the hearing of a fool,
  for he will despise the wisdom of your words.
[10]Do not remove an ancient landmark
  or enter the fields of the fatherless;
[11]for their Redeemer is strong;
  he will plead their cause against you.
[12]Apply your mind to instruction
  and your ear to words of knowledge.
[13]Do not withhold discipline from a child;
  if you beat him with a rod, he will not die.
[14]If you beat him with the rod
  you will save his life from Sheol.
[15]My son, if your heart is wise,
  my heart too will be glad.
[16]My soul will rejoice
  when your lips speak what is right.
[17]Let not your heart envy sinners,
  but continue in the fear of the LORD all the
    day.
[18]Surely there is a future,
  and your hope will not be cut off.

[19]Hear, my son, and be wise,
  and direct your mind in the way.
[20]Be not among winebibbers,
  or among gluttonous eaters of meat;
[21]for the drunkard and the glutton will come to
    poverty,
  and drowsiness will clothe a man with rags.

[22]Listen to your father who begot you,
  and do not despise your mother when she is old.
[23]Buy truth, and do not sell it;
  buy wisdom, instruction, and understanding.
[24]The father of the righteous will greatly rejoice;
  he who begets a wise son will be glad in him.
[25]Let your father and mother be glad,
  let her who bore you rejoice.

[26]My son, give me your heart,
  and let your eyes observe[n] my ways.
[27]For a harlot is a deep pit;
  an adventuress is a narrow well.
[28]She lies in wait like a robber
  and increases the faithless among men.

[29]Who has woe? Who has sorrow?
  Who has strife? Who has complaining?
  Who has wounds without cause? Who has
    redness of eyes?
[30]Those who tarry long over wine,
  those who go to try mixed wine.
[31]Do not look at wine when it is red,
  when it sparkles in the cup
  and goes down smoothly.
[32]At the last it bites like a serpent,
  and stings like an adder.
[33]Your eyes will see strange things,
  and your mind utter perverse things.
[34]You will be like one who lies down in the midst
    of the sea,
  like one who lies on the top of a mast.[o]
[35]"They struck me," you will say,[p] "but I was not
    hurt;
  they beat me, but I did not feel it.
When shall I awake?
  I will seek another drink."

23:6 a man who is stingy: Literally, "an evil eye". The idiom refers to one who shows a culpable lack of generosity toward others (Deut 15:9).

23:10 landmark: On this, see note on 22:28.

23:11 plead their cause: Yahweh looks after the fatherless orphan as a divine Father (Ps 68:5) and calls his people to do the same (Jas 1:27).

23:13 if you beat him: Proverbs neither advocates nor endorses the physical abuse of children. Non-injurious forms of corporal discipline are in view here and elsewhere in the book. See notes on 13:24 and 20:30.

23:14 Sheol: The realm of the dead. See note on 1:12.

23:15 My son: Recalls the parental speeches that appear often in Prov 1–9. See note on 1:8.

23:17 envy sinners: A temptation especially for the young, in whose eyes transgressors seem to prosper and enjoy the full zest and excitement of life. The desire to live solely for pleasure and personal interest is also discouraged in 3:31, 24:1, 20, and more extensively in Ps 37:1–40 and 73:1–28. **fear of the LORD:** The first step toward wisdom and the overarching theme of Proverbs. See note on 1:7.

23:23 Buy truth: The price of truth is the effort one must expend to gain wisdom for upright and responsible living.

23:27 harlot: The dangers that prostitutes and other promiscuous women pose to young men are discussed several times in Proverbs (2:16–19; 5:1–23; 7:1–27) (CCC 2355).

23:29–35 The folly of drunkenness is vividly depicted. Among its painful consequences, it causes sorrow and strife (23:29), produces strange and embarrassing behavior (23:33), and can even lead to poverty (23:21). No less tragically, the drunkard becomes a slave to his alcohol, for no sooner does he recover from his intoxication than his heart desires "another drink" (23:35) (CCC 2290).

23:31 Do not look at wine: An enticement to the alcoholic. • The Greek LXX reads instead, "Do not get drunk with wine" and is quoted by Paul in Eph 5:18. • Be not friends with someone who will make you displeasing to God. Such a one is an enemy both to himself and to you. If you make yourself and your companion drunk, a man will be your friend, but God will be your enemy (St. Caesarius of Arles, *Sermons* 46, 4).

23:32 bites like a serpent: By implication, one should avoid excessive drink as one flees from a poisonous snake (Sir 21:2).

23:34 the midst of the sea: The meaning of this saying is uncertain. Perhaps the proverb is comparing a drunken hangover to seasickness (cf. Ps 107:27).

---

[m]Heb obscure.
[n]Another reading is *delight in.*
[o]Heb obscure.
[p]Gk Syr Vg Tg: Heb lacks *you will say.*

24

Be not envious of evil men,
nor desire to be with them;
[2] for their minds devise violence,
and their lips talk of mischief.

[3] By wisdom a house is built,
and by understanding it is established;
[4] by knowledge the rooms are filled
with all precious and pleasant riches.
[5] A wise man is mightier than a strong man,[q]
and a man of knowledge than he who has
strength;
[6] for by wise guidance you can wage your war,
and in abundance of counselors there is
victory.
[7] Wisdom is too high for a fool;
in the gate he does not open his mouth.
[8] He who plans to do evil
will be called a mischief-maker.
[9] The devising of folly is sin,
and the scoffer is an abomination to men.

[10] If you faint in the day of adversity,
your strength is small.
[11] Rescue those who are being taken away to death;
hold back those who are stumbling to the
slaughter.
[12] If you say, "Behold, we did not know this,"
does not he who weighs the heart perceive it?
Does not he who keeps watch over your soul
know it,
and will he not repay man according to his
work?

[13] My son, eat honey, for it is good,
and the drippings of the honeycomb are sweet
to your taste.
[14] Know that wisdom is such to your soul;
if you find it, there will be a future,
and your hope will not be cut off.

[15] Lie not in wait as a wicked man against the
dwelling of the righteous;
do not violence to his home;
[16] for a righteous man falls seven times, and rises
again;
but the wicked are overthrown by calamity.

[17] Do not rejoice when your enemy falls,
and let not your heart be glad when he stumbles;
[18] lest the LORD see it, and be displeased,
and turn away his anger from him.

[19] Fret not yourself because of evildoers,
and be not envious of the wicked;
[20] for the evil man has no future;
the lamp of the wicked will be put out.

[21] My son, fear the LORD and the king,
and do not disobey either of them;[r]
[22] for disaster from them will rise suddenly,
and who knows the ruin that will come from
them both?

[23]   These also are sayings of the wise.

Partiality in judging is not good.

24:1 Be not envious: On this theme, see note on 23:17. **to be with them:** The assumption is that "Bad company ruins good morals" (1 Cor 15:33). Related to this is the danger of peer pressure, which is warned against in 1:11 and 13:20.

24:3 By wisdom: Similar to the statements in 9:1 and 14:1. **a house is built:** The concrete image of a home under construction is a figure for one's life. In Hebrew, the term for "house" can also refer to a "household" or "family". • The house is the Church built by Christ, and its storerooms, filled with every splendid thing, are the hearts of believers who live as he did. In other words, their hearts abound in goodness of thought, word, and deed (St. John Chrysostom, *Commentary on Proverbs* 24).

24:4 riches: A blessing sometimes given to those who pursue wisdom (8:18) and are generous toward others (11:24–25).

24:5 wise ... strong: Mind prevails over muscle when it prudently accepts wise counsel (20:18; 24:6; Eccles 9:16).

24:7 the gate: The ancient equivalent of a courtroom. Here the fool can only be silent, for he lacks the insight and discernment necessary to manage the affairs of civic life. See note on 22:22.

24:9 scoffer: One who refuses correction from others and mocks the discipline of living wisely (9:7; 13:1; 15:12).

24:11 Rescue: A call to intervene on behalf of someone unjustly sentenced to death. As implied in 24:12, this should be done if information proving the innocence of the con-

demned is known. Otherwise the Lord will count inaction as a sin of omission (Jas 4:17; CCC 1853).

24:12 weighs the heart: Perhaps an image borrowed from Egyptian texts that envision the hearts of the dead being weighed in a balance to determine their destiny in the afterlife. **he who keeps watch:** The all-seeing and all-knowing Lord. See note on 15:3.

24:13 honey: Represents wisdom as something delightful and desirable (16:24). The law of the Lord is described in these terms in Ps 19:10.

24:16 seven times: Signifies "many times" (as in Lk 17:4). **rises again:** The righteous show determination rather than despair when life's hardships knock them down.

24:17 Do not rejoice: Gloating over the misfortune of an enemy or wrongdoer is forbidden (17:5). Over and above this standard, Christians are urged to be compassionate to all and to "weep with those who weep" (Rom 12:15).

24:19 be not envious: Repeats the warning of 23:17 and 24:1.

24:20 lamp ... put out: An image of a person's life or well-being snuffed out by some calamity (13:9; 20:20).

24:21 fear the LORD: The first step toward a life of wisdom and the overarching theme of Proverbs. See note on 1:7. **and the king:** Obedience to civil authority is commended both in the OT (Eccles 8:2–5) and in the NT (Rom 13:1–7; 1 Pet 2:17) (CCC 2238–40).

24:22 Following this verse, the Greek LXX includes five additional verses that do not appear in the Hebrew text of Proverbs.

24:23 sayings of the wise: A title for the short collection of proverbs in 24:23–34, which serves as an appendix to the

---

[q] Gk Compare Syr Tg: Heb *is in strength.*
[r] Gk: Heb *do not associate with those who change.*

²⁴He who says to the wicked, "You are innocent,"
　　will be cursed by peoples, abhorred by nations;
²⁵but those who rebuke the wicked will have
　　delight,
　　and a good blessing will be upon them.
²⁶He who gives a right answer
　　kisses the lips.

²⁷Prepare your work outside,
　　get everything ready for you in the field;
　　and after that build your house.

²⁸Be not a witness against your neighbor without
　　cause,
　　and do not deceive with your lips.
²⁹Do not say, "I will do to him as he has done
　　to me;
　　I will pay the man back for what he has
　　done."

³⁰I passed by the field of a sluggard,
　　by the vineyard of a man without sense;
³¹and behold, it was all overgrown with thorns;
　　the ground was covered with nettles,
　　and its stone wall was broken down.
³²Then I saw and considered it;
　　I looked and received instruction.
³³A little sleep, a little slumber,
　　a little folding of the hands to rest,
³⁴and poverty will come upon you like a robber,
　　and want like an armed man.

Further Wise Sayings of Solomon

25 These also are proverbs of Solomon which
the men of Hezeki′ah king of Judah copied.

²It is the glory of God to conceal things,
　　but the glory of kings is to search things
　　out.
³As the heavens for height, and the earth for depth,
　　so the mind of kings is unsearchable.
⁴Take away the dross from the silver,
　　and the smith has material for a vessel;
⁵take away the wicked from the presence of the
　　king,
　　and his throne will be established in
　　righteousness.
⁶Do not put yourself forward in the king's presence
　　or stand in the place of the great;
⁷for it is better to be told, "Come up here,"
　　than to be put lower in the presence of the
　　prince.

　What your eyes have seen
⁸　do not hastily bring into court;
　forˢ what will you do in the end,
　　when your neighbor puts you to shame?
⁹Argue your case with your neighbor himself,
　　and do not disclose another's secret;
¹⁰lest he who hears you bring shame upon you,
　　and your ill repute have no end.

¹¹A word fitly spoken
　　is like apples of gold in a setting of silver.
¹²Like a gold ring or an ornament of gold
　　is a wise reprover to a listening ear.
¹³Like the cold of snow in the time of harvest
　　is a faithful messenger to those who send
　　him,
　　he refreshes the spirit of his masters.

---

larger collection in 22:17—24:22. **Partiality:** Showing favoritism in the courtroom is a violation of justice. God, the supreme Judge, is perfectly impartial (Deut 10:17), and human judges are expected to act according to the same standard (Deut 1:17; 16:19). The Mosaic Law forbids taking bribes (Ex 23:8) and even showing favor to the poor and powerless when judging their innocence (Lev 19:15).

24:24 You are innocent: Acquitting the guilty of their crimes is "an abomination to the LORD" (17:15).

24:26 kisses the lips: Honest words are like the affectionate gesture of a spouse or trusted friend.

24:27 Prepare: Thoughtful planning is advised, not only for building a house in which to live, but for contracting a marriage and building a family. See note on 24:3.

24:28–29 The proverb prohibits not only false testimony in the courtroom but also the misuse of the legal system as a means for personal reprisal. Scripture commands us to restrain the impulse to exact revenge by surrendering the matter to God (20:22; Rom 12:19).

24:32 I ... considered it: Reflecting on the foolish mistakes of others (e.g., 24:30–31) is one of the classic ways of learning wisdom.

24:33 folding of the hands: An image of the sluggard crossing his arms in preparation for a relaxing nap (6:10).

25:1 proverbs of Solomon: A heading for the sayings that appear in 25:1—29:27. This is the third collection of Solomonic proverbs in the book after 1:1—9:18 and 10:1—22:16. **men of Hezekiah:** Presumably royal scribes whose duties included the preservation of ancient wisdom traditions. Promoting the teaching of Solomon may have been part of the religious reform launched by King Hezekiah during his reign from ca. 715 to 686 B.C. (2 Kings 18:1–5; 2 Chron 29:1–36).

25:2 glory of God: Manifest in the mystery of his divine ways and thoughts, which far exceed human comprehension (Job 26:14; Is 55:8–9; Rom 11:33). **glory of kings:** Manifest in the righteous governance of their kingdoms (16:12; 20:28) and the wise administration of justice among their subjects (29:14; 1 Kings 3:16–28).

25:6–7 Advice about proper etiquette around powerful people. It is a mark of humility to know one's place, whereas presumption and self-promotion end in shame (Sir 13:9–11). A similar lesson is taught in Jesus' parable of the Marriage Feast in Lk 14:7–11.

25:8 hastily: A warning that rash judgment (based on appearances, 25:7b) followed by rushing into litigation will end in regret. It is better to sort out personal differences in private than to face public humiliation (25:9).

25:9 disclose another's secret: Not only a betrayal of trust (11:13) but a sin of detraction committed by "one who speaks foolishly" (20:19; CCC 2477–79, 2489).

25:11 fitly spoken: The right thing said at the right time (15:23).

25:12 a listening ear: Stands for the person who is open to correction and instruction from others (15:31–32).

25:13 the cold of snow: A sign of refreshment, similar to the "cold water" in 25:25. **the time of harvest:** The grueling days of late summer.

ˢCn: Heb *lest*.

¹⁴Like clouds and wind without rain
    is a man who boasts of a gift he does not give.

¹⁵With patience a ruler may be persuaded,
    and a soft tongue will break a bone.
¹⁶If you have found honey, eat only enough for you,
    lest you be sated with it and vomit it.
¹⁷Let your foot be seldom in your neighbor's house,
    lest he become weary of you and hate you.
¹⁸A man who bears false witness against his
        neighbor
    is like a war club, or a sword, or a sharp
        arrow.
¹⁹Trust in a faithless man in time of trouble
    is like a bad tooth or a foot that slips.
²⁰He who sings songs to a heavy heart
    is like one who takes off a garment on a cold
        day,
    and like vinegar on a wound.ᵗ
²¹If your enemy is hungry, give him bread to eat;
    and if he is thirsty, give him water to drink;
²²for you will heap coals of fire on his head,
    and the LORD will reward you.
²³The north wind brings forth rain;
    and a backbiting tongue, angry looks.
²⁴It is better to live in a corner of the housetop
    than in a house shared with a contentious
        woman.

²⁵Like cold water to a thirsty soul,
    so is good news from a far country.
²⁶Like a muddied spring or a polluted fountain
    is a righteous man who gives way before the
        wicked.
²⁷It is not good to eat much honey,
    so be sparing of complimentary words.ᵘ
²⁸A man without self-control
    is like a city broken into and left without
        walls.

26 Like snow in summer or rain in harvest,
    so honor is not fitting for a fool.
²Like a sparrow in its flitting, like a swallow in
        its flying,
    a curse that is causeless does not alight.
³A whip for the horse, a bridle for the donkey,
    and a rod for the back of fools.
⁴Answer not a fool according to his folly,
    lest you be like him yourself.
⁵Answer a fool according to his folly,
    lest he be wise in his own eyes.
⁶He who sends a message by the hand of a
        fool
    cuts off his own feet and drinks violence.
⁷Like a lame man's legs, which hang useless,
    is a proverb in the mouth of fools.
⁸Like one who binds the stone in the sling
    is he who gives honor to a fool.

25:21, 22: Rom 12:20.

📖 **25:14 clouds and wind without rain:** Symbolic of disappointed expectations, as when the weather seems to promise needed rainfall, but no precipitation is forthcoming. • The NT uses this imagery for false teachers, whom it calls "waterless clouds, carried along by winds" (Jude 12).
25:15 break a bone: Accentuates the effectiveness of gentle persistence.
25:16 lest you be sated: A warning against overindulgence in good things (Sir 37:29–31). The same message appears in 25:27.
25:17 weary of you: Overstaying one's welcome can weaken relationships and even make enemies out of friends. Moderation applied to visitation is thus advocated as a form of social wisdom.
25:18 false witness: Lying or misleading testimony given under oath (24:28). This is forbidden by the eighth commandment of the Decalogue (Ex 20:16; CCC 2476).
25:20 like vinegar: Merriment in times of sorrow and loss only increases the anguish of those who suffer (Sir 22:6).
📖 **25:21–22** The proverb promotes kindness toward enemies. It is disputed whether the **coals of fire** refer to the burning sense of shame and remorse that wins over the evildoer or to the fiery judgment that God will bring upon him, as in Ps 140:10. Either way, retaliation and revenge are discouraged (CCC 2262). • Paul quotes this saying in Rom 12:20 in the context of urging believers not to avenge themselves on persecutors but to overcome evil by doing good to all (Rom 12:14–21).
25:24 It is better: The same proverb appears in 21:9.
25:26 who gives way: The righteous give bad witness when they compromise their moral and religious principles, for they must "never be moved" (12:3; Ps 55:22). The pressure to

accept bribes and pervert justice may be in view (17:8; 29:4; Is 1:23).
25:28 without walls: I.e., vulnerable to the assaults of temptation.
26:1–28 Four clusters of sayings touching on the subjects of fools (26:1–12), sluggards (26:13–16), quarrels (26:17–21), and harmful speech (26:22–28). Thematic as well as verbal links bind these units together.
26:1 rain: Most rainfall in Palestine comes during the winter months.
26:2 does not alight: A curse does not take effect against one who is innocent.
26:3 rod: An instrument of moral correction and training (10:13; 19:29). Associating the rod with a "whip" and "bridle" hints that the fool is comparable to a senseless beast.
26:4–5 Two proverbs that appear to be contradictory on the surface but actually apply to different situations. In certain contexts, the wise do well to avoid conversation with fools as they may be provoked to respond in kind to their thoughtless and inflammatory comments (26:4). In other contexts, such as when fools wish to appear intelligent and sophisticated, their errors ought to be refuted and corrected (26:5). The first saying cautions the wise against stooping to the level of fools; the second aims to keep fools from getting conceited.
26:6 cuts off his own feet: Trusting an unreliable messenger can thwart the sender's ability to communicate with others. On the woes associated with untrustworthy couriers, see also 10:26 and 13:17. **drinks violence:** The meaning of this metaphor is obscure.
26:7 hang useless: The fool may be able to recite a proverb, but it gives him no benefit because he fails to apply its wisdom to his life.
26:8 binds the stone: Illustrates the futility of honoring fools (26:1).

ᵗGk: Heb *lye.*
ᵘCn Compare Gk Syr Tg: Heb *searching out their glory is glory.*

⁹Like a thorn that goes up into the hand of a
  drunkard
    is a proverb in the mouth of fools.
¹⁰Like an archer who wounds everybody
    is he who hires a passing fool or drunkard.ᵛ
¹¹Like a dog that returns to his vomit
    is a fool who repeats his folly.
¹²Do you see a man who is wise in his own eyes?
    There is more hope for a fool than for him.
¹³The sluggard says, "There is a lion in the road!
    There is a lion in the streets!"
¹⁴As a door turns on its hinges,
    so does a sluggard on his bed.
¹⁵The sluggard buries his hand in the dish;
    it wears him out to bring it back to his mouth.
¹⁶The sluggard is wiser in his own eyes
    than seven men who can answer discreetly.
¹⁷He who meddles in a quarrel not his own
    is like one who takes a passing dog by the ears.
¹⁸Like a madman who throws firebrands,
    arrows, and death,
¹⁹is the man who deceives his neighbor
    and says, "I am only joking!"
²⁰For lack of wood the fire goes out;
    and where there is no whisperer, quarreling
    ceases.
²¹As charcoal to hot embers and wood to fire,
    so is a quarrelsome man for kindling strife.
²²The words of a whisperer are like delicious
  morsels;
    they go down into the inner parts of the body.

²³Like the glazeʷ covering an earthen vessel
    are smoothˣ lips with an evil heart.
²⁴He who hates, dissembles with his lips
    and harbors deceit in his heart;
²⁵when he speaks graciously, believe him not,
    for there are seven abominations in his heart;
²⁶though his hatred be covered with guile,
    his wickedness will be exposed in the assembly.
²⁷He who digs a pit will fall into it,
    and a stone will come back upon him who
    starts it rolling.
²⁸A lying tongue hates its victims,
    and a flattering mouth works ruin.

27 Do not boast about tomorrow,
    for you do not know what a day may
    bring forth.
²Let another praise you, and not your own mouth;
    a stranger, and not your own lips.
³A stone is heavy, and sand is weighty,
    but a fool's provocation is heavier than both.
⁴Wrath is cruel, anger is overwhelming;
    but who can stand before jealousy?
⁵Better is open rebuke
    than hidden love.
⁶Faithful are the wounds of a friend;
    profuse are the kisses of an enemy.
⁷He who is sated loathes honey,
    but to one who is hungry everything bitter is
    sweet.
⁸Like a bird that strays from its nest,
    is a man who strays from his home.

26:11: 2 Pet 2:22.

26:10 archer who wounds: Hiring a fool can only harm the business interests of the employer.

26:11 returns to his vomit: The fool never changes his ways and refuses to learn from his senseless mistakes (27:22). His repulsive behavior is comparable to that of an animal. • The proverb is quoted in 2 Pet 2:22 to describe one who repents and believes in the gospel only to turn back to embrace a sinful life-style.

26:12 wise in his own eyes: A temptation to pride faces those who cultivate wisdom. Essential to the biblical concept of wisdom is the virtue of humility (3:7; 15:33).

26:13 lion in the road: The lazy person's ridiculous excuse for not going to work, as also in 22:13.

26:15 buries his hand: Nearly identical to the proverb at 19:24.

26:17 dog by the ears: A senseless and potentially dangerous move. One is just as likely to get "bitten" as a result of interfering in a conflict between others.

26:19 I am only joking: The excuse of the prankster, whose careless deceptions only make people angry.

26:20 whisperer: A gossip (16:28).

26:22 words of a whisperer: A duplicate of the proverb at 18:8.

26:23 smooth lips: The translation of the Greek LXX. The Hebrew text reads, "burning lips", such as those of the evil plotter in 16:27.

26:25 seven abominations: I.e., many hateful intentions, which are concealed beneath a veneer of hypocrisy.

26:27 digs a pit: Similar sayings appear at Ps 7:15 and Eccles 10:8.

26:28 lying ... flattering: Sins of speech that are also denounced in 6:16–17; 10:18; 29:5.

27:1–27 Several proverbs in this chapter are grouped together in pairs because they touch on similar themes or share a significant word in common. The final verses, however, stand apart as a discrete unit (27:23–27).

27:1 Do not boast: Because the future is uncertain, it is presumptuous to brag about what the days ahead will bring (Lk 12:18–20; Jas 4:13–16).

27:2 Let another praise you: People are overly prone to judge themselves worthy of applause, overlooking their faults and failures in the process. For this reason, others, especially the Lord, often stand in a better position to judge our actions objectively (16:2; 21:2).

27:5 open rebuke: A sign of true affection when it aims at correcting another for his own good (cf. 3:11–12; 15:31–32). **hidden love:** A cowardly form of love that fails to admonish the friend or family member who is living foolishly.

27:6 wounds: Words of correction or rebuke, though painful experiences, can nevertheless be an expression of genuine friendship (28:23; Ps 141:5). **kisses:** A potentially deceptive sign of affection. A kiss can be a means of seducing into sin (7:13) or disguising malicious intentions (Mt 26:47–49).

27:7 loathes honey: The result of overindulgence in something good (see 25:16, 27).

27:8 strays: To distance oneself from family is to expose oneself to many dangers, not least the temptation to compromise moral principles and spiritual beliefs (cf. Lk 15:11–19).

ᵛThe Hebrew text of this verse is uncertain.
ʷCn: Heb *silver of dross*.
ˣGk: Heb *burning*.

⁹Oil and perfume make the heart glad,
    but the soul is torn by trouble.ʸ
¹⁰Your friend, and your father's friend, do not
    forsake;
    and do not go to your brother's house in the
    day of your calamity.
  Better is a neighbor who is near
    than a brother who is far away.
¹¹Be wise, my son, and make my heart glad,
    that I may answer him who reproaches me.
¹²A prudent man sees danger and hides himself;
    but the simple go on, and suffer for it.
¹³Take a man's garment when he has given surety
    for a stranger,
    and hold him in pledge when he gives surety
    for foreigners.ᶻ
¹⁴He who blesses his neighbor with a loud voice,
    rising early in the morning,
    will be counted as cursing.
¹⁵A continual dripping on a rainy day
    and a contentious woman are alike;
¹⁶to restrain her is to restrain the windᵃ
    or to grasp oil in one's right hand.
¹⁷Iron sharpens iron,
    and one man sharpens another.
¹⁸He who tends a fig tree will eat its fruit,
    and he who guards his master will be honored.
¹⁹As in water face answers to face,
    so the mind of man reflects the man.
²⁰Sheol and Abad'don are never satisfied,
    and never satisfied are the eyes of man.

²¹The crucible is for silver, and the furnace is for
    gold,
    and a man is judged by his praise.
²²Crush a fool in a mortar with a pestle
    along with crushed grain,
    yet his folly will not depart from him.

²³Know well the condition of your flocks,
    and give attention to your herds;
²⁴for riches do not last for ever;
    and does a crown endure to all generations?
²⁵When the grass is gone, and the new growth
    appears,
    and the herbage of the mountains is gathered,
²⁶the lambs will provide your clothing,
    and the goats the price of a field;
²⁷there will be enough goats' milk for your food,
    for the food of your household
    and maintenance for your maidens.

The Wicked and the Righteous Contrasted

28 The wicked flee when no one pursues,
    but the righteous are bold as a lion.
²When a land transgresses
    it has many rulers;
  but with men of understanding and knowledge
    its stability will long continue.
³A poor man who oppresses the poor
    is a beating rain that leaves no food.
⁴Those who forsake the law praise the wicked,
    but those who keep the law strive against
    them.

27:10 not ... your brother's: Friends are sometimes more loyal than family members (18:24). Generally, however, relatives are supposed to be dependable in good times and in bad (17:17).

27:11 that I may answer: Children who are raised well bring honor to their parents and constitute living testimony to their wisdom (Sir 30:2–3).

27:12 A prudent man: A duplicate of the proverb at 22:3.

27:13 Take a man's garment: A duplicate of the proverb at 20:16.

27:15 continual dripping: A source of nagging irritation. **contentious woman:** One of several proverbs that bemoan the trials of living with a disagreeable wife (19:13; 21:9, 19; 25:24). Similar comments could certainly be made about the strains placed upon marriage by a husband who is temperamental or given to quarrelling.

27:17 sharpens another: Literally, "sharpens the face of his friend". One person's ability to help shape the character of another appears to be in view. This likely entails such things as offering advice, encouragement, and admonishment.

27:19 the mind: Literally, "the heart", considered as a mirror of one's true self. Knowledge of this sort may be discovered by introspection (Sir 37:14) or disclosed to others through speech (Mt 12:34).

27:20 Sheol and Abaddon: Hebrew terms signifying "death and destruction". See note on 15:11. **never satisfied:** The insatiable appetite of Sheol is elsewhere described in 30:16; Is 5:14; Hab 2:5. **the eyes of man:** Perpetually lust after the wealth and possessions of this world (Eccles 4:8; 1 Jn 2:16).

27:21–22 The imagery of these verses is often associated with the trials of divine testing and chastisement (17:3; Wis 3:5–6; Sir 2:5; 1 Pet 1:6–7).

27:21 judged by his praise: Public acclaim is viewed as a test of character to see whether a person will become proud or maintain a humble estimation of self.

27:22 folly will not depart: The headstrong fool is ultimately unteachable (26:11; 29:1).

27:23–27 Practical wisdom for the herdsman, for whom grazing animals are his principal form of wealth (27:24) as well as a primary source of food and clothing (27:26–27) (CCC 2417). Tasks associated with these household provisions are mentioned later in connection with the praiseworthy wife (see 31:13–16).

27:24 riches do not last: Also a topic of reflection in 23:4–5 and Eccles 5:13–17.

28:1 wicked ... righteous: A typical distinction based on moral and spiritual conduct. Fearfulness versus fearlessness is another aspect of this classic contrast, for "wickedness is a cowardly thing" (Wis 17:11).

28:2 many rulers: Frequent changes in national leadership can be an indicator, not only of political unrest, but of moral disintegration in society at large. **stability:** The result of wise and just governance (29:4).

28:3 a beating rain: Oppression of the poor is like a torrential downpour that erodes the soil and damages crops.

28:4 the law: Mentioned four times in 28:4–9. Interpreters differ over its precise meaning in this context, where it may refer to (1) the Law of Moses or (2) the wisdom instruction of the Book of Proverbs. On the one hand, numerous sayings in Proverbs are simply an application of Mosaic precepts. On the other, legal language is regularly used in Proverbs for parental teaching offered to young people. See note on 13:13. **praise the wicked:** The sin of adulation (Rom 1:32).

ʸGk: Heb *the sweetness of his friend from hearty counsel.*
ᶻVg and 20:16: Heb *a foreign woman.*
ᵃHeb obscure.

⁵Evil men do not understand justice,
   but those who seek the Lord understand it
      completely.
⁶Better is a poor man who walks in his integrity
   than a rich man who is perverse in his ways.
⁷He who keeps the law is a wise son,
   but a companion of gluttons shames his father.
⁸He who augments his wealth by interest and
      increase
   gathers it for him who is kind to the poor.
⁹If one turns away his ear from hearing the law,
   even his prayer is an abomination.
¹⁰He who misleads the upright into an evil way
   will fall into his own pit;
   but the blameless will have an excellent
      inheritance.
¹¹A rich man is wise in his own eyes,
   but a poor man who has understanding will
      find him out.
¹²When the righteous triumph, there is great glory;
   but when the wicked rise, men hide
      themselves.
¹³He who conceals his transgressions will not
      prosper,
   but he who confesses and forsakes them will
      obtain mercy.
¹⁴Blessed is the man who fears the Lord always;
   but he who hardens his heart will fall into
      calamity.
¹⁵Like a roaring lion or a charging bear
   is a wicked ruler over a poor people.

¹⁶A ruler who lacks understanding is a cruel
      oppressor;
   but he who hates unjust gain will prolong his
      days.
¹⁷If a man is burdened with the blood of another,
   let him be a fugitive until death;
   let no one help him.
¹⁸He who walks in integrity will be delivered,
   but he who is perverse in his ways will fall
      into a pit.ᵇ
¹⁹He who tills his land will have plenty of bread,
   but he who follows worthless pursuits will
      have plenty of poverty.
²⁰A faithful man will abound with blessings,
   but he who hastens to be rich will not go
      unpunished.
²¹To show partiality is not good;
   but for a piece of bread a man will do wrong.
²²A miserly man hastens after wealth,
   and does not know that want will come upon
      him.
²³He who rebukes a man will afterward find more
      favor
   than he who flatters with his tongue.
²⁴He who robs his father or his mother
   and says, "That is no transgression,"
   is the companion of a man who destroys.
²⁵A greedy man stirs up strife,
   but he who trusts in the Lord will be enriched.
²⁶He who trusts in his own mind is a fool;
   but he who walks in wisdom will be delivered.

28:6 Better . . . than: Substantially the same as the proverb at 19:1. The assumption in both is that moral evil is worse than material poverty.

28:8 wealth by interest: Collecting interest on assistance loans is prohibited by the Mosaic Law (Ex 22:25; Lev 25:35–36). Usury was permitted for an Israelite only when the borrower was a Gentile (Deut 23:20). **increase:** Most likely the injustice of raising prices on goods and services without due cause. **for him who is kind:** Seems to say that God will eventually place ill-gotten wealth into the hands of people who give generously to the less fortunate (cf. 13:22).

28:9 abomination: Prayer can be rendered ineffective by sin (Ps 66:18; Jas 4:3; 1 Pet 3:7). See note on 15:8. • Petition the Lord in faith, without doubting. Be worthy of being heard by living well. One who recalls transgressing the Lord's commands rightly fails to hope that the Lord will answer his prayers (St. Bede, *Commentary on James* 1, 6).

28:11 wise in his own eyes: The self-delusion of the fool (26:12). **find him out:** The wise man knows the truth of the matter.

28:12 when the wicked rise: Partially identical to the proverb at 28:28.

28:13 He who conceals: Harboring unconfessed sin can result in painful psychological trials (Ps 32:3–4). **He who confesses:** Confession of sin is the ordinary means of receiving God's forgiveness (Ps 32:5). In OT times, this could take place in the private context of prayer (1 Kings 8:36) or in the public context of Israel's liturgy, where one's transgressions were made known to a priest and the appropriate sacrifice was offered (Lev 5:5–6; Num 5:5–10) (CCC 1455–58). For similar practices implied in the NT, see note on 1 Jn 1:9.

28:14 Blessed: See word study: *Blessed* at Ps 1:1. **fears the Lord:** A reverential fear of God is the most essential component of wisdom and the overarching theme of Proverbs. See note on 1:7. **hardens his heart:** The stubborn refusal to comply with the revealed will of God. The expression recalls Pharaoh's obstinacy before Israel's escape from bondage in Egypt (Ex 8:15, 32; 9:34).

28:17 burdened with the blood: Bloodguilt weighs heavily on the conscience of a murderer. **a fugitive:** Like Cain, the first to commit murder in the Bible (Gen 4:8–12).

28:19 He who tills: Similar to the proverb at 12:11.

28:20 hastens to be rich: In this context, wealth quickly attained is dishonestly attained.

28:21 partiality is not good: I.e., in judging legal cases. See note on 24:23. **piece of bread:** Used to bribe the poor.

28:22 miserly: Literally, "evil of eye". See note on 22:9. **want:** The tragic irony that results from obsession with money and possessions.

28:23 He who rebukes: Verbal correction is recommended for its ability to foster moral maturity and wise decision making (19:25; 25:12; 26:5; 27:5).

28:24 He who robs: Obviously violates the fourth commandment to "Honor your father and your mother" (Ex 20:12). Other offenses against parents condemned in Proverbs include abusing (19:26), cursing (20:20), shaming (28:7), and mocking them (30:17) (CCC 2197–2200).

28:25 stirs up strife: The same is said of the hot-tempered person (29:22). **enriched:** Wealth honestly obtained can be a blessing from the Lord (10:22).

28:26 trusts in his own mind: The fool's confidence is placed in himself. In contrast, the wise are urged to "Trust in the Lord" and not to rely on their "own insight" (3:5).

ᵇSyr: Heb *in one*.

²⁷He who gives to the poor will not want,
    but he who hides his eyes will get many a curse.
²⁸When the wicked rise, men hide themselves,
    but when they perish, the righteous increase.

29
He who is often reproved, yet stiffens his neck,
    will suddenly be broken beyond healing.
²When the righteous are in authority, the people rejoice;
    but when the wicked rule, the people groan.
³He who loves wisdom makes his father glad,
    but one who keeps company with harlots
      squanders his substance.
⁴By justice a king gives stability to the land,
    but one who exacts gifts ruins it.
⁵A man who flatters his neighbor
    spreads a net for his feet.
⁶An evil man is ensnared in his transgression,
    but a righteous man sings and rejoices.
⁷A righteous man knows the rights of the poor;
    a wicked man does not understand such
      knowledge.
⁸Scoffers set a city aflame,
    but wise men turn away wrath.
⁹If a wise man has an argument with a fool,
    the fool only rages and laughs, and there is no
      quiet.
¹⁰Bloodthirsty men hate one who is blameless,
    and the wicked[c] seek his life.
¹¹A fool gives full vent to his anger,
    but a wise man quietly holds it back.

¹²If a ruler listens to falsehood,
    all his officials will be wicked.
¹³The poor man and the oppressor meet together;
    the Lord gives light to the eyes of both.
¹⁴If a king judges the poor with equity
    his throne will be established for ever.
¹⁵The rod and reproof give wisdom,
    but a child left to himself brings shame to his
      mother.
¹⁶When the wicked are in authority, transgression
    increases;
    but the righteous will look upon their
      downfall.
¹⁷Discipline your son, and he will give you rest;
    he will give delight to your heart.
¹⁸Where there is no prophecy the people cast off
    restraint,
    but blessed is he who keeps the law.
¹⁹By mere words a servant is not disciplined,
    for though he understands, he will not give
      heed.
²⁰Do you see a man who is hasty in his words?
    There is more hope for a fool than for him.
²¹He who pampers his servant from childhood,
    will in the end find him his heir.[d]
²²A man of wrath stirs up strife,
    and a man given to anger causes much
      transgression.
²³A man's pride will bring him low,
    but he who is lowly in spirit will obtain
      honor.

28:27 He who gives: Generosity to those in need is often rewarded by the Lord with a greater abundance of material blessings (11:24-25). **many a curse:** Possibly from God but certainly from the embittered poor (Sir 4:5-6).

28:28 When the wicked rise: Identical in part to the proverb at 28:12.

29:1 stiffens his neck: Like an ox that resists the yoke of the plowman, the fool refuses to yield to the teaching of wisdom (cf. Sir 51:26). Despite reprimands, he is unwilling to change his ways (27:22). **suddenly be broken:** The fate of the wicked man according to 6:15.

29:2 righteous ... in authority: Similar statements appear in 11:10 and 28:12. **when the wicked rule:** Compare with 28:28 and 29:16.

29:3 squanders his substance: A father is dishonored twice over when an undisciplined son misspends his inheritance on prostitutes. Exactly this situation is described in Jesus' parable of the Prodigal Son (Lk 15:13).

29:4 stability: A similar saying appears in 28:2.

29:5 flatters: Or, possibly, "deceives". **spreads a net:** Premeditated sin leads to self-entrapment (1:17-18) and even self-destruction (26:27).

29:7 rights of the poor: Providing both legal protection and tangible assistance to the poor is a prominent concern in Proverbs (19:17; 21:13; 22:22; 29:14).

29:8 Scoffers: Here refers to troublemakers who sow division and strife among others (26:21).

29:9 rages and laughs: Debates with a stubborn fool are entirely unproductive, which is one reason why the wise should avoid getting drawn into them (26:4).

29:10 hate ... seek his life: The righteous are despised by the wicked because the good oppose and denounce their evil ways (see Wis 2:12-20).

29:11 holds it back: Controlling one's temper is a hallmark of the wise man (12:16; 14:17, 29; 16:32).

29:13 light to the eyes: Means that God the Creator gives "life" to the oppressed and oppressor alike, and so both are accountable to him. A similar affirmation appears in 22:2.

29:15 rod and reproof: On the subject of child rearing in Proverbs, see note on 13:24.

29:17 Discipline: A similar exhortation appears at 19:18. **Rest ... delight:** Peace of mind and joy of heart are the well-earned fruits of wise parenting (10:1).

29:18 prophecy: Or, "prophetic vision" (cf. Ezek 7:26). **cast off restraint:** The same verb describes how the Israelites "had broken loose" to indulge in sinful revelry before the golden calf at Mt. Sinai (Ex 32:25). **the law:** For possible meanings of this, see note on 28:4.

29:19 not disciplined: The proverb expresses skepticism that verbal correction alone is effective in changing the insubordinate behavior of a household servant. No alternative is mentioned, but if corporal discipline is insinuated, this would have to be kept within the bounds of the law, i.e., it must not be injurious (Ex 21:26-27) or, still less, lethal (Ex 21:20).

29:20 hasty in his words: One who is quick to speak is susceptible to making thoughtless comments and rash promises (10:19; 20:25). By contrast, one who is wise "restrains his words" (17:27) and is "slow to speak" (Jas 1:19). **more hope for a fool:** Identical to the second line of the proverb at 26:12.

29:22 stirs up strife: The same is said of the greedy person in 28:25. **given to anger:** On the perils of yielding to a hot temper, see 14:17, 29; 15:18; 19:19.

29:23 bring him low: The outcome of pride, also noted in 16:18. **honor:** The outcome of humility, also noted in 15:33.

---

[c]Cn: Heb *upright*.
[d]The meaning of the Hebrew word is uncertain.

²⁴The partner of a thief hates his own life;
  he hears the curse, but discloses nothing.
²⁵The fear of man lays a snare,
  but he who trusts in the LORD is safe.
²⁶Many seek the favor of a ruler,
  but from the LORD a man gets justice.
²⁷An unjust man is an abomination to the
    righteous,
  but he whose way is straight is an
    abomination to the wicked.

Sayings of Agur

30 The words of Agur son of Ja′keh of
    Mas′sa.ᵉ
  The man says to Ith′iel,
    to Ithiel and U′cal:ᶠ
²Surely I am too stupid to be a man.
  I have not the understanding of a man.
³I have not learned wisdom,
  nor have I knowledge of the Holy One.
⁴Who has ascended to heaven and come down?
  Who has gathered the wind in his fists?
Who has wrapped up the waters in a garment?
  Who has established all the ends of the earth?
What is his name, and what is his son's name?
  Surely you know!

⁵Every word of God proves true;
  he is a shield to those who take refuge in him.

⁶Do not add to his words,
  lest he rebuke you, and you be found a liar.

⁷Two things I ask of you;
  deny them not to me before I die:
⁸Remove far from me falsehood and lying;
  give me neither poverty nor riches;
  feed me with the food that is needful for me,

⁹lest I be full, and deny you,
  and say, "Who is the LORD?"
or lest I be poor, and steal,
  and profane the name of my God.

¹⁰Do not slander a servant to his master,
  lest he curse you, and you be held guilty.

¹¹There are those who curse their fathers
  and do not bless their mothers.
¹²There are those who are pure in their own
    eyes
  but are not cleansed of their filth.
¹³There are those—how lofty are their eyes,
  how high their eyelids lift!
¹⁴There are those whose teeth are swords,
  whose teeth are knives,
to devour the poor from off the earth,
  the needy from among men.

29:24 hears the curse: In biblical times, a curse was called down upon anyone who witnessed or had knowledge of a crime but who refused to come forward to testify against the perpetrator (Lev 5:1; Judg 17:2). To remain silent was to bear the guilt of an accomplice.

29:25 trusts in the LORD: Confidence in God and his protection (18:10) can help to overcome the fear of mortal men (30:5; Is 51:12–16).

30:1–33 Different divisions of this chapter are possible, depending on how far the "words of Agur" (30:1) extend. It is perhaps best to take 30:1–14 as the teaching of Agur and to take 30:15–33 as an anonymous collection of numerical proverbs interspersed with admonitions (30:17, 20, 32–33). The Greek LXX treats the first 14 verses as a unit and places them earlier in the book, before 24:23.

30:1 Agur: Otherwise unknown, but seemingly a non-Israelite. If so, he is like Job, who is often identified as an Arabian or Edomite wise man. See note on Job 1:1. **Massa:** Located in northern Arabia and named after one of the sons of Ishmael (Gen 25:14). The word could also be translated "an oracle". **Ithiel and Ucal:** Understood as proper nouns by the RSV (the names of two of Agur's students?). However, since the Hebrew is difficult to decipher, others think the text has suffered corruption, i.e., scribes must have miscopied this line at an early point in the process of transmission (see textual note *f*).

30:2–4 Rhetorical questions implying that the power and wisdom of God are beyond the reach of human understanding. The same technique is used in Job 38–39, Sir 1:2–6, and Is 40:12–15. Similar statements about the Lord's sovereignty over the natural world appear in Job 38:8–9 and Ps 135:7.

30:3 the Holy One: A title for Yahweh occurring only here and at 9:10.

30:4 Who has ascended: Implies that no man has acquired the divine wisdom that resides in heaven (Bar 3:29). No one could make such a claim for himself except Jesus Christ (Jn 3:13). **his son's name:** The question is difficult to understand, both in light of the context and within the overall framework of OT faith. The Greek LXX reads "the name of his sons", which may be a reference to angels, who are known in Scripture as "the sons of God" (Job 1:6; 38:7; Ps 29:1). • Christian readers can rightly detect a hint that God has an eternal Son, later revealed through the Incarnation (Mt 14:33; Lk 1:35; Jn 1:14). **Surely you know!:** A sarcastic rebuke (Job 38:5, 18).

30:5 proves true: Literally, "is tested", which implies that every utterance of God proves to be trustworthy (CCC 215). The same point is made in Ps 18:30, a passage that closely resembles this verse. **a shield:** A metaphor for God's protecting grace (2:7; Gen 15:1; Ps 3:3).

30:6 Do not add: Similar prohibitions are found in Deut 4:2, regarding the terms of Israel's covenant with Yahweh, and in Rev 22:18, regarding inspired Christian prophecy about the future.

30:8 nor riches: Yet another indication in Proverbs that material wealth is not life's greatest blessing (see also 11:28; 15:16; 16:8). **food that is needful for me:** Literally, "the bread of my portion", referring to one's sufficient daily sustenance (cf. Mt 6:11; Lk 11:3).

30:9 lest I be full: Times of plenty can make us forget about our total dependence upon God for the necessities of life (Deut 31:20; Rev 3:17). **lest I . . . steal:** Theft is a violation of the seventh commandment of the Decalogue (Ex 20:15; Deut 5:19; CCC 2401).

30:11 curse their fathers: A capital crime in ancient Israel (Ex 21:15).

30:12 pure in their own eyes: Persons convinced of their own righteousness (16:2; Lk 18:11). See note on 14:12.

30:13 lofty are their eyes: A sign of arrogance (6:17; 21:4).

30:14 teeth are swords: Symbolizes ruthless and heartless greed.

ᵉOr *the oracle*.
ᶠThe Hebrew of this verse is obscure.

15The leech^g has two daughters;
  "Give, give," they cry.
 Three things are never satisfied;
  four never say, "Enough":
16Sheol, the barren womb,
  the earth ever thirsty for water,
  and the fire which never says, "Enough."^h

17The eye that mocks a father
  and scorns to obey a mother
 will be picked out by the ravens of the valley
  and eaten by the vultures.

18Three things are too wonderful for me;
  four I do not understand:
19the way of an eagle in the sky,
  the way of a serpent on a rock,
 the way of a ship on the high seas,
  and the way of a man with a maiden.

20This is the way of an adulteress:
  she eats, and wipes her mouth,
  and says, "I have done no wrong."

21Under three things the earth trembles;
  under four it cannot bear up:
22a slave when he becomes king,
  and a fool when he is filled with food;
23an unloved woman when she gets a husband,
  and a maid when she succeeds her mistress.

24Four things on earth are small,
  but they are exceedingly wise:
25the ants are a people not strong,
  yet they provide their food in the
    summer;
26the badgers are a people not mighty,
  yet they make their homes in the
    rocks;
27the locusts have no king,
  yet all of them march in rank;
28the lizard you can take in your hands,
  yet it is in kings' palaces.

29Three things are stately in their tread;
  four are stately in their stride:
30the lion, which is mightiest among beasts
  and does not turn back before any;
31the strutting cock,ⁱ the he-goat,
  and a king striding before^j his people.

32If you have been foolish, exalting yourself,
  or if you have been devising evil,
  put your hand on your mouth.
33For pressing milk produces curds,
  pressing the nose produces blood,
  and pressing anger produces strife.

Sayings of Lemuel's Mother; Praise of a Good Wife

31 The words of Lem′uel, king of Massa,^k
  which his mother taught him:

30:15–33 Numerical proverbs, which state the numbers "three" and "four" in parallel lines and then list four examples that illustrate the observation being made. The same formula appears using the numbers "six" and "seven" in 6:16–19.

30:15–16 An observation about four insatiable things. **Sheol** always has an appetite for the dead; the **barren womb** longs to bear children; the **earth** continually absorbs water; and **fire** seeks only to consume. See notes on 1:12 and 27:20.

30:15 two daughters: Refers to the bloodsuckers at each end of the leech's body.

30:17 eye: Often associated with generosity ("good eye") or a culpable lack of it ("evil eye"). See note on 22:9. **Ravens ... vultures:** To be left unburied was to suffer the indignity of being food for carrion birds (1 Kings 14:11).

30:18–19 An observation about four inscrutable things. The movements of the **eagle**, the **serpent**, and the **ship** in the realms of sky, land, and sea are as wondrous as the mystery of attraction between a **man** and woman in the sphere of human relationships. • The way of an eagle flying is the Ascension of Christ; the way of a serpent on a rock is the devil finding no sin in Christ; the way of a ship in the sea is the way of the Church in this world; and the way of a man in his youth is the way of him who was born of the Holy Spirit and the Virgin (St. Hippolytus, *On Proverbs* fragment).

30:20 I have done no wrong: The adulteress exploits her victims without remorse because she considers herself guiltless. For the dangers posed by a promiscuous married woman, see 7:1–27.

30:21–23 An observation about four intolerable things. Each is thought to turn the proper order of the world upside down. Typically a **slave** rises to power only when a revolution overthrows an existing government; when a **fool** eats sumptuously, he is probably guilty of unjust gain; when an **unloved woman** gets a spouse, it is because she was divorced and left to remarry; and a **maid** stands in the place of her mistress when she bears children that the mistress could not (as in Gen 16:1–6).

30:24–28 An observation about four intelligent things. These are animals that display wisdom and orderliness in life that is often lacking in men. Even **ants** know how to plan for their future; **badgers** know how to protect themselves from enemies; **locusts** know how to move and work together toward a common purpose; and the **lizard** can live where most people cannot, i.e., in a royal palace. See note on 6:6.

30:29–31 An observation about four impressive things. Much as the **lion**, the **cock**, and the **he-goat** strut with confidence among their kind, so a **king** displays strength and leadership by the way he presents himself before his subjects.

30:32 hand on your mouth: Silence is urged for the person who brags about himself or his sinister plans.

30:33 pressing anger: Provocation such as speaking harsh words (15:1) or lashing out in anger against another (29:22).

31:1 Lemuel: An Arabian monarch not otherwise known. Peoples neighboring Israel who were renowned for their wisdom in biblical times include Arabians and other "people of the east" (1 Kings 4:30) such as Job and his friends (Job 1:1, 2:11). **Massa:** Located in northern Arabia and named after one of the sons of Ishmael (Gen 25:14). **his mother taught him:** The admonitions of Proverbs 31 are those of a Queen Mother offered to her royal son. She cautions him against the snares of women and wine (31:3–7), encourages him to stand up for the poor (31:8–9), and counsels him on the benefits of a good wife (31:10–31). See essay: *Queen Mother* at 1 Kings 2.

---

^gThe meaning of the Hebrew word is uncertain.
^hHeb obscure.
ⁱGk Syr Tg Compare Vg: Heb obscure.
^jThe meaning of the Hebrew is uncertain.
^kOr *King Lemuel, the oracle.*

²What, my son? What, son of my womb?
    What, son of my vows?
³Give not your strength to women,
    your ways to those who destroy kings.
⁴It is not for kings, O Lem′uel,
    it is not for kings to drink wine,
    or for rulers to desire¹ strong drink;
⁵lest they drink and forget what has been
        decreed,
    and pervert the rights of all the afflicted.
⁶Give strong drink to him who is perishing,
    and wine to those in bitter distress;
⁷let them drink and forget their poverty,
    and remember their misery no more.
⁸Open your mouth for the mute,
    for the rights of all who are left desolate.ᵐ
⁹Open your mouth, judge righteously,
    maintain the rights of the poor and needy.

¹⁰Who can find a good wife?
    She is far more precious than jewels.
¹¹The heart of her husband trusts in her,
    and he will have no lack of gain.
¹²She does him good, and not harm,
    all the days of her life.
¹³She seeks wool and flax,
    and works with willing hands.
¹⁴She is like the ships of the merchant,
    she brings her food from afar.
¹⁵She rises while it is yet night
    and provides food for her household
    and tasks for her maidens.
¹⁶She considers a field and buys it;
    with the fruit of her hands she plants a
        vineyard.
¹⁷She clothes her loins with strength
    and makes her arms strong.

31:2 son of my vows: Perhaps like Hannah, the mother of Samuel, she prayed for a son and vowed to dedicate him to God if her prayer was answered (1 Sam 1:9–11).

31:3 women: The king is urged to guard himself against palace intrigues and sexual indulgence, both of which are dangers posed by the ladies of the royal harem. **those who destroy kings:** One is reminded of the foreign wives who corrupted the heart of King Solomon, paving the way for his downfall (1 Kings 11:1–11).

31:4 strong drink: On the folly of drunkenness, see 20:1 and 23:29–35. The point here is that alcohol will impair a ruler's ability to defend his neediest subjects (31:8–9; Is 28:7).

31:6–7 Recommending **strong drink** to lessen the **misery** of the afflicted later developed into the Jewish custom of offering sour wine to victims of crucifixion (Mt 27:34; Mk 15:36).

31:8 the mute: Those who have no spokesman or advocate among the ruling class.

31:10–31 The epilogue to Proverbs praises the value of a "good wife" (31:10). It is an acrostic poem in which the first word in each of its 22 verses begins with a consecutive letter of the Hebrew alphabet (made up of 22 consonants). This technique was popular among Hebrew writers, as indicated by its regular occurrence in the OT (e.g., Ps 9–10; 25; 34). Not only did the alphabetic format facilitate memorization, but its purpose was to suggest that a complete presentation of the poem's topic was being given—everything from A to Z, so to speak. Here it unfolds the range of virtues that characterize the praiseworthy wife. Several lines echo earlier verses in the book, hinting that the wife of the poem is an exemplar of wisdom (see notes on 31:10 and 31:11).

31:10 Who can find...?: Finding an excellent wife is comparable to finding wisdom, for both bring "favor from the LORD" (compare 8:35 with 18:22). **more precious than jewels:** The same is said of wisdom in 3:15 and 8:11. • Not only since the coming of the Lord has the Catholic Church been preached, but from the beginning she was prefigured by hidden mysteries. Indeed, Solomon speaks of her when he says, "Who shall find a worthy wife?" That courageous woman is the Church (St. Caesarius of Arles, *Sermons* 139).

31:11 no lack of gain: Anticipates the various ways that the wife of the poem contributes to meeting the needs of her household (31:16, 18–19, 24). The statement also recalls how wisdom, expressed as trust in the Lord, brings prosperity (8:21; 28:25).

31:13 wool and flax: Materials spun into thread for making clothing (31:19). Wool is for winter garments (31:21), and the fibers of flax straw can be made into fine linen (31:22, 24).

31:14 food from afar: May imply that her family enjoys a diversified diet that includes imported foods.

31:15 rises ... night: Unselfish love awakens her before sunrise and keeps her going until long after dark (31:18). Such discipline is lacking in the foolish sluggard (6:9–10; 26:14).

31:16 considers ... buys: An exercise in good judgment and the foresight that sees potential for profit. It confirms that the husband's trust in his wife is well placed (31:11). Ordinarily the male head of the household would be involved in the purchase of property.

Word Study

Good Wife (31:10)

'Eshet ḥayil (Heb.): translated in the RSV as "a woman of worth" (Ruth 3:11) or "a good wife" (Prov 12:4; 31:10). Neither constitutes a faulty rendering of the Hebrew, but the term *ḥayil* tends to be stronger in meaning than merely "good" or "worthy". Generally the word conveys the notion of strength, be it physical strength (Ps 33:17), financial strength (Deut 8:18), or the strength of character that makes one fit for an important task (Ex 18:21). Often the term is found in military contexts, where warriors are described as men of "valor" (Josh 1:14; Judg 6:12; 2 Kings 5:1; 2 Chron 13:3); it can even refer to an entire "army" or "host" of soldiers (Ex 15:4; Is 36:2; Jer 32:2; Ezek 17:17). Given this usage, it seems best to render the expression in Prov 31:10 as "a valiant wife" or "a courageous wife" (the Greek LXX and the Latin Vulgate both opt for the latter). She is described as being resourceful (31:13–14), disciplined (31:15), enterprising (31:16, 24), productive (31:19, 22, 27), generous (31:20), wise (31:26), and God-fearing (31:30). More than merely good or noble, the woman of Proverbs 31 shows heroic strength of character in serving the Lord and her family.

---

¹Cn: Heb *where*.
ᵐHeb *are sons of passing away*.

¹⁸She perceives that her merchandise is profitable.
    Her lamp does not go out at night.
¹⁹She puts her hands to the distaff,
    and her hands hold the spindle.
²⁰She opens her hand to the poor,
    and reaches out her hands to the needy.
²¹She is not afraid of snow for her household,
    for all her household are clothed in scarlet.
²²She makes herself coverings;
    her clothing is fine linen and purple.
²³Her husband is known in the gates,
    when he sits among the elders of the land.
²⁴She makes linen garments and sells them;
    she delivers sashes to the merchant.
²⁵Strength and dignity are her clothing,
    and she laughs at the time to come.

²⁶She opens her mouth with wisdom,
    and the teaching of kindness is on her
    tongue.
²⁷She looks well to the ways of her household,
    and does not eat the bread of idleness.
²⁸Her children rise up and call her blessed;
    her husband also, and he praises her:
²⁹"Many women have done excellently,
    but you surpass them all."
³⁰Charm is deceitful, and beauty is vain,
    but a woman who fears the Lord is to be
    praised.
³¹Give her of the fruit of her hands,
    and let her works praise her in the gates.

31:18 profitable: The woman's labor as a seamstress is a cottage industry that earns income for the benefit of her family (31:24).

31:19 distaff ... spindle: Instruments for spinning and weaving thread into fabric.

31:20 opens her hand: Compassionate and generous, the wise wife offers material assistance to the less fortunate (14:21; 22:9). In light of 11:24–25, this may be said to add to her family's financial abundance.

31:21 in scarlet: The Hebrew term can also be vocalized to mean "twofold" or "doubly", which is how the Greek LXX and Latin Vulgate read it. Reference to **snow** in the preceding line makes this alternative translation attractive.

31:22 coverings: Some type of sheets or blankets for a couch (7:16). **fine linen and purple:** Typically worn by persons of wealth or nobility (Gen 41:42; Judg 8:26; Lk 16:19). She has become a woman of means by her strong work ethic, for "the hand of the diligent makes rich" (10:4).

31:23 Her husband is known: His honored reputation is supported by the effective home management of his wife, which is known and praised by others (31:31). **the gates:** The main entryways into a walled village where town leaders conducted business and judged legal cases.

31:25 laughs: An expression of confident optimism regarding the future.

31:27 looks well: The Hebrew is *ṣophiyyah*, which some think is a play on the Greek term *sophia*, meaning "wisdom". This is not impossible, but neither is it certain. In any case, it is a very slim basis upon which to date the Book of Proverbs as late as the Hellenistic period, as some propose.

31:28 call her blessed ... praises her: The devoted wife and mother earns the respect and acclaim of her family. Her sacrificial love is neither unappreciated nor taken for granted.

31:29 excellently: Or, "valiantly" (as in Num 24:18).

31:30 Charm is deceitful: Gracious speech and mannerisms can sometimes hide the true intentions of the heart (5:3–4; 7:21; 26:23–25). **beauty is vain:** Good looks lack the permanence and practical significance that can sustain a marriage over the long term. This is not to say that a husband cannot take delight in the physical attractiveness of his bride (see 5:18). **fears the Lord:** The good wife is a godly wife. Pious reverence for the Almighty is the preeminent virtue of the wise. See note on 1:7.

Study Questions
Proverbs

Chapter 1

For understanding
1. **Word Study: Proverb.** What kinds of literary forms does the Hebrew word *mashal* encompass? What negative connotation does it sometimes have? What does it most commonly denote? As observations, on what are proverbs based?
2. **1:7.** What does Proverbs teach about the fear of the Lord? In practical terms, what does fear of the Lord mean? According to St. John Chrysostom, where does sin have its beginning? What kinds of fear does St. Bede describe in his *Commentary on Proverbs*?
3. **1:8.** Where was the primary setting for moral and religious instruction in biblical Israel? When does direct evidence for Jewish schools materialize in Palestine? What other societies present fathers instructing their sons in proper behavior?
4. **1:15.** As an overarching metaphor in Proverbs, for what does "the way" stand? How many roads may one travel in life, and where do they lead?

For application
1. **1:7b–8.** When you were a child, how receptive were you to the formation and instruction of your parents or those who educated you? What were the main areas of resistance? How do you regard their instruction now?
2. **1:11–16.** When you were an adolescent, what influence did your peers have on your behavior, whether for good or ill? What influence did you have on the behavior of your peers? How did your peer relationships help or harm your faith in God?
3. **1:19.** Have you ever stolen anything, either openly or secretly? If you have stolen repeatedly, what were your motives? How do things gained that way take away the lives of their possessors, according to the proverb?
4. **1:29–32.** How deadly are the consequences of a serious sin, such as a sin against the fifth, sixth, seventh, or eighth commandment? How is the sinner killed by his sin, even if he remains physically alive?

Chapter 2

For Understanding
1. **2:1–22.** On what are these verses a discourse? Once possessed, what will wisdom give young men?
2. **2:6.** To whom is wisdom given? What, therefore, is essential in its pursuit besides study, reflection, and learning? Who provides living proof of this?
3. **2:16.** Who is the "loose woman" here? What does she betray? Why is it crucial to avoid her?
4. **2:17.** What was marriage considered to be in ancient Israel? What does adultery violate in addition to the covenant with one's spouse?

For application
1. **2:3.** When you pray for wisdom, how do you recognize its arrival? Why is it better to pray for wisdom regularly than only at those moments when you especially need it?
2. **2:5–15.** Over the course of your life, has an "instinct" for right behavior ever preserved you from situations or people that might have proven dangerous even though you did not recognize the danger at the time? Did you gain wisdom as a result?
3. **2:7–8.** Read these verses carefully. What do they tell you about the character of the person who attains wisdom?
4. **2:20–22.** In an age when it seems that the wicked inherit the land and the treacherous gain all the wealth, what needs to change in the culture for the truth of these verses to become apparent?

Chapter 3

For understanding
1. **3:1–35.** What are the four main units of this chapter? What does each section propose?
2. **3:5.** What does wisdom urge one to recognize? What does the biblical notion of wisdom include?
3. **3:11–12.** How is divine discipline experienced as a form of fatherly training? For what purpose does the book of Hebrews quote these verses? What is the aim of such painful ordeals?
4. **3:18.** What does Proverbs intend to depict by evoking memories of the tree of life from Genesis 2:9? In effect, what do those who find wisdom receive? How does Origen of Alexandria apply the image of the tree of life to the Eucharist?
5. **3:34.** To whom is the Lord's favor shown in answered prayer? According to St. Jerome, why is pride evil and not "a trifling sin"?

For application
1. **3:5–7.** What does Proverbs typically call the person who is wise in his own eyes? If you have expertise in a certain area, is it possible both to use it and to trust in the Lord with all your heart at the same time?
2. **3:9–10.** Read the note for these verses. What percentage of your income do you contribute to the Church? Have you tried tithing—that is, giving 10 percent of your income? If not, why not? If so, what has been the fruit?
3. **3:11–12.** How has the discipline of the Lord shown itself in your life? What have you learned about yourself and your relationship with the Lord from it? Have you sought his discipline or tried to avoid it?
4. **3:27–28.** Related to the issue of tithing is that of almsgiving. Do you regularly give alms, particularly when someone in your parish community needs help that you can provide? In addition to donations of money, what other types of aid are you in a position to give?

Chapter 4

For understanding
1. **4:6–9.** How is wisdom personified in these verses? What is she doing?
2. **4:18.** What increases over time for the righteous?
3. **4:20–27.** For what is the father appealing in these verses? How are his words reinforced in a tangible way?
4. **4:27.** From what is the young man cautioned not to swerve? Using similar language, what do other biblical exhortations urge readers to observe?

For application
1. **4:1–4.** Describe your relationship with your father, guardian, or mentor. What kinds of things did he try to teach you? Regardless of a child's gender, how important is a father figure in his life? Why?
2. **4:14–15.** In your environment, what does "the path of the wicked" look like? For example, do you face an environment where experimentation with drugs, casual sex, aggressive partying, gang activity, and the like are prevalent? What enticements to this type of behavior present themselves to you? How do you avoid them?
3. **4:19.** If "the path of the wicked" is so much fun, why is *night* the time to take it? Why is daytime used to describe the "path of the righteous"?
4. **4:24.** Read CCC 2482–2487, about lying. Why is "crooked speech" and "devious talk" so harmful? Whom does it harm?

Chapter 5

For understanding
1. **5:1–23.** With what are the dangers of adultery contrasted? What does involvement with a "loose woman" bring? What does fidelity to one's wife bring? With what does the chapter combine practical advice?
2. **5:15–18.** For what is the *well* or *fountain* a poetic image? How does this image apply to the protection of one's wife? What does part of this protection involve?
3. **5:19.** What can fanning the flames of marital love do to a marriage?
4. **5:21.** If the prospect of shame and remorse are not enough to dissuade the young man from an adulterous affair, what will?

For application
1. **5:8.** What, besides direct personal contact, are some of the ways of going "near the house" of the "loose woman"? For example, what are some of the pornographic temptations that surround you? How do you avoid them? If you have children, how do you protect them?
2. **5:11–12.** How likely is the threat of falling victim to a sexually transmitted disease to deter someone from sexual promiscuity or infidelity? Once sexual integrity has been lost, what can be done to restore it?
3. **5:18–19.** In your experience, why do spouses who have been married some years become dissatisfied with each other and begin to think of straying? If love in a marriage becomes stale, how can it be rejuvenated?
4. **5:23.** Is marital infidelity merely a lack of discipline? How should a spouse exercise sexual self-control when temptations against fidelity arise?

Chapter 6

For understanding
1. **6:1–35.** What are young men urged to avoid in this chapter?
2. **6:6.** Why should the young man pay attention to a tiny insect like the ant? According to St. Basil, how does wise Solomon praise labor? What will he who gave us the ability to work require?
3. **6:16–19.** What kind of proverb is here, and what does it do? What does this proverb catalogue? With what are most of these sins associated?
4. **6:30.** How are thievery and adultery associated in the biblical world? What is the difference in terms of making amends?

For application
1. **6:1–5.** If you co-sign on a loan, what happens if the primary borrower defaults? What kinds of precautions should you take before agreeing to co-sign?
2. **6:10–11.** If a relative or acquaintance repeatedly asks you for money or other support, how do you determine whether the requests arise from laziness instead of a genuine need? What are some charitable ways you can stop supporting a person who should be supporting himself?
3. **6:16–19.** What do these seven abominable attitudes have in common? What kind of person do they describe? How many of them do you see in yourself?
4. **6:25.** Compare Deut 5:21 with Mt 5:27–28. When does appreciation for the beauty of another's spouse become "adultery in the heart"? If *fighting* an adulterous desire is not an appropriate way to handle temptation, what is?

Chapter 7

For understanding
1. **7:1–27.** Against what do these verses warn? What does the father recount here?
2. **7:2.** What is the "apple" of the eye?
3. **7:4.** For whom is the epithet "my sister" sometimes used? Who should the most intimate companion in life be?
4. **7:14.** What might be the meaning of the harlot's statement about offering sacrifices? Either way, how does she try to appear and why?

For application
1. **7:1–5.** How can the eager pursuit of divine wisdom be an effective deterrent against sexual temptation? How might it help you when you face such temptation?
2. **7:6–9.** How might one, consciously or not, actually *court* sexual temptation?
3. **7:10.** Read the definition of modesty in CCC 2521. How do today's clothing fashions accord with that definition? How might clothing that is itself reasonably modest be worn so as to suggest an immodest attitude?
4. **7:13–27.** Seduction, especially sexual seduction, probes for weak points in a person's character, such as a need to be found attractive or a desire for power or adventure. What are some weak points where an effort to seduce might attract you? How should you protect yourself?

Chapter 8

For understanding
1. **8:1–36.** How does the woman Wisdom portray herself in these verses? To whom is she appealing, and what is she urging? In addition to her gifts, what other mention is made about her origin? How does the Church's tradition read these wisdom speeches in Proverbs?
2. **8:22–31.** Before the world and history came into being, where was Wisdom? How is she related to God? What is her role in creation? For what revelation does her personification in the OT prepare in the NT, and how does it relate to Jesus? According to St. Bede, why does the Lord possess Wisdom at the beginning of his ways?
3. **8:22.** What description of Wisdom suggests the alternative translation of the Lord "begetting" Wisdom? How is the Greek LXX wording reflected in Revelation? According to St. Ambrose, how is this verse a prophecy of the Incarnation?
4. **8:24.** What does Wisdom mean by saying that she was "brought forth" when there were no depths?

For application
1. **8:7.** Since Wisdom deals with practical *decisions*, what kind of *truth* does the mouth of Wisdom utter? How is this kind of truth opposed to wickedness?
2. **8:12.** Read CCC 1806 on the cardinal virtue of prudence. What is "practical reason"? According to the Catechism, how does the prudent person determine and direct his conduct?
3. **8:13.** What does "hatred" mean in this verse? Is it an intense dislike for or a rejection of evil?
4. **8:14.** Read CCC 1808 on the cardinal virtue of fortitude. Given the growing opposition to Christian moral teaching in our society, how necessary is this virtue for you? How might you grow in moral fortitude?

Chapter 9

For understanding
1. **9:1–18.** How does this chapter begin and end? How is the contrast between Wisdom and Folly brought out? What do their two banquets represent?
2. **9:1.** What are two ways to understand the metaphor of Wisdom's house? According to St. Augustine, what sort of house has Wisdom built, and how has she set her table?
3. **9:2.** Why does Wisdom mix her wine? Of what does her banquet consist?
4. **9:17.** To what might the image of stolen water refer, and, in this case, what might be in view? With what prospect is the seductress luring the foolish man?

For application
1. **9:1–6.** Compare these verses with Jn 7:37–39. How should accepting the invitation of Wisdom to her banquet slake the kind of thirst about which Jesus is talking?
2. **9:10.** About what kind of knowledge does this verse talk? How does one come to know the Holy One?
3. **9:13–17.** Since both Wisdom and Folly in this chapter have their attractions and make similar appeals to the fool, to what does each appeal in order to win him over?

Chapter 10

For understanding
1. **10:1–22:16.** Of what does this second main collection of wisdom instructions consist? What does the number of sayings match? How are the several clusters of sayings in this section grouped? With what topics do they deal, and what do they imply about wisdom and foolishness?
2. **Essay: Wisdom Literature in the Bible.** Which books are included in the wisdom writings of the Old Testament? Expressed in didactic poetry, with what do they deal? What are some of the historical reasons for the existence of wisdom literature? What may be the evangelical reasons for the existence of wisdom literature? How do these considerations account for Solomon's inspiration of the wisdom tradition in Israel?
3. **10:12.** What can a spirit of charity and mercy absorb? For what is the notion of "covering" sins and offenses an idiom? Where does a paraphrase of this verse appear in the New Testament?
4. **10:19.** What is meant by the warning against "many words"? What characterizes the speech of the wise man?

For application
1. **10:1.** If you are a parent, what are some signs of emotional or moral maturity that you expect to see as your children grow? What character traits do you encourage in them?
2. **10:4–5.** How do you encourage children to mature in doing work consistently well? How do you assign chores, and how do you discipline children in regard to their performance?

3. **10:10.** What is the difference between a stern disciplinarian and a strict one? As someone who must occasionally discipline others through correction, which of these types are you? How do you think your corrections are received?
4. **10:18.** Read CCC 2477–79 and 2484. How would you evaluate the justice and charity of critical remarks you make about other people? Even when criticisms are justified, are you able to maintain charity in speech about others? How is it possible to accomplish this?

Chapter 11

For understanding
1. **11:1.** What is a "false balance"? How was it frequently used by sellers? What does Scripture demand, and what does it condemn?
2. **11:4.** What is the "day of wrath"?
3. **11:22.** What is the point of the proverb about a gold nose ring? What lesson about reading and memorizing Scripture does St. John Cassian derive from this proverb?
4. **11:30.** What does the "tree of life" symbolize here? What influence does it have? According to St. Hippolytus, who is the tree of life, and what does he bring forth?

For application
1. **11:1.** In a competitive business environment like ours, what challenges do Christian entrepreneurs face in conducting their business affairs honestly? What are some of the Christian goals of running a business?
2. **11:13.** When you have been entrusted with a secret, how well do you keep it? According to CCC 2491, when should a professional secret be kept, and when would it become necessary to reveal it?
3. **11:24–25.** On what basis do you determine how much to contribute to your parish's financial needs? How do you regard your responsibility to support the Church financially? If finances are a concern, how else do you contribute (e.g., by volunteering)?
4. **11:30.** Read the note for this verse. How might your pursuit of holiness be an encouragement to others? By the same token, how might your failure to pursue it impede others' pursuit of holiness?

Chapter 12

For understanding
1. **12:1.** To what does "discipline" refer here? In this connection, what is the difference between how the wise and the foolish man receive correction?
2. **12:10.** How does the wise man treat animals? How does that treatment differ from the treatment given by the wicked?
3. **12:23.** What does prudence recognize about silence? How does imprudence display itself?
4. **12:27.** Whom does this proverb appear to rebuke?

For application
1. **12:4.** How does a good marriage serve as a witness to an age that either denigrates or despises traditional marriage? How can the honor and respect of spouses for each other contribute to that witness, especially to their children?
2. **12:10.** Read CCC 2416–18. How does the attitude toward animals expressed in the Catechism compare or contrast with current attitudes toward animals, animal rights, and particularly toward pets?
3. **12:16.** How do you respond to an insult (real or imagined), especially from a family member? What is your responsibility to forgive? When is it important to forbear an insult in order to keep the lines of communication open, and when might it be prudent to cut communication off?
4. **12:25.** How have friends or considerate strangers helped you deal with your anxieties by their verbal or practical encouragement? Have you ever tried to encourage others who are anxious (e.g., by helping a mother anxious about the care of her first baby or a neighbor just dismissed from his job)?

Chapter 13

For understanding
1. **13:3.** How does the wise man guard his mouth? Who is the one who "opens wide his lips"?
2. **13:11.** What is the literal translation of riches "hastily gotten"? To what does it presumably refer? What are the benefits of diligence and industry?
3. **13:20.** What is this proverb about? What does the saying imply?
4. **13:24.** What does it mean to "spare the rod"? Why is neglect of a child's formation a grave disservice? What is the rod of discipline said to do elsewhere in Proverbs? How do parents who lovingly discipline their children imitate God?

For application
1. **13:4.** How might this proverb apply to the problem of urban crime; for example, when someone with no money commits a crime to obtain a pair of designer sunglasses or shoes? How might "the diligent" prevent such crime?
2. **13:11.** What is the wisdom of prudent investing instead of relying on lotteries or gambling for wealth, even if one were to strike it rich? What are some of the dangers in gambling, both for the gambler, his family, and the society at large?
3. **13:20.** Of all the companions with whom you have associated in your life, which are the ones who were most beneficial and which were the most harmful? What did you learn about yourself from your association with those in each group?
4. **13:24.** What was the approach to corporal punishment taken by your parents? If you are a parent or guardian of minors, what is your approach to it? What should be the purpose of corporal punishment, and how can it be administered in a loving way?

Chapter 14

For understanding
1. **14:1.** To whom does "Wisdom" in this proverb refer? Whom does the saying appear to praise?
2. **14:12.** To what fact does this proverb point? What effect does sin have on the intellect in this case?
3. **14:17.** To what are persons who have quick tempers prone? What does the wise man do, and why? Why does St. Ambrose suggest becoming angry with oneself when easily roused?
4. **14:34.** On what does the welfare of a nation depend? How does Israel stand as a premier example of this in the Bible?

For application
1. **14:2.** What kinds of activity (such as credit card purchases) do you tend to hide from those nearest to you, such as a spouse or superior? What does devious behavior ultimately do to those relationships? What does it do to your relationship with the Lord?
2. **14:4.** What moral responsibility do you have for maintaining your personal resources, such as automobiles or other equipment or property, and for whose benefit? What is your moral responsibility for handling the resources belonging to others, such as your employer, that are provided for your use?
3. **14:12.** Read the note for this verse. Have you ever been aware of deceiving yourself about the rightness of a course of action? How did you convince yourself to take that course? What were the consequences? What did you learn about yourself?
4. **14:29–30.** How would you describe your temper? For example, are you quickly or slowly aroused and quick or slow to calm down? How do you treat others when you become angry? How quick are you to ask forgiveness if your temper gets out of hand?

Chapter 15

For understanding
1. **15:6.** How does God sometimes favor the upright? What ancient theory underlies this idea? What will additional revelation in the OT and the NT show?
2. **15:8.** To what does the Lord expect our worship to be joined? What does Scripture insist about the liturgical and ethical aspects of life? What type of man is the wise man?
3. **15:11.** To what do Sheol and Abaddon refer? If the realm of deceased souls is visible to the Lord, toward what does the proverb reason from that fact?
4. **15:24.** In what way might a prolonged life be one of the blessings of wise conduct? Once belief in an afterlife had clearly formed in Israel's theology, what did sayings like this suggest?

For application
1. **15:1.** In a heated argument, what is the most effective way to calm tensions? If someone pushes you with accusations or sarcasm, how can you pull back so as to disarm his attack? Have you ever tried such tactics in the past?
2. **15:3, 11.** How is your conduct affected by the knowledge that God sees your every move, hears your thoughts, and knows your intentions? Have you ever tried to hide your thoughts from him or avoid his eyes (e.g., as depicted on a statue or a painting) so that he would not see what you were doing?
3. **15:13.** Read 2 Cor 3:7–18. How might an experience of the closeness of God change one's countenance? What truth lies behind the idea that one's face begins eventually to resemble the image upon which he continually gazes?
4. **15:33.** How is humility related to fear of the Lord? As one grows in fear of the Lord, properly understood, how does one's view of himself change?

Chapter 16

For understanding
1. **16:1.** To what mystery does this proverb seem to refer?
2. **16:6.** To what do the terms "loyalty" and "faithfulness" refer here? If good works do not absolve the eternal guilt of our sins, how do they "atone for iniquity"? How does St. Cyprian apply the act of almsgiving to persons polluted after the grace of baptism?
3. **16:9.** What two things does Scripture affirm here? What is the theological mystery about how the two operate together?
4. **16:32.** What do the wise know how to control, and what virtue do they know how to exercise? How does St. Gregory the Great interpret this proverb?
5. **16:33.** To what does "the lot" perhaps allude here? What were Urim and Thummim, and how were they used?

For application
1. **16:2.** How easy is it for you to rationalize the purity of your motives? How often do you ask the Holy Spirit to purify them—even to convict you of sin so you can repent where needed?
2. **16:3.** As you commit your way to the Lord, how does your planning change direction? Compare your answer with the proverb in verse 9.
3. **16:18.** Have there been occasions when you presumed you knew what God's will in a situation was? Though in theory you may have been correct, what was the actual outcome? What did you learn about yourself from it?
4. **16:32.** Read the note for this verse. How do you understand the virtue of meekness? Assuming that one definition of it is "the attitude of a person who refuses to defend himself" (or of one who chooses God for his defender), how close do you come to that standard?

Chapter 17

For understanding

1. **17:3.** How does the Lord test the genuineness of our faith? What does a comparison between trials and the smelting of metals suggest? What else do we learn in Proverbs about what God does with the human heart?
2. **17:5.** Why is callous disdain for the needy an offense against God? How does this proverb differ from the one in 14:31? By contrast, what is honored by the Lord?
3. **17:14.** What are readers advised to do in a quarrel? How should one act if locked in a disagreement with another?
4. **17:24.** What does the proverb mean by saying that the eyes of a fool are on the ends of the earth? Where is the fool's attention directed?

For application

1. **17:3.** Certain sufferings are trials of character and the genuineness of one's spiritual life. Can *all* trials be used this way? When trials come, how do you typically respond to them? What would it take for you to respond in a better spirit?
2. **17:6.** In what way is one's father the glory of his child? What has your relationship with your father been like? If you do not relate well to your father, how can you relate well with your Heavenly Father?
3. **17:17.** What is one quality of a true friend? Do you have friends like that? How have you been a friend to others who are going through difficult times?
4. **17:22.** This proverb talks about a spirit that is *habitually* cheerful or downcast. If you are habitually depressed, what have you done to get help? What is the difference between psychological depression and spiritual dryness? What are some remedies for the latter?

Chapter 18

For understanding

1. **18:8.** Why is the spreading of rumors and gossip a dangerous activity?
2. **18:10–11.** What contrast is implied in the juxtaposition of these two verses about the Lord and about wealth? What does the proverb say about the value of riches?
3. **18:13.** What mark of a fool is described here? What should one do instead?
4. **18:22.** What about marriage is being affirmed here? What is the husband being called to do? On a theological level, to what is the value of "finding a wife" compared, and what does one obtain in both cases?

For application

1. **18:2.** Have you ever engaged in a conversation about spiritual things? What marks the skill of a good conversationalist, especially in such matters? On what should sound opinions about spiritual things be based?
2. **18:4.** Whom do you know who seems to have a good understanding of spiritual matters? What advantage do you take of that person's understanding? What opportunities do you have to share your own?
3. **18:14.** What ministries of spiritual healing are available in your parish? Have you ever taken advantage of them? Have you ever been able to help those whose spirits seem to be broken by death, illness, or misfortune?
4. **18:22.** Discussing the role of the woman as a "helpmate" in marriage, CCC 1605 says that she "represents God from whom comes our help". How often have you seen husbands treat their wives that way? How would marriages change if both spouses treated each other as a representative of God?

Chapter 19

For understanding

1. **19:4.** How is poverty a burden twice over? What does wisdom counsel us to do?
2. **19:5.** Of what is giving false testimony a violation? If dishonesty like this goes undetected by others, what will the Lord do?
3. **19:17.** How does one who is kind to the poor lend to the Lord? How does the Lord promise to reward our works of mercy? How does St. Cyril of Alexandria explain the reward of lending to the Lord?
4. **19:24.** How does this proverb poke fun at laziness? On what custom is it based?

For application

1. **19:3.** Have you ever become angry at God? What were the circumstances? How did you resolve your anger? If you are still angry at God, what are you doing to reconcile with him?
2. **19:13.** What kind of damage does frequent or continual bickering do to a marriage? What does it say about the relationship between spouses? What does it teach the children?
3. **19:17.** What does it mean for the Church to exercise a "preferential option for the poor"? As a member of the Church, how do you exercise such a preferential option?
4. **19:21.** The Catechism, in paragraphs 303–14, discusses the workings of divine Providence, especially in situations of great physical and moral evil (e.g., natural disasters, wholesale massacres). What trust do you place in God's Providence for yourself? for others affected by such evils?

Chapter 20

For understanding

1. **20:9.** What does this rhetorical question mean to imply? What does only God have the power to do?
2. **20:10.** To what do the "weights" and the "measures" in this verse refer? How might sellers cheat the buyer of grain?
3. **20:22.** May one exact personal revenge? What should people do with their (non-criminal) grievances?

4. **20:25.** How could money or valuables be dedicated to the Lord's sanctuary? Because items set apart for religious service became holy, what would have been preferable to making a vow and then changing one's mind?
5. **20:30.** To what do the blows that cleanse away evil refer? To what two forms of discipline is this principle applicable? How should the term "wounding" be taken?

For application
1. **20:1.** Have you had any experience of your own with alcoholism or other forms of substance abuse? How has it affected yourself and your family? What kinds of treatment were available, and how effective have they been? How can intercessory prayer help?
2. **20:9.** How difficult is it for you to prepare for the Sacrament of Reconciliation? What makes it so hard to identify sins to confess? What does that difficulty reveal about one's relationship with God?
3. **20:20.** What is the difference between an expletive spoken in anger and a curse? If someone truly intends to ask God to bring harm to another, how is God likely to respond?
4. **20:22.** In paragraph 2302, the Catechism describes anger as a desire for revenge. Why does Jesus teach that anyone who is angry with his brother will be liable to divine judgment (see Mt 5:22)? If vengeance belongs to God, who will repay (Rom 12:19)? What kind of vengeance does God ultimately desire the sinner to receive?

Chapter 21

For understanding
1. **21:1.** What does the stream of water in the king's heart symbolize? What does it suggest about the political life of nations and their rulers?
2. **21:13.** For what is giving help to the poor and underprivileged a condition for receiving? What can the merciless expect? How does St. Cyril of Alexandria view almsgiving and charity?
3. **21:18.** What is the application of this saying? How might the Exodus event illustrate its meaning?
4. **21:22.** What does the wise man's scaling of the stronghold of the mighty represent? How can those who are wise accomplish such a feat? In general terms, what is the lesson here?

For application
1. **21:1.** Read the note for this verse. How willing are you to acknowledge that the will of God is being worked out through the political life of our nation? Where do you see that will most active? Where do you see the need for intercessory prayer?
2. **12:3.** Because sacrifice is directed to the Lord and righteousness and justice are directed to the neighbor, what does this proverb say about God's priorities? What should it say about your own?
3. **12:23.** How is it best to keep peace in a Christian community when issues arise where legitimate disagreement is possible? When should one avoid confrontation, and when should one seek it? How does one maintain love in the face of disagreement?
4. **12:26.** Why do some people steal when they have the means to pay? What change of heart is needed for the covetous?

Chapter 22

For understanding
1. **22:7.** Against what does this observational proverb warn? In the biblical world, what could happen to a debtor until the balance of a loan was paid off?
2. **22:17—24:34.** What have scholars detected about this section of Proverbs? What is the *Instruction of Amenemope*? How may it have influenced this section of Proverbs? Why is it no surprise that Israel should appropriate insights from other Near Eastern cultures?
3. **Word Study: Thirty Sayings.** What does the Hebrew adverb *shalishiwm* mean? Because of its unusual form and possible relationship to an Egyptian work that is divided into 30 sections, to what do many scholars propose the word should be changed? Why? How does the Greek Septuagint translate the word? Despite arguments in favor of emending the text, about what do scholars disagree?
4. **22:22.** What is the importance of the gate of a walled town?

For application
1. **22:6.** If you are a parent who has trained a child in the faith, how do you respond when the child departs from it? What hope is provided by the example of saints like St. Monica (St. Augustine's mother), who prayed for decades for her son's conversion?
2. **22:11.** What is purity of heart? To what areas of life besides sexual purity does it extend? How does it benefit relationships with others as well as with God?
3. **22:15.** How would you describe your approach to disciplining a child? If the expression "rod of discipline" need not refer to corporal punishment, how can discipline remain strict without being overbearing, on the one hand, or lax, on the other?
4. **22:19.** How do you encourage yourself to trust the Lord when times get difficult? For example, are there hymns that you sing, or Scripture passages that you recall? How do you "evangelize yourself"?

Chapter 23

For understanding
1. **23:2.** Why does this proverb recommend that a man given to appetite put a knife to his throat? What does the virtue of temperance promote in this case?
2. **23:13.** When it comes to physical discipline of children, what does Proverbs neither advocate nor endorse? What is in view here and elsewhere in the book?

3.   **23:29–35.** What do these verses vividly depict? What are among its painful consequences? What happens when the drunkard recovers from his intoxication?

4.   **23:31.** Why should the alcoholic not *look* at wine? How does the Greek Septuagint translate this verse? According to St. Caesarius of Arles, what happens when you become friends with someone who is displeasing to God?

For application

1.   **23:1–3.** How often have you been in the company of important or influential people? How did you conduct yourself? Why, if you do not know them well, is it necessary to guard your conduct and your speech in their presence?

2.   **23:13.** The administration of corporal punishment is a subject of controversy these days. What is your philosophy? How do you best train a child to recognize wrongdoing, repent of it, and seek forgiveness?

3.   **23:17.** Read CCC 2538–40. In what ways do you envy the good fortune of others? Of all the capital sins, why is envy singled out as "diabolical" (CCC 2539)? How can one struggle against it?

4.   **23:29–35.** To what are you addicted? What have been the consequences for you and for your relationship with God? What resources (including prayer) are available for you to use in order to become free of the addiction? How serious have you been in taking advantage of them?

Chapter 24

For understanding

1.   **24:3.** Of what is a home under construction a concrete image? In Hebrew, to what can the term for "house" also refer? According to St. John Chrysostom, for what do the house and its storerooms stand?

2.   **24:11.** What is this proverb a call to do? As implied in 24:12, when should this be done? If it is not done, what kind of sin is it?

3.   **24:23.** Of what is showing favoritism in the courtroom a violation? According to what standard are human judges expected to act? In this regard, what two things does the Mosaic Law forbid?

4.   **24:28–29.** What two things does this proverb prohibit? How, according to Scripture, can we restrain the impulse to exact revenge?

For application

1.   **24:11–12.** Have you ever been aware of a wrong being done (such as spousal or child abuse) but either ignored it or claimed to know nothing about it? What type of sin might this be?

2.   **24:16.** How often have you failed to overcome a significant temptation to sin? Despite occasional failure, how often have you resumed the battle? How have you dealt with the temptation to give up? What have you done to give the problem over to the Lord?

3.   **24:17–18.** Why would the Lord be displeased at your pleasure over the fall of an enemy? What attitude should you take at the fall of an enemy? (Compare your answer with Mt 5:44–45.)

4.   **24:23.** How might a parent or an employer show partiality in judging a child or an employee? What kind of example does this set for the person judged and for others who are aware of the partiality?

Chapter 25

For understanding

1.   **25:1.** Who, presumably, are the "men of Hezekiah"? What did promoting the teachings of Solomon have to do with King Hezekiah?

2.   **25:2.** How does this proverb say the glory of God is manifested? How is the glory of kings manifested?

3.   **25:14.** Of what are clouds and wind without rain symbolic? How does the NT use this imagery?

4.   **25:21–22.** What does this proverb promote? To what might the "coals of fire" refer? Either way, what actions are discouraged here? In what context does Paul quote this saying in Romans 12:20?

For application

1.   **25:7b–10.** What is your opinion of lawsuits brought by one Christian against another? How would you respond to St. Paul's statement in 1 Cor 6:1–7 that Christians ought to allow themselves to be cheated rather than bring suit against another Christian in a civil court?

2.   **25:14.** Have you ever promised, either explicitly or implicitly, something you failed to deliver? How significant was the promise? What if any were the moral implications of the promise?

3.   **25:21–22.** Read the note for this verse. What does Jesus say (e.g., in Mt 5:44) about our attitude toward enemies? What does the Lord's Prayer imply about it? How have you fulfilled these injunctions?

4.   **25:27.** According to CCC 2480, flattery can be a mortal or a venial sin, depending on the circumstances. What circumstances does the Catechism mention? When is it right to compliment others?

Chapter 26

For understanding

1.   **26:4–5.** Though these two proverbs appear contradictory on the surface, to what do they apply? In certain contexts, how do the wise do well to avoid conversations with fools? In other contexts, such as when fools appear intelligent and sophisticated, what should the wise do? What does each saying aim to do?

2.   **26:7.** Though the fool may be able to recite a proverb, why does it give him no benefit?

3.   **26:11.** How is the fool's behavior comparable to that of a dog returning to its vomit? What does 2 Pet 2:22 describe by quoting this proverb?

4.   **26:12.** What temptation faces those who cultivate wisdom? What virtue is essential to the biblical concept of wisdom?

For application
1. **26:4.** When you find a conversation turning toward criticism of someone else, what should be your response? What do the cardinal virtues have to do with engaging in criticism of others?
2. **26:5.** When you find a conversation turning toward criticism of someone else and you believe that the speakers are wrong, what should be your response? Again, how do you apply the cardinal virtues in this situation?
3. **26:11.** When does foolish behavior (such as viewing pornography) turn into an addiction? What are some loving ways to deal with someone who is addicted to self-destructive behavior?
4. **26:18–19.** What is rationalization? When you are caught in a lie or in dishonest behavior, how do you tend to explain your conduct? What does a tendency to rationalize say about one's character?

Chapter 27

For understanding
1. **27:1–27.** Why are several proverbs in this chapter grouped in pairs? What about the final verses?
2. **27:5.** When is an open rebuke a sign of true affection? What is meant by "hidden love" here?
3. **27:6.** Why are words of correction or rebuke described as the wounds of a friend? How are kisses potentially deceptive signs of affection?
4. **27:23–27.** How does the practical wisdom in these verses benefit the herdsman with his flock?

For application
1. **27:5.** If fraternal correction is supposed to be part of the Christian life, why do so few Christians practice it? If we turn from evil out of a fear of others' anger, what does that say about ourselves? (Refer to CCC 1828–29.)
2. **27:8.** Read the note for this verse. What are some of the moral and spiritual dangers that young people face when they first leave home, e.g., for college? How can you prepare them?
3. **27:10.** If you need help, especially long-term help, on whom would you rely for it—your family or your friends? What resources do you have if you need care?
4. **27:17.** What are your friendships like? What are their strengths and limitations? How do they improve or hinder your relationship with the Lord (even if they are not particularly religious)?

Chapter 28

For understanding
1. **28:4.** How do interpreters differ over the precise meaning of "the law" in the context of this verse? In what two ways is legal language regularly used in Proverbs?
2. **28:8.** How does the Mosaic Law regard collecting interest on assistance loans? When was usury permitted for an Israelite? To what does "increase" (in addition to interest) most likely refer? What does the proverb seem to say that God will do with ill-gotten wealth?
3. **28:9.** What can render prayer ineffective? How does St. Bede recommend that one pray?
4. **28:13.** What can harboring unconfessed sin do to a person? What is the ordinary way of receiving God's forgiveness? In OT times, what were two ways in which this might take place?

For application
1. **28:5.** How does seeking the Lord increase one's understanding of justice? By calling St. Joseph a "just man" (Mt 1:19), what is Scripture saying about his relationship with the Lord? What would it say about yours?
2. **28:8.** What do you think Solomon would say about the modern practice of buying on credit and accumulating enormous debts? What is your own level of financial indebtedness, and what do you think God wants you to do about your own borrowing habits?
3. **28:9.** Although one's conscience can make mistakes, when can a person be held morally responsible for a mistaken judgment of conscience? How serious is the obligation to form one's conscience?
4. **28:13.** When you go to confession, how often do you find yourself confessing the same sins over and over again? If they are venial sins, how seriously do you take them? What have you done to correct habitual patterns of sin?

Chapter 29

For understanding
1. **29:3.** How is a father dishonored twice over by an undisciplined son? Which parable of Jesus describes this situation?
2. **29:20.** To what is one who is quick to speak susceptible? By contrast, what does one who is wise do?
3. **29:24.** In biblical times, on whom could a curse be called down? What did remaining silent mean if one had knowledge about a crime?

For application
1. **29:3.** How should Christian parents respond when they learn that one or more of their children have not only left the faith but have adopted ways of life opposed to the principles by which they were raised? What should such parents do with their own grief? How should they relate to their dissenting children?
2. **29:10.** What stories of Christian martyrs have you read? What effect do such stories have on your faith? Do you see yourself as a Christian witness in today's social and political environment? If so, in what way?
3. **29:11.** What most typically makes you angry, and how do you express anger? How do you try to control your anger? What does it mean to be angry without sinning (see Eph 4:26)?
4. **29:18.** If prophecy is not merely foretelling the future, what is it? On whose behalf does the prophet speak? Why does St. Paul recommend that Christians seek the spiritual gift of prophecy (1 Cor 14:1ff.)?

Chapter 30

For understanding
1. **30:1.** Who is Agur? How is he like Job? Where is Massa, and after whom was that location named? How does the RSV understand the names Ithiel and Ucal? What makes some scholars believe that the text has suffered corruption?
2. **30:4.** What does the rhetorical question about ascending into heaven imply? Who can make the claim of having done it? Who is meant by the reference to "his son's name"? What hint can Christian readers rightly detect about God?
3. **30:9.** What can times of plenty make us do? How does theft profane the name of God?
4. **30:15–33.** How do these numerical proverbs work?
5. **30:21–23.** How does each of the four intolerable things in these verses turn the world upside down?

For application
1. **30:2–3.** If it is true that one who thinks he has acquired the virtue of humility has just lost it, how does one learn humility? What can the realization that one never completely grows up do to advance one's relationship with the Lord?
2. **30:5.** Paragraphs 109–14 of the Catechism provide principles for interpreting Scripture. How might these principles help you apply the word of God profitably to your life?
3. **30:8b–9a.** Why is prosperity dangerous to a living faith in God? Why are suffering and persecution often good for it?

Chapter 31

For understanding
1. **31:1.** Who is Lemuel? What people neighboring Israel were renowned for their wisdom in biblical times? From whom do the admonitions of Proverbs 31 come, and to whom are they addressed? About what does she caution him, what does she encourage him to do, and about what does she counsel him?
2. **31:10–31.** What does this epilogue to Proverbs praise? What kind of poem is this, and how does it work? Why would Hebrew writers create poems in this alphabetic format? As it unfolds the virtues of the praiseworthy wife (echoing several lines earlier in the book), at what does it hint regarding her?
3. **Word Study: The Good Wife.** Although translating *'eshet hayil* as "a woman of worth" or "a good wife" is not inaccurate, what does the word *hayil* generally convey? Where is the term often found? Given the military usage, how might one best render the expression in Proverbs 31:10? Which of her strengths are singled out for mention? What kind of character does she actually show?
4. **31:10.** To what is finding an excellent wife comparable? According to St. Caesarius of Arles, who is the "worthy wife"?
5. **31:30.** How is charm deceitful, and how are good looks vain? Should the husband disregard the physical attractiveness of his wife? What kind of wife is the good wife? What is the preeminent virtue of the wise?

For application
1. **31:2–3.** What cautions did your parents give you about relations with the opposite sex? About what were they concerned? What do daughters learn about men from their fathers, and what do sons learn about women from their mothers? What *should* they be learning from them?
2. **31:10.** In an era of soaring divorce, for what should one look in a prospective spouse? Even if divorce is part of the family history, how does one prevent it from determining the direction of one's own marriage?
3. **31:11.** How vital to a marriage is trust between the spouses? In what areas is trust likely to become an issue? If trust is once violated, how can it be repaired? How important is forgiveness for the spouse who has been wronged?
4. **31:28–29.** What benefits accrue to a marriage when a husband honors his wife? How are modest displays of affection between spouses beneficial to the children?

Author and Date Ecclesiastes claims to relate the words of an unnamed "son of David" who reigned as "king in Jerusalem" (1:1). Jewish and Christian scholars have long identified this figure as King Solomon, the renowned wise man of OT times whose name is attached to similar writings in the Bible such as Proverbs (Prov 1:1) and the Song of Solomon (Song 1:1). Several comments in the book support this traditional ascription to Solomon: the author describes himself as "king over Israel" (1:12; 1 Kings 4:1), as a man of "great wisdom" (1:16; 1 Kings 4:29–34), as a builder of "houses" (2:4; 1 Kings 6:1; 7:1–8), as a planter of "vineyards" (2:4; Song 8:11), as an owner of "slaves" (2:7; 1 Kings 9:21), as a student and composer of "proverbs" (12:9; 1 Kings 4:32), and as one who accumulated "great possessions" (2:7; 1 Kings 10:23), including "silver and gold" (2:8; 1 Kings 10:2, 14, 22, 25), "singers" (2:8; 1 Kings 10:12), and a harem of "concubines" (2:8; 1 Kings 11:3). So, too, the themes of the book are consistent with a Solomonic composition. For instance, the enormously wealthy and powerful Solomon was eminently qualified to speak on the vanity of worldly power, pleasure, and possessions in a way that the vast majority of Israelites were not. Indeed, the author's disillusionment with even the finest luxuries in life is a state of mind that one might expect of Solomon as he experienced the Lord's discipline in the declining years of his reign. On the basis of this traditional view of authorship, the book would have been written in the tenth century, between Solomon's rise to kingship in 970 B.C. and his death in 930 B.C.

Much of modern scholarship contests the Solomonic authorship of Ecclesiastes and maintains that the book was written by an unknown author in the postexilic period. Among the reasons for this critical assessment are the following. First, the author informs us in 1:1 of his title ("the Preacher"), his lineage ("son of David"), his position ("king"), and his location ("in Jerusalem"), but he never discloses his name. The option for anonymity is said to be inconsistent with the ready appearance of Solomon's name in other wisdom texts of the OT (Prov 1:1; 10:1; 25:1; Song 1:1). Second, the comment at 1:16, where the writer claims to surpass "all who were over Jerusalem before me", sounds odd and even improbable on the lips of Solomon, since only his father David ruled before him as king of Israel in the holy city. Third, apart from chapters 1–2, where most of the Solomonic allusions are found, the author seems to speak from the perspective of a subject rather than from that of a king. To take one example, the writer laments that no one steps forward to oppose the injustice of oppression (4:1), even though a king such as Solomon was obligated to correct abuses and ensure that justice was served throughout his realm. Fourth, linguistic studies suggest that Ecclesiastes was written in the Persian period or later, i.e., sometime after 530 B.C. The appearance of Persian loanwords in 2:5 and 8:11 points in this direction, but even more persuasive is the regular occurrence of Aramaic patterns of speech that are reproduced in the Hebrew text, several of which are not attested before Persian times, when Aramaic rose to prominence as the international language of the wider Near East. Ecclesiastes thus has more grammatical affinities with texts written in the postexilic period than with classical Hebrew writings dating back to the time of Solomon.

Since all agree that Ecclesiastes presents itself as a book of Solomonic wisdom, the question is whether it goes back to Solomon himself or whether a later author employed the literary technique of impersonating Solomon in order to lend prestige to his own teaching. The matter would seem to be settled by indications that Ecclesiastes was written half a millennium or more after the time of Solomon. However, the date one assigns to the book's final form is not a decisive argument against a modified view of Solomonic authorship. It could be the case, for instance, that Ecclesiastes contains authentic teaching from Solomon that scribes (e.g., the "men of Hezekiah" in Prov 25:1) preserved through the centuries and that a postexilic sage later recast in his own contemporary idiom. An original collection of Solomonic sayings that was modernized and possibly expanded after the Babylonian Exile could account for the internal evidence of the text as well as for the external evidence of Jewish and Christian tradition. Nevertheless, most scholars today hold that the "persona" of Solomon projected by the author is simply a literary device (as in chaps. 6–9 of the Book of Wisdom) and that the composition of the book should be dated somewhere between 500 and 200 B.C. Ecclesiastes could not have been written much later than this since fragments of the book found among the Dead Sea Scrolls have been dated to the middle of the second century B.C.

Title Ecclesiastes bears the title *Qoheleth*, a Hebrew term that occurs seven times in the book and appears to mean "one who assembles". Some think it a pseudonym or pen name, while others suggest that it serves as a title for "one who presides over an assembly". The Greek Septuagint (LXX) translates it *Ekklēsiastēs*, which designates "a member of a civic assembly". The Latin Vulgate transliterates the Greek title with the expanded heading *Liber Ecclesiastes*, "Book of Ecclesiastes", from which the English title is derived. It was Saint Jerome who established the tradition that *Qoheleth* means "Preacher" (Lat., *concionator*), the influence of which carries over into the RSV's translation of the term throughout the book (see 1:1–2, 12; 7:27; 12:8–10).

Structure There is no one division of Ecclesiastes that commands universal agreement. Some even deny that the book has an overall structure that extends beyond short clusters of sayings that share a common theme. Nevertheless, a basic distinction is commonly made between the main body of the work, which is expressed in the first person (1:12—12:8), and a short prologue and epilogue, both of which are written in the third person (1:1–11 and 12:9–14). Deciding on the internal structure of the book is the more challenging task. Simple but serviceable is a twofold division of the main speech: first, 1:12—6:9 deals with Qoheleth's various quests to find meaning in life; and, second, 7:1—12:8 relates Qoheleth's advice on how to cope with life's inevitabilities, concluding with a reflection on aging and death. In between stands 6:10–12, which serves as a bridge between the two halves.

Place in the Canon There was some dispute in early Judaism over whether or not to include Ecclesiastes in the canon of the Bible (Mishnah, *'Eduyot* 5, 3), but the matter was eventually resolved in its favor. In the Hebrew Bible, Ecclesiastes is grouped among the five scrolls, called the *Megilloth*, which were traditionally read on Jewish feast days (the four others being the Song of Solomon, Ruth, Lamentations, and Esther). Ecclesiastes was read at the yearly feast of Tabernacles, celebrating the end of the harvest season, perhaps because of passages that speak of "a time to laugh" (3:4) and that say "it is God's gift to man that every one should eat and drink and take pleasure" (3:13). In the Greek Septuagint and Latin Vulgate, as in most modern translations, Ecclesiastes stands between Proverbs and the Song of Solomon. Behind this arrangement is the tradition that all three works were authored by King Solomon. The Church seems to have accepted the scriptural status of Ecclesiastes from the start.

Themes and Characteristics Ecclesiastes is the most philosophical book of the Bible. It looks at the world almost exclusively from the standpoint of human reason, experience, and observation. The existence of God is assumed, and his sovereignty over history and the world is affirmed, but man's relationship with God is not examined in great detail. From this limited perspective, in which faith is often left out of the picture, the author can only conclude that everything is "vanity" (1:2; 12:8). One could say that Ecclesiastes reveals the problem to which the rest of the Bible offers the solution, namely, that life is meaningless if death is our ultimate destiny and if man has no hope for happiness that reaches beyond the grave.

Given this somber outlook, the author of Ecclesiastes (Qoheleth or "the Preacher") is frequently described as a despairing skeptic or an incurable pessimist. He is a man sorely disillusioned by the harsh realities of the world. So far as Qoheleth can see, man is engaged in endless toil, yet it seems to bring him minimal "gain" (1:3; 2:11; 3:9; 5:11). Eventually man will leave this world with nothing (5:15–17), and the fruits of his labor will pass to another (2:18–23). In the meantime, oppression flourishes unopposed (3:16; 4:1-3; 5:8; 8:9), and sin corrupts the hearts of all, even the righteous (7:20; 9:3). Despite his earnest search for wisdom, Qoheleth ends up frustrated (1:13–18) by the fact that God's ways remain a mystery (3:11; 8:16–17; 11:5) and the future is hidden from sight (3:22; 6:12; 8:7; 10:14). Despite experiencing the finest pleasures the world has to offer, he is left unfulfilled (2:1–11) and comes to see that wealth can bring no stable satisfaction (4:7–8; 5:10).

Life is pronounced vain and meaningless primarily because death is inescapable. For Qoheleth, death is the "great equalizer" that levels all distinctions between people. Because of it, the wise appear to have no advantage over the foolish (2:14–17), the righteous seem to fare no better than the wicked (7:15–18; 8:14), and the rich are no different from the poor insofar as they cannot enjoy their wealth (6:1–6). Besides this, the end of man and beast is the same: when their life-breath is taken away, their bodies dissolve into dust (3:18–20). This destiny is the more bitter because it lies beyond man's control. Unlike God, who appoints times of prosperity and adversity (7:14), man has no "authority over the day of death" (8:8). The best he can do, says Qoheleth, is to enjoy the good things in life as much as his circumstances allow (2:24; 3:12, 22; 8:15).

God fits into this picture in important but limited ways. As the Creator (12:1), he determines all times and seasons of life (3:1–8), and its intermittent joys are acknowledged as his gift (2:24–26; 3:13; 5:18–20; 9:7). Because God is also Judge and will hold man accountable for his actions (3:17; 11:9; 12:14), Qoheleth urges readers to fear him (5:7; 12:13), to keep his commandments (12:13), and to avoid thoughtless expressions of prayer and worship (5:2–3). He is convinced that "it will be well with those who fear God" (8:12). Less clear is man's relationship with God at death. Qoheleth holds that man's spirit returns to God when it leaves the mortal body (12:7), but he seems to have no vision of ongoing life or happiness after death (9:5, 10). This is where the limitations of human understanding and observation stand out most clearly. Apart from supernatural revelation, philosophy is hard-pressed to make firm judgments about the ultimate destiny of man, and so its perception of "the meaning of life" is necessarily incomplete. Ecclesiastes is included in the Bible to teach precisely this lesson.

Christian Perspective The New Testament never quotes the Book of Ecclesiastes directly, although it may allude to a few of its memorable statements (see notes on 1:3; 7:20; 11:5). This does not mean that Christians found the book unpalatable or devoid of spiritual insight. On the contrary, Ecclesiastes was thought to be written so that man would yearn in his heart for another kind of life (St. Augustine, *City of God* 20, 3). In fact, from the time of Origen of Alexandria in the third century, it was held that the wisdom books attributed to Solomon (Proverbs, Ecclesiastes, the Song of Solomon) represented

three stages of spiritual growth. This was famously expressed by St. Bonaventure, who said that Proverbs teaches us how to live wisely in the world, that Ecclesiastes teaches contempt for worldly things, and that the Song of Solomon teaches us love for heavenly things (see Bonaventure's introduction to his *Commentary on Ecclesiastes*). Nevertheless, theologians down through the ages struggled to explain several passages in Ecclesiastes that seemed to contradict the revealed tenets of Christian faith. A common approach was to read 12:13–14 as Solomon's own perspective and to consider seemingly unorthodox statements earlier in the book as unsound opinions that are ultimately rejected. Even today, scholars have entertained the notion that more than one "voice" seems to be speaking in Ecclesiastes, although the task of isolating which words represent the author's view and which represent the objectionable views of someone else is extremely difficult.

OUTLINE OF ECCLESIASTES

1. Prologue (1:1–11)

2. Part One: The Vanities of Life (1:12—6:9)
    A. Vanity of Wisdom (1:12–18)
    B. Vanity of Pleasures and Toil (2:1–26)
    C. Times and Seasons of Life (3:1–15)
    D. Vanity of Life and Death (3:16—4:16)
    E. Fear of God (5:1–7)
    F. Vanity of Wealth and Desire (5:8—6:9)

3. Transitional Verses (6:10–12)

4. Part Two: The Mysteries of Life (7:1—12:8)
    A. The "Better" Part of Wisdom (7:1–14)
    B. Mysteries of Recompense and Sin (7:15–29)
    C. Practical Maxims for Courtiers (8:1–5)
    D. The Inscrutability of God's Ways (8:6–17)
    E. Universality of Death, Unfairness of Life (9:1–12)
    F. Advantages of Wisdom (9:13—10:20)
    G. Uncertainty of the Future (11:1–6)
    H. Youth and Old Age (11:7—12:8)

5. Epilogue (12:9–14)

THE BOOK OF
ECCLESIASTES

All Is Vanity

1 The words of the Preacher,[a] the son of David,
king in Jerusalem.
2 Vanity of vanities, says the Preacher,
vanity of vanities! All is vanity.
3 What does man gain by all the toil
at which he toils under the sun?
4 A generation goes, and a generation
comes,
but the earth remains for ever.
5 The sun rises and the sun goes down,
and hastens to the place where it rises.

6 The wind blows to the south,
and goes round to the north;
round and round goes the wind,
and on its circuits the wind returns.
7 All streams run to the sea,
but the sea is not full;
to the place where the streams flow,
there they flow again.
8 All things are full of weariness;
a man cannot utter it;
the eye is not satisfied with seeing,
nor the ear filled with hearing.

1:1 The words of: Identifies the work as a collection of wise sayings or proverbs (as in Prov 30:1; 31:1). **the Preacher:** The Hebrew is *Qoheleth*, a term that appears to mean "one who assembles" or "one who gathers". It is not certain whether this was a pen name or a professional title; also unclear is whether the author was mainly a gatherer of wisdom or a gatherer of people to be instructed in wisdom (12:9). **son of David:** Royal title for one of David's dynastic heirs who succeeded him on the throne. Most take this as a reference to Solomon, although his name never appears in the book. An allusion to Solomon is supported by several details in 1:12—2:11.

1:2 vanity of vanities!: The expression has a superlative meaning ("the utmost vanity!"). The author signals these words as the book's leading motif by making them the first (1:2) and last words of his main discourse (12:8). **All is vanity:** Applies to all things that constitute man's life and labor in this world. Qoheleth's sweeping pronouncement does not cover matters related to God and his activity, as these have an ultimate value (3:14; 12:13).

1:3–11 The endless cycles of nature illustrate man's failure to make permanent progress. Qoheleth has come to question whether anything new ever happens in the world and to think that "the more things change, the more they stay the same." Oftentimes old things only seem new because of our tendency to forget the past.

1:3 What does man gain: Implies that no human undertaking is really profitable or lasting in the grand scheme of life. • Jesus echoes this sentiment when he states that even gaining the whole world will profit man nothing unless God is the focus of his life and pursuits (Mt 16:26; Mk 8:36). • What would it profit us to memorize the whole Bible and the teachings of the philosophers if we lived without grace and the love of God? Vanity of vanities and all is vanity

except to love and serve God alone (Thomas à Kempis, *Imitation of Christ* 1, 1).

1:4 earth remains for ever: In contrast to the shortness of human life (2:3; Jas 4:14). The statement is exaggerated for emphasis; elsewhere Scripture teaches that the present form of this world will pass away (2 Pet 3:10; 1 Jn 2:17; Rev 21:1).

1:5 sun rises ... goes down: Not a scientific statement but a phenomenological description of how the natural world appears to the senses. See note on Gen 1:6.

1:8 full of weariness: Poetically speaking, the world is tired of the monotony of nature's repeated operations. **not satisfied:** Suggested by the constant sensation of the eyes and ears, which are ever restless to experience more and more of the world.

Word Study

Vanity (1:2)

Hebel/Habel (Heb.): literally denotes a "breath" or "vapor" (Prov 21:6; Is 57:13). As such it is often used in the Bible to signify something that is fleeting or passes away quickly (Job 7:16; Ps 39:5; 144:4), something that is pointless, without advantage, or amounts to wasted effort (Is 49:4; Jer 10:15; Lam 4:17), or something that is empty of meaning or senseless from the standpoint of conventional wisdom (Eccles 5:7; Zech 10:2). The term is also used for vain idols (2 Kings 17:15; Ps 31:6). Roughly half of its occurrences in the OT are found in Ecclesiastes, which has as its theme the exclamation: "All is vanity" (Eccles 1:2, 14; 2:17; 12:8). Among the experiences of life pronounced vain are such things as worldly pleasure (Eccles 2:1), wealth (Eccles 5:10) and wisdom (Eccles 2:15), as well as the vigor of youth (Eccles 11:10) and the inevitability of death (Eccles 3:19; 11:8). Various nuances have been proposed for the meaning of vanity in Ecclesiastes, ranging from "brevity" to "futility" to "absurdity". Interestingly, the numerical value of the Hebrew term *hebel* is 37, which is precisely the number of times the word appears in the book.

The name is the Greek rendering of the Hebrew, Qoheleth, which means "one who convenes or speaks in an assembly." Hence the name: the Preacher. By a literary device the book is ascribed to Solomon, but in fact it was written after the Exile, probably in the third century B.C. There is no knowledge in the book of any idea of rewards and punishments after this life, thus much the same problem is met with here as in the book of Job. Why do the good suffer and the wicked flourish? Belief and experience do not harmonize. Ecclesiastes has to insist on God's goodness and power and providence even though experience seems at times to show the contrary. He has no solution to offer other than faith in God and trust that he will, in his own way and time, punish evil and reward good; cf. 3:17; 8:12–13. He constantly emphasizes the vanity of created things, which can never satisfy the heart of man. Thus he gives us something more than an unsolved problem and stimulates faith and trust in God in spite of appearances which might influence us to the contrary.

[a] Heb *Qoheleth*.

⁹What has been is what will be,
and what has been done is what will be done;
and there is nothing new under the sun.
¹⁰Is there a thing of which it is said,
"See, this is new"?
It has been already,
in the ages before us.
¹¹There is no remembrance of former things,
nor will there be any remembrance
of later things yet to happen
among those who come after.

Vanity in Seeking Wisdom

12 I the Preacher have been king over Israel in Jerusalem. ¹³And I applied my mind to seek and to search out by wisdom all that is done under heaven; it is an unhappy business that God has given to the sons of men to be busy with. ¹⁴I have seen everything that is done under the sun; and behold, all is vanity and a striving after wind.ᵇ
¹⁵What is crooked cannot be made straight,
and what is lacking cannot be numbered.

16 I said to myself, "I have acquired great wisdom, surpassing all who were over Jerusalem before me; and my mind has had great experience of wisdom and knowledge." ¹⁷And I applied my mind to know wisdom and to know madness and folly. I perceived that this also is but a striving after wind.

¹⁸For in much wisdom is much vexation,
and he who increases knowledge increases
sorrow.

Vanity in Self-indulgence

2 I said to myself, "Come now, I will make a test of pleasure; enjoy yourself." But behold, this also was vanity. ²I said of laughter, "It is mad," and of pleasure, "What use is it?" ³I searched with my mind how to cheer my body with wine—my mind still guiding me with wisdom—and how to lay hold on folly, till I might see what was good for the sons of men to do under heaven during the few days of their life. ⁴I made great works; I built houses and planted vineyards for myself; ⁵I made myself gardens and parks, and planted in them all kinds of fruit trees. ⁶I made myself pools from which to water the forest of growing trees. ⁷I bought male and female slaves, and had slaves who were born in my house; I had also great possessions of herds and flocks, more than any who had been before me in Jerusalem. ⁸I also gathered for myself silver and gold and the treasure of kings and provinces; I got singers, both men and women, and many concubines,ᶜ man's delight.

9 So I became great and surpassed all who were before me in Jerusalem; also my wisdom remained

---

1:9 under the sun: The expression means "in the world of human experience" and appears frequently in the book (1:14; 2:11, 17, 18, 19, 20, etc.).

1:12–18 Qoheleth's pursuit of wisdom ends in disappointment. His satisfaction of mind is frustrated by the inscrutable puzzles of life, which taunt reason's limited ability to make sense of the world (7:23–24). Besides that, a life of wisdom affords no more protection against death than a life of folly (2:14–16).

1:12 king over Israel: An allusion to Solomon, who reigned over all Israel in the tenth century B.C. (1 Kings 4:1).

1:13 my mind: Literally, "my heart", which is closely associated with the intellect in ancient Hebrew thought. See word study: *Heart* at Deut 30:6. **by wisdom:** By reason, reflection, and observation. **unhappy business:** Even the quest to acquire wisdom is a toilsome burden.

1:14 a striving after wind: A favorite expression of the author (1:17; 2:11, 17, 26; 4:4, 6, 16; 6:9). Since one cannot even see rushing air, much less take hold of it, the saying refers to any elusive goal or futile effort. Ancient Greek and Latin translations understand the expression differently, e.g., the LXX translates it "a choice of [one's] spirit", and the Vulgate renders it "an affliction of [one's] spirit".

1:16 great wisdom: Possessed by no one more than Solomon in OT times (1 Kings 4:29–34; 10:23–24; Sir 47:14–17). **all who were over Jerusalem before me:** Often read as a hint that Solomon was not the real author of the book but only the literary persona adopted by a later author. The reason for this view lies in the word "all", which seems exaggerated, since David was the only king of Israel to reign in the holy city before Solomon. Others argue that Solomon is claiming to be wiser than any former ruler of Jerusalem, including its pre-Israelite kings such as Melchizedek (see note on Gen 14:18).

1:17 madness and folly: Investigation into the value of wisdom would not be complete without learning something of its opposite.

2:1–11 Qoheleth reports on his experiment with pleasure. He found that indulging in sensual delights and amassing wealth failed to provide the key to happiness. Somehow these experiences left him unfulfilled; instead, they proved to be merely distractions from the haunting reality that life seems to have no ultimate meaning. • Why are vast and overflowing riches vain? Because they have no useful purpose. Riches are vain when they purchase luxury, but they cease to be vain when they go forth to the needy (St. John Chrysostom, *Homilies on Ephesians* 12). • Like writing in water, enjoyments disappear in their doing. When the activity stops, the pleasure stops, and nothing is laid up for the future, nor is any trace of happiness left behind. There is no advantage for those who labor for what is vain (St. Gregory of Nyssa, *Homilies on Ecclesiastes* 4).

2:3 my mind still guiding: The king experienced the joys of wine with conscious restraint, i.e., without descending into drunkenness. **what is good:** In the sense of "advantageous" or "profitable".

2:4 built houses: Solomon's greatest architectural achievements included construction of the Temple, called "the house of the LORD", and a complex of royal palaces (1 Kings 6:1; 7:1-8). **vineyards:** Planted on Solomon's royal estates (Song 8:11; cf. 1 Chron 27:27).

2:5 gardens and parks: Places of peaceful retreat and recreation. In the Song of Solomon, the king's garden serves as a lover's paradise (Song 6:2; 8:13).

2:8 silver and gold: Acquired by Solomon on an unprecedented scale (1 Kings 9:28; 10:1, 14, 22, 25, 27). **provinces:** Tribute-paying nations subject to Israel are probably in view. Several surrounding peoples were made vassals of the Israelite kingdom through the conquests of David (2 Sam 8:1–14). **singers:** Solomon had a retinue of vocalists and court musicians (1 Kings 10:12). **concubines:** Solomon is said to have had a harem of 300 such women, not including his 700 wives (1 Kings 11:3).

ᵇOr *a feeding on wind*. See Hos 12:1.
ᶜThe meaning of the Hebrew word is uncertain.

with me. [10]And whatever my eyes desired I did not keep from them; I kept my heart from no pleasure, for my heart found pleasure in all my toil, and this was my reward for all my toil. [11]Then I considered all that my hands had done and the toil I had spent in doing it, and behold, all was vanity and a striving after wind, and there was nothing to be gained under the sun.

Vanity of Folly and Toil

12 So I turned to consider wisdom and madness and folly; for what can the man do who comes after the king? Only what he has already done. [13]Then I saw that wisdom excels folly as light excels darkness. [14]The wise man has his eyes in his head, but the fool walks in darkness; and yet I perceived that one fate comes to all of them. [15]Then I said to myself, "What befalls the fool will befall me also; why then have I been so very wise?" And I said to myself that this also is vanity. [16]For of the wise man as of the fool there is no enduring remembrance, seeing that in the days to come all will have been long forgotten. How the wise man dies just like the fool! [17]So I hated life, because what is done under the sun was grievous to me; for all is vanity and a striving after wind.

18 I hated all my toil in which I had toiled under the sun, seeing that I must leave it to the man who will come after me; [19]and who knows whether he will be a wise man or a fool? Yet he will be master of all for which I toiled and used my wisdom under the sun. This also is vanity. [20]So I turned about and gave my heart up to despair over all the toil of my labors under the sun, [21]because sometimes a man who has toiled with wisdom and knowledge and skill must leave all to be enjoyed by a man who did not toil for it. This also is vanity and a great evil. [22]What has a man from all the toil and strain with which he toils beneath the sun? [23]For all his days are full of pain, and his work is a vexation; even in the night his mind does not rest. This also is vanity.

24 There is nothing better for a man than that he should eat and drink and find enjoyment in his toil. This also, I saw, is from the hand of God; [25]for apart from him[d] who can eat or who can have enjoyment? [26]For to the man who pleases him God gives wisdom and knowledge and joy; but to the sinner he gives the work of gathering and heaping, only to give to one who pleases God. This also is vanity and a striving after wind.

Everything Has a Season

3 For everything there is a season, and a time for every matter under heaven:
[2]a time to be born, and a time to die;
a time to plant, and a time to pluck up what is planted;

2:10 whatever my eyes desired: Given his vast resources, Solomon could afford to spare no expense in gratifying his every passion.

2:12–17 Qoheleth partly endorses and partly disputes the traditional notion that wisdom is always better than folly. It is true that wise conduct has some practical advantages over foolish behavior in life, but death seems to cancel these benefits by reducing all to the same fate. It is hard to refute Qoheleth's logic from a this-worldly standpoint, unless one accepts that God will balance the scales of justice in an afterlife (see 12:14).

2:12 after the king: Meaning obscure. Perhaps it implies that Solomon's conclusions in 1:12—2:11 can hardly be disputed by men with lesser wisdom and fewer opportunities for pleasure. Others see this as a reference to the king's royal heirs.

2:13 light ... darkness: Often symbolizes the alternatives of righteousness and sinfulness as two opposing ways of life (Job 12:25; Prov 6:23; 1 Thess 5:4–8; 1 Jn 1:6–7).

2:16 no enduring remembrance: An honorable reputation that lived on in the memory of one's descendants was highly esteemed in Israel (Prov 10:7; Sir 41:12–13). However, seen through the lens of Qoheleth's pessimism, even this is eventually forgotten (1:11).

2:17 I hated life: Insofar as life seemed to him hopelessly unfair.

2:18–23 Qoheleth bemoans the fact that everything acquired in life passes to a successor at death. Moreover, one cannot be certain whether his belongings will go to a worthy heir who will appreciate what comes to him or to an unworthy heir who will squander it away. It is certain only that death will force us to part with the material goods and comforts we have earned through our labors (Ps 49:10).

2:21 a great evil: Not a moral evil but a painful reality that is difficult to accept.

2:24 eat and drink: Stands for the good things in life that gladden the heart and provide some relief from its many trials and difficulties. These experiences are gifts from God (3:13; 5:18; 8:15; 9:7). The statement is not an endorsement of hedonism, nor is it evidence that Qoheleth was influenced by the Greek philosophy of Epicureanism, which held that maximizing pleasure was the supreme good in life. On the contrary, Qoheleth has already tested the worth of sensual indulgence and found it wanting (2:2). Thus, his point is not that feasting and merrymaking give life its ultimate significance; rather, they are high points for man as he struggles against the vanity that overshadows so much of his existence. See note on 8:15. **enjoyment in his toil:** God has arranged that a measure of happiness and a sense of accomplishment may be found in one's work (3:22; 5:19).

2:26 God gives wisdom: According to the RSV, God distributes his gifts on the basis of personal merit ("to the man who pleases him"). Many commentators, however, understand the Hebrew text to mean that God confers his blessings on the basis of his sovereign will ("to whatever man he pleases"). The RSV translation does not accord with the author's perspective that the righteous do not always prosper and the wicked do not always suffer hardship (7:15; 8:10), whereas the alternative translation coheres with Ecclesiastes' view that God's will cannot be thwarted (3:14; 7:13).

3:1–8 A litany of times and seasons ordained by God, who is sovereign over history and human affairs (Ps 31:15; Sir 33:13). Man can neither control nor fully comprehend these arrangements, so he must accept that God determines the seasons of life and must order his expectations accordingly. In short, he is called to "fear" God, whose purposes are both mysterious (3:11) and immutable (3:14).

3:2 born ... die: Birth and death, which constitute the boundaries of human life, are the most obvious experiences that lie beyond human control. • In baptism one dies and is born in the same moment, the saving water being both a grave and a mother. The saying of Solomon "a time for dying and a time for being born" applies to this one moment, which accomplishes both (St. Cyril of Jerusalem, *Mystagogical Catechesis* 2, 4).

---

[d]Gk Syr: Heb *apart from me.*

³a time to kill, and a time to heal;
 a time to break down, and a time to build up;
⁴a time to weep, and a time to laugh;
 a time to mourn, and a time to dance;
⁵a time to cast away stones, and a time to gather
 stones together;
 a time to embrace, and a time to refrain from
 embracing;
⁶a time to seek, and a time to lose;
 a time to keep, and a time to cast away;
⁷a time to tear, and a time to sew;
 a time to keep silence, and a time to speak;
⁸a time to love, and a time to hate;
 a time for war, and a time for peace.
⁹What gain has the worker from his toil?

God-given Tasks

10 I have seen the business that God has given to the sons of men to be busy with. ¹¹He has made everything beautiful in its time; also he has put eternity into man's mind, yet so that he cannot find out what God has done from the beginning to the end. ¹²I know that there is nothing better for them than to be happy and enjoy themselves as long as they live; ¹³also that it is God's gift to man that every one should eat and drink and take pleasure in all his toil. ¹⁴I know that whatever God does endures for ever; nothing can be added to it, nor anything taken from it; God has made it so, in order that men should fear before him. ¹⁵That which is, already has been; that which is to be, already has been; and God seeks what has been driven away.

Judgment and the Future Belong to God

16 Moreover I saw under the sun that in the place of justice, even there was wickedness, and in the place of righteousness, even there was wickedness. ¹⁷I said in my heart, God will judge the righteous and the wicked, for he has appointed a time for every matter, and for every work. ¹⁸I said in my heart with regard to the sons of men that God is testing them to show them that they are but beasts. ¹⁹For the fate of the sons of men and the fate of beasts is the same; as one dies, so dies the other. They all have the same breath, and man has no advantage over the beasts; for all is vanity. ²⁰All go to one place; all are from the dust, and all turn to dust again. ²¹Who knows whether the spirit of man goes upward and the spirit of the beast goes down to the earth? ²²So I saw that there is nothing better than that a man should enjoy his work, for that is his lot; who can bring him to see what will be after him?

3:3 time to kill: Such things as hunting, warfare, and criminal executions seem to be in view. The killing of innocent persons is always forbidden in the Bible (Ex 20:13; Deut 5:17).

3:5 cast away: The work of the farmer, who must clear his field of stones before plowing and planting it. **gather:** The work of the builder, who collects stones for the purpose of erecting walls and livestock enclosures. **Embrace ... refrain from embracing:** Perhaps times of sexual intimacy and abstinence are meant. Refraining from marital relations can be determined by legal prescriptions (Lev 18:19), disciplinary customs (1 Sam 21:5), and consensual agreement between spouses (1 Cor 7:3–5).

3:7 keep silence ... speak: The matter of when to talk and when to listen is the subject of several wisdom instructions in the Bible (Prov 17:27–28; Sir 20:6–7; Jas 1:19).

3:8 time to love ... time to hate: An observation that just as love between people tends to flourish in times of tranquility (**peace**), so hatred for violence and its perpetrators tends to abound in times of invasion and armed conflict (**war**).

3:9 What gain ... toil: A rhetorical question implying a negative answer. See note on 1:3.

3:11 eternity: The Hebrew term denotes "perpetuity" or "duration". The statement has been taken to mean different things, such as (1) that God has programmed *the times and seasons* of 3:1–8 into the heart of man, giving him a sense of heaven's sovereignty over his life in the world, or (2) that God has implanted in man a *desire for eternity* that no creature or experience in this world can satisfy and that keeps him from being content with this life. The divine gift does not include an understanding of the grand designs of the Almighty, for these remain undiscoverable to man apart from divine revelation. • The Lord moves us to take pleasure in praise, for he has made us for himself, and our heart is restless until it rests in him (St. Augustine, *Confessions* 1, 1). **man's mind:** Literally, "man's heart". See word study: *Heart* at Deut 30:6. **so that:** Or, "with the result that".

3:12 nothing better: For this theme, see note on 2:24.

3:14 nothing can be added: Divine works and decrees are immutable (Sir 18:5–6). Man must not try to add to or subtract from them (Deut 4:2; Prov 30:6; Rev 22:18–19).

3:15 already has been: Recalls the climax of the introductory poem in 1:10. **what has been driven away:** A poetic description of the past, which God seems to retrieve each time we experience another one of life's recurring cycles (3:1–8).

3:17 God will judge: Men are accountable to God for their actions, whether good or evil, private or public, and no injustice will be overlooked by God (see 11:9; 12:14). Unfortunately, Qoheleth never specifies when he expects the **appointed** time for judgment to occur. Early in the OT period, it was believed that divine blessings and curses were meted out in the course of history (Deut 28:1–68), but eventually the belief emerged that divine rewards and punishments would also be given after death (Dan 12:2; 2 Mac 7:9). • Christian faith teaches that each person will face a particular judgment by God after death (Heb 9:27) and that all peoples and nations will undergo a universal judgment at the end of time (Mt 25:31–46; Rev 20:11–15) (CCC 678–79).

3:19 the same breath: The "breath of life", which God gives to man (Gen 2:7) and animals alike (Gen 7:21–22). **no advantage:** Experience teaches that all bodily creatures eventually die. Mortality is yet another instance of vanity's grip on the world.

3:20 one place: Either the ground, which is the grave of all (Sir 40:11), or Sheol, which is the biblical name for the realm of the dead (9:10; CCC 633). See word study: *Sheol* at Num 16:30. **the dust:** Biblical imagery for the material substance that makes up a body (Gen 2:7; Sir 33:10) and to which it returns at death (12:7; Gen 3:19; Ps 104:29).

3:21 Who knows...?: The question sounds as though Qoheleth is addressing a dispute among his contemporaries. That death involves a separation of spirit or breath from the body appears to be a given in the debate; it is the destiny of the spirit that is contested. Qoheleth holds that the spirit of man ascends to God once it leaves the body (12:7).

3:22 nothing better: For this theme, see note on 2:24.

Injustice of Life

4 Again I saw all the oppressions that are practiced under the sun. And behold, the tears of the oppressed, and they had no one to comfort them! On the side of their oppressors there was power, and there was no one to comfort them. [2]And I thought the dead who are already dead more fortunate than the living who are still alive; [3]but better than both is he who has not yet been, and has not seen the evil deeds that are done under the sun.

4 Then I saw that all toil and all skill in work come from a man's envy of his neighbor. This also is vanity and a striving after wind.

5 The fool folds his hands, and eats his own flesh.

6 Better is a handful of quietness than two hands full of toil and a striving after wind.

7 Again, I saw vanity under the sun: [8]a person who has no one, either son or brother, yet there is no end to all his toil, and his eyes are never satisfied with riches, so that he never asks, "For whom am I toiling and depriving myself of pleasure?" This also is vanity and an unhappy business.

Value of Friendship

9 Two are better than one, because they have a good reward for their toil. [10]For if they fall, one will lift up his fellow; but woe to him who is alone when he falls and has not another to lift him up. [11]Again, if two lie together, they are warm; but how can one be warm alone? [12]And though a man might prevail against one who is alone, two will withstand him. A threefold cord is not quickly broken.

13 Better is a poor and wise youth than an old and foolish king, who will no longer take advice, [14]even though he had gone from prison to the throne or in his own kingdom had been born poor. [15]I saw all the living who move about under the sun, as well as that[f] youth, who was to stand in his place; [16]there was no end of all the people; he was over all of them. Yet those who come later will not rejoice in him. Surely this also is vanity and a striving after wind.

Reverence, Humility, Enjoyment

5 [g]Guard your steps when you go to the house of God; to draw near to listen is better than to offer the sacrifice of fools; for they do not know that they are doing evil. [2][h]Be not rash with your mouth, nor let your heart be hasty to utter a word before God, for God is in heaven, and you upon earth; therefore let your words be few.

3 or a dream comes with much business, and a fool's voice with many words.

4 When you vow a vow to God, do not delay paying it; for he has no pleasure in fools. Pay what you vow. [5]It is better that you should not vow than that you should vow and not pay. [6]Let not your

---

4:1–3 Qoheleth laments injustices perpetrated against the poor. In view of such crimes, he considers future generations more fortunate than the living and the dead, for at least persons not yet conceived are untouched by the evil of the world. Some consider Qoheleth's perspective on oppression as evidence that he cannot really be King Solomon, for he speaks as though he is powerless to correct abuses that victimize the less fortunate.

4:4–8 Different perspectives on human labor, which is better than laziness (4:5) but can be tainted by competitiveness (4:4) or covetousness (4:7–8).

4:4 envy: Or, better, "jealous rivalry", which seeks to outdo another in accomplishments or possessions.

4:5 folds his hands: An image of the sluggard who crosses his arms to take a nap. Such a person would rather sleep than work for a living (Prov 6:10; 24:33). **eats his own flesh:** Exaggerated language to say that slothful behavior is self-destructive, for it leads to hunger and eventually a decline in health.

4:6 handful of quietness: A measure of peaceful enjoyment in life is better than endless toil and productivity (Prov 15:16).

4:8 has no one: I.e., has no family or offspring to leave with an inheritance. **eyes:** Sometimes associated with greed or covetous desire (2:10; Sir 14:9; 1 Jn 2:16).

4:9–12 The practical advantage of partnerships. In view are several challenges in life that are more readily overcome with the help of a companion. By way of illustration, a rope made of three strands is stronger than any single strand by itself (4:12). • The rope is faith in the truth that is woven from knowledge of the Trinity (St. Gregory the Great, *Moralia in Job* 33, 18).

4:13–16 The popularity of a king shifting to his successor illustrates how even the benefits of wisdom can fade over time. The rise from poverty to royal power may not allude to an actual historical event, but many have noted similarities with the story of Joseph, who went from prison to high political office in Egypt on the merits of his wisdom (Gen 37–41).

4:13 no longer take advice: It is wisdom to accept counsel and reproof from others (Prov 12:15; 13:10; 15:5).

4:16 those who come later: The next generation of subjects.

5:1 Guard your steps: Readers are advised to approach God with a prayerful and teachable heart. **the house of God:** The Lord's Temple in Jerusalem. **listen:** The Hebrew notion of "hearing" includes the idea of "heeding" or "obeying". **sacrifice of fools:** Liturgy and life form a unity in biblical religion, so much so that one's worship is not acceptable to God unless one's conduct is upright (1 Sam 15:22; Prov 21:3, 27; Is 1:12–17).

5:2 let your words be few: Overuse of words in prayer comes with the danger that many will be empty, thoughtless words (5:7; Sir 7:14). • Jesus expressed a similar view in his own teaching on prayer: "Do not heap up empty phrases as the Gentiles do; for they think that they will be heard for their many words" (Mt 6:7).

5:3 dream: Caused by the many concerns of the businessman. **many words:** If fools are overly talkative, the wise are restrained in their speech (Prov 10:19; 13:3; 21:23; Jas 1:19).

5:4 a vow to God: Imposes a grave obligation with serious consequences for negligence or nonfulfillment (Num 30:2; Deut 23:21–23). Careful consideration should thus be given to the matter before such a pledge is made (Prov 20:25; Sir 18:22–23) (CCC 2102–3). **Pay what you vow:** I.e., fulfill what you have promised to do.

5:6 the messenger: The officiating priest (Mal 2:7) who makes atonement for the one who sins unwittingly (Num 15:27–28). Instead of "the messenger", the Greek LXX reads "the face of God". **it was a mistake:** The excuse of one who

---

[f]Heb *the second.*
[g]Ch 4:17 in Heb.
[h]Ch 5:1 in Heb.

mouth lead you into sin, and do not say before the messenger[1] that it was a mistake; why should God be angry at your voice, and destroy the work of your hands?

7 For when dreams increase, empty words grow many:[j] but you must fear God.

8 If you see in a province the poor oppressed and justice and right violently taken away, do not be amazed at the matter; for the high official is watched by a higher, and there are yet higher ones over them. [9]But in all, a king is an advantage to a land with cultivated fields.[k]

10 He who loves money will not be satisfied with money; nor he who loves wealth, with gain: this also is vanity.

11 When goods increase, they increase who eat them; and what gain has their owner but to see them with his eyes?

12 Sweet is the sleep of a laborer, whether he eats little or much; but the surfeit of the rich will not let him sleep.

13 There is a grievous evil which I have seen under the sun: riches were kept by their owner to his hurt, [14]and those riches were lost in a bad venture; and he is father of a son, but he has nothing in his hand. [15]As he came from his mother's womb he shall go again, naked as he came, and shall take nothing for his toil, which he may carry away in his hand. [16]This also is a grievous evil: just as he came, so shall he go; and what gain has he that he toiled for the wind, [17]and spent all his days in darkness and grief,[1] in much vexation and sickness and resentment?

18 Behold, what I have seen to be good and to be fitting is to eat and drink and find enjoyment in all the toil with which one toils under the sun the few days of his life which God has given him, for this is his lot. [19]Every man also to whom God has given wealth and possessions and power to enjoy them, and to accept his lot and find enjoyment in his toil—this is the gift of God. [20]For he will not much remember the days of his life because God keeps him occupied with joy in his heart.

Frustration of Desires

6 There is an evil which I have seen under the sun, and it lies heavy upon men: [2]a man to whom God gives wealth, possessions, and honor, so that he lacks nothing of all that he desires, yet God does not give him power to enjoy them, but a stranger enjoys them; this is vanity; it is a sore affliction. [3]If a man begets a hundred children, and lives many years, so that the days of his years are many, but he does not enjoy life's good things, and also has no burial, I say that an untimely birth is better off than

---

claims to have sinned inadvertently. Another possibility is that 5:6 continues the discussion of 5:4–5, in which case the excuse comes from one who took a vow rashly and wishes to avoid the consequences of failing to live up to his pledge (cf. Lev 5:4). See note on Num 15:22–31.

5:7 fear God: One's most basic religious obligation (3:14; 7:18; 8:12–13; 12:13). See note on Prov 1:7.

5:8 high . . . higher: An acknowledgment that government bureaucracies sometimes do more to enable corruption than to prevent it.

5:9 a king is an advantage: The statement, perhaps a proverb, is notoriously difficult to interpret. It can also be rendered: "Land is an advantage over it all, a king to a cultivated field" (see also textual note *k*). It remains uncertain whether the benefit is seen (1) in having a monarch, (2) in owning productive farmland, or (3) in some combination of the two.

5:10–17 Sayings on the vanity of wealth. Financial abundance is not an ultimate good, says Qoheleth, because the rich are often left unsatisfied, anxious, and at risk of incurring severe losses on investments (CCC 2424, 2536).

5:15 naked: Without money or possessions of any kind (Job 1:21; 1 Tim 6:7).

5:18 eat and drink: On this advice, see note on 2:24.

5:20 occupied with joy: Happy times can be a welcome distraction from the shortness and difficulties of life.

6:2 a stranger: Perhaps he acquires the estate of a wealthy man who dies without an heir among his kin (cf. 2:18–21). Qoheleth can see no benefit in "having it all" if one has no opportunity to enjoy it.

6:3 children . . . years: Having a large family and a long life were among the most treasured blessings in biblical Israel (Ps 127:3–5; Prov 3:16; 9:11). **no burial:** A supremely dishonorable end to life (Jer 14:16; Ezek 29:5). **an untimely birth:** A stillborn baby, who never sees the light of day (Job 3:16; Ps 58:8). From the jaded perspective of Qoheleth, at least the lifeless infant is spared the troubles that afflict our world (4:2–3).

Word Study

Lot (5:18)

Ḥeleq (Heb.): denotes a "portion" or "share" of something. The Bible uses the term for such things as a share of the spoils of war (Gen 14:24), a portion of a family inheritance (Gen 31:14), and an allotment of land that is parceled out for settlement (Josh 18:5; Ezek 45:7). In the realm of personal and spiritual relationships, Israel can be described as the Lord's portion (Deut 32:9), just as Yahweh himself can be called the portion that Israel's priests and Levites are privileged to inherit (Num 18:20; Deut 10:9). Occasionally, *ḥeleq* designates the dreadful "fate" that awaits the wicked (Job 27:13; Is 17:14). In Ecclesiastes, where the word appears eight times, several shades of meaning are evident. In one passage, reference is made to a "portion" or piece of bread to be shared with others (Eccles 11:2). Elsewhere, one's lot is either the "reward" that comes from work, be it pleasure or possessions (Eccles 2:10, 21), or the circumstances in which God has placed a person, with its varied opportunities for enjoyment (Eccles 3:22; 5:18; 9:9). According to Qoheleth, one can do no better than accept his lot in life, for in doing so he accepts gifts apportioned to him by God (Eccles 5:19).

---

[1]Or *angel*.
[j]Or *For in a multitude of dreams there is futility, and ruin in a flood of words.*
[k]Or *The profit of the land is among all of them; a cultivated field has a king.*
[1]Gk: Heb *all his days also he eats in darkness.*

he. ⁴For it comes into vanity and goes into darkness, and in darkness its name is covered; ⁵moreover it has not seen the sun or known anything; yet it finds rest rather than he. ⁶Even though he should live a thousand years twice told, yet enjoy no good—do not all go to the one place?

7 All the toil of man is for his mouth, yet his appetite is not satisfied. ⁸For what advantage has the wise man over the fool? And what does the poor man have who knows how to conduct himself before the living? ⁹Better is the sight of the eyes than the wandering of desire; this also is vanity and a striving after wind.

10 Whatever has come to be has already been named, and it is known what man is, and that he is not able to dispute with one stronger than he. ¹¹The more words, the more vanity, and what is man the better? ¹²For who knows what is good for man while he lives the few days of his vain life, which he passes like a shadow? For who can tell man what will be after him under the sun?

Wisdom and Folly Compared

7 A good name is better than precious ointment; and the day of death, than the day of birth. ²It is better to go to the house of mourning than to go to the house of feasting;

for this is the end of all men,
and the living will lay it to heart.
³Sorrow is better than laughter,
for by sadness of countenance the heart is made glad.
⁴The heart of the wise is in the house of mourning;
but the heart of fools is in the house of mirth.
⁵It is better for a man to hear the rebuke of the wise
than to hear the song of fools.
⁶For as the crackling of thorns under a pot,
so is the laughter of the fools;
this also is vanity.
⁷Surely oppression makes the wise man foolish,
and a bribe corrupts the mind.
⁸Better is the end of a thing than its beginning;
and the patient in spirit is better than the proud in spirit.
⁹Be not quick to anger,
for anger lodges in the bosom of fools.
¹⁰Say not, "Why were the former days better than these?"
For it is not from wisdom that you ask this.
¹¹Wisdom is good with an inheritance,
an advantage to those who see the sun.

6:6 one place: Either the grave or the netherworld of Sheol. See note on 3:20.

6:7 for his mouth: Much of human labor is aimed at acquiring food for survival (Prov 16:26). This never-ending quest is emblematic of our desire for the goods of the world: just as the body is never satisfied for long after eating, so the spirit quickly grows restless to acquire more and more possessions even after it is indulged (4:7-8). • The passage may be understood of one who is learned in Scripture but whose soul is not satisfied because he always desires to learn more (St. Jerome, *Commentary on Ecclesiastes 6, 7*).

6:8 what advantage: From the perspective of this world, the benefits of wisdom over folly are real but limited (7:11-12, 19), though eventually these appear to be cancelled out by death (2:13-16).

6:9 the sight of the eyes: What one already possesses. **the wandering of desires:** Greed that is left to covet the things of the world unchecked.

6:10-12 Transitional verses that form a bridge between the first half of the book and the second. Several themes developed in later chapters are introduced in this short section (e.g., the limitations of man, his knowledge, and his life-span).

6:10 named ... known: By God. **one stronger than he:** God, whose sovereignty over man and his situation cannot be contested by mere creatures.

6:11 what is man the better?: Or, "what does it profit man?" The question is similar to 1:3.

6:12 who knows: Qoheleth is rightly skeptical that man, given his considerable limitations, can have a clear perception of the meaning of life or of what the future will bring by an exercise of his own intelligence (i.e., apart from divine revelation). **shadow:** An image for the shortness of human life (Job 8:9; Ps 102:11; cf. Jas 4:14).

7:1-14 A collection of wisdom sayings that take up the question of "what is good for man" from 6:12. The Hebrew term for "good" (*ṭob*) recurs several times in this section (7:1-3, 5, 8, 10-11, 14), though it is variously translated ("good", "precious", "better", "prosperity"). Using exagger-

ated language, Qoheleth contends that, because death casts its shadow over the whole of life, it is foolish to ignore the fact while abandoning oneself to merriment. The wise understand that life has no unmixed joys this side of the grave (Prov 14:13).

7:1 name ... ointment: A wordplay in Hebrew between *shem* (name) and *shemen* (oil). Though the fragrance of ointment lingers after it is applied, an honorable reputation long outlives the person who acquired it. A good reputation was highly valued in biblical times (Prov 10:7), yet eventually it fades from memory, according to Qoheleth (2:16).

7:2 the end of all men: Death is the one inescapable certainty in life.

7:3 the heart is made glad: Difficult to interpret. Generally speaking, the proverb is taken to mean either (1) that the look on one's face can sometimes disguise the interior state of the heart (a contrast between inside and outside) or (2) that misfortunes in life, though occasions for sadness, can make one wiser and happier in the days to come (a contrast between present and future).

7:5 rebuke of the wise: Affords the opportunity for the erring fool to change his ways and to improve himself. Humbly accepting reproof is one of the hallmarks of wisdom, according to the Bible (Prov 12:1; 13:18; 17:10).

7:6 the crackling of thorns: The sound of brushwood burning beneath a cooking kettle. Perhaps the point is that the fool's **laughter** (i.e., his self-satisfaction) is destined to be just as quickly consumed (cf. Lk 6:25).

7:7 oppression ... bribe: The result and cause of a manipulated justice system (Deut 16:19; Prov 16:8).

7:8 proud in spirit: Presumptuous overconfidence regarding the future is meant (Jas 4:13-16).

7:9 Be not quick to anger: It is wisdom to control one's temper rather than to be controlled by it. See note on Prov 14:17.

7:10-11 A rare instance in which Qoheleth extols the benefits of wisdom (see also 7:19).

7:11 good with an inheritance: Or, possibly, "as good as an inheritance".

¹²For the protection of wisdom is like the protection
 of money;
  and the advantage of knowledge is that
   wisdom preserves the life of him who has it.
¹³Consider the work of God;
  who can make straight what he has made
   crooked?

14 In the day of prosperity be joyful, and in the
day of adversity consider; God has made the one
as well as the other, so that man may not find out
anything that will be after him.

Inequalities of Life

15 In my vain life I have seen everything; there is
a righteous man who perishes in his righteousness,
and there is a wicked man who prolongs his life in
his evil-doing. ¹⁶Be not righteous overmuch, and
do not make yourself overwise; why should you
destroy yourself? ¹⁷Be not wicked overmuch, neither
be a fool; why should you die before your time? ¹⁸It
is good that you should take hold of this, and from
that withhold not your hand; for he who fears God
shall come forth from them all.

19 Wisdom gives strength to the wise man more
than ten rulers that are in a city.

20 Surely there is not a righteous man on earth
who does good and never sins.

21 Do not give heed to all the things that men
say, lest you hear your servant cursing you; ²²your
heart knows that many times you have yourself
cursed others.

23 All this I have tested by wisdom; I said, "I will
be wise"; but it was far from me. ²⁴That which is,
is far off, and deep, very deep; who can find it out?
²⁵I turned my mind to know and to search out and
to seek wisdom and the sum of things, and to know
the wickedness of folly and the foolishness which is
madness. ²⁶And I found more bitter than death the
woman whose heart is snares and nets, and whose
hands are fetters; he who pleases God escapes her,
but the sinner is taken by her. ²⁷Behold, this is
what I found, says the Preacher, adding one thing
to another to find the sum, ²⁸which my mind has
sought repeatedly, but I have not found. One man
among a thousand I found, but a woman among all
these I have not found. ²⁹Behold, this alone I found,
that God made man upright, but they have sought
out many devices.

Obedience to Rulers

8 Who is like the wise man?
 And who knows the interpretation of a thing?
A man's wisdom makes his face shine,
 and the hardness of his countenance is changed.

7:13–14 Good and bad times alike are appointed by God. But insofar as the divine plan is a mystery, life is more or less unpredictable (3:22; 6:12); one can only accept what comes, knowing that the future will unfold according to the designs of Providence (Sir 33:13).

7:15 righteous man who perishes: Qoheleth gives reason to question the conventional theory of rewards and punishments, according to which God always blesses the saints with prosperity and longevity and always curses sinners with misfortune and premature death. Experience shows this scheme to be too rigid and mechanical: examples can be found to support the theory, but counterexamples can be found as well (8:14; Job 21:29–30). • Christian faith affirms the OT doctrine of divine retribution (Prov 24:12; Jer 17:10) but realizes that not all rewards and punishments are given by God in this life. Not until after death is justice fully satisfied as each person is requited according to his works (Mt 16:27; Rom 2:6–10; 2 Cor 5:10; 1 Pet 1:17).

7:16 righteous overmuch: Various interpretations are given of this verse. (1) Some read the passage as a warning against proud self-righteousness or against pretending to be more righteous that one really is. (2) Others read the passage as a warning against an excessive preoccupation with justice or righteousness, which can make one rigidly unmerciful toward others. (3) Still others hear an appeal for restraint motivated by self-interest, the idea being that moral heroism can be personally disadvantageous, e.g., if one forfeits his life or well-being in trying to be overly righteous. This last view makes sense only if, like Qoheleth, one has no clear expectation of life or divine rewards after death.

7:17 die before your time: In some cases, an untimely death can be a divine punishment for sin (1 Sam 2:31; Ps 55:23; Prov 10:27).

7:18 this ... that: Refer back to the two sayings in 7:16–17, which Qoheleth urges readers to adopt as practical advice. **fears God:** One of the themes of the book. See note on 5:7.

7:19 more than ten rulers: The proverb extols wisdom over power (9:16; Prov 21:22; 24:5).

7:20 never sins: No one, however righteous, is untouched by sin and its effects on the human race (except the Virgin Mary: see note on Rom 3:23 and CCC 491). It was clear even in OT times that no one could pass through life innocent of all transgression (1 Kings 8:46; Ps 14:1–3; Sir 19:16) (CCC 386–87, 402–9). • Paul similarly insists that all peoples have fallen under the power of sin (Rom 3:9–18) and are thereby subject to the penalty of death (Rom 5:12–14).

7:23–29 An experiment with wisdom yielding disappointing results. See note on 1:12–18.

7:26 the woman: Reminiscent of the warnings against promiscuous women in the Book of Proverbs (Prov 2:16–19; 5:1–23; 6:23–35; 7:6–27). Qoheleth's words are not an attack on the female sex in general.

7:28 among a thousand: A rhetorical way of saying that trustworthiness and sincerity are extraordinarily rare among people (cf. Prov 20:6).

7:29 God made man upright: Man was created sinless and just in the beginning, and so his Creator cannot be held responsible for the sin and evil that subsequently invaded the world. See note on Gen 3:1–24. • The Church teaches that, before the Fall of the human race, the first man and woman possessed the grace of original justice, i.e., they were morally and spiritually righteous, living in a state of friendship with God (CCC 374–79). **sought out many devices:** Fallen man has shown himself creative in inventing new ways of doing evil (Rom 1:30).

8:1–17 Qoheleth insists again that wisdom eludes the searching mind. Some things can be clearly perceived ("I know", 8:12), yet God and his ways often remain a mystery beyond the reach of natural reason (8:16–17). It is a reminder that God has revealed some things for us to know, while other things remain hidden from our view (Deut 29:29). The latter fact is often noted in Ecclesiastes (3:11, 22; 6:12; 7:14).

8:1 makes his face shine: An idiom meaning that wisdom makes one benevolent or gracious toward others (Num 6:25; Prov 16:15).

2 Keep[m] the king's command, and because of your sacred oath be not dismayed; ³go from his presence, do not delay when the matter is unpleasant, for he does whatever he pleases. ⁴For the word of the king is supreme, and who may say to him, "What are you doing?" ⁵He who obeys a command will meet no harm, and the mind of a wise man will know the time and way. ⁶For every matter has its time and way, although man's trouble lies heavy upon him. ⁷For he does not know what is to be, for who can tell him how it will be? ⁸No man has power to retain the spirit, or authority over the day of death; there is no discharge from war, nor will wickedness deliver those who are given to it. ⁹All this I observed while applying my mind to all that is done under the sun, while man lords it over man to his hurt.

God's Ways Are Inscrutable

10 Then I saw the wicked buried; they used to go in and out of the holy place, and were praised in the city where they had done such things. This also is vanity. ¹¹Because sentence against an evil deed is not executed speedily, the heart of the sons of men is fully set to do evil. ¹²Though a sinner does evil a hundred times and prolongs his life, yet I know that it will be well with those who fear God, because they fear before him; ¹³but it will not be well with the wicked, neither will he prolong his days like a shadow, because he does not fear before God.

14 There is a vanity which takes place on earth, that there are righteous men to whom it happens according to the deeds of the wicked, and there are wicked men to whom it happens according to the deeds of the righteous. I said that this also is vanity. ¹⁵And I commend enjoyment, for man has no good thing under the sun but to eat and drink and enjoy himself, for this will go with him in his toil through the days of life which God gives him under the sun.

16 When I applied my mind to know wisdom, and to see the business that is done on earth, how neither day nor night one's eyes see sleep; ¹⁷then I saw all the work of God, that man cannot find out the work that is done under the sun. However much man may toil in seeking, he will not find it out; even though a wise man claims to know, he cannot find it out.

Acceptance of Life As It Comes

9 But all this I laid to heart, examining it all, how the righteous and the wise and their deeds are in the hand of God; whether it is love or hate man does not know. Everything before them is vanity,[n] ²since one fate comes to all, to the righteous and the

---

8:2–5 Prompt obedience to the king is recommended for royal servants. For similar advice on court etiquette, see Prov 14:35; 16:14; 24:21; 25:6-7.

8:2 sacred oath: Literally, "oath to God", whose name is invoked when fidelity is sworn to a king (1 Chron 29:24).

8:5 no harm: Government power is not a threat to loyal, law-abiding citizens (Rom 13:1-4). **time and way:** Literally, "time and judgment", which may be a reference to the prudent action of the wise, i.e., their doing the right thing at the right time.

8:7 what is to be: The future is veiled from the sight of unaided reason (6:12; 7:14; 10:14).

8:8 retain the spirit: Means either "hold back the wind" or, more likely, "keep hold of the breath [of life]" (3:21; 12:7). God alone has absolute authority over life and death (Wis 16:13) and determines the timing of both (3:2). **no discharge from war:** The violence of war is inescapable once an enemy engages. In this sense, too, man has limited control over life and death.

8:9 lords it over man: The third time Qoheleth laments the abuse of ruling power (4:1-3; 5:8).

8:10 buried: Indicates that the person is honored in death as in life. **the holy place:** The Jerusalem Temple. **praised in the city:** Undeserved because the public piety of the wicked concealed the evils of their private life (Mt 23:25-28).

8:11 not executed speedily: For some, delayed justice can be an occasion for continued injustice. In reality, the patience of God is not a sign of his indifference toward sin but a mercy that gives the sinner time to repent (Rom 2:4; 2 Pet 3:9).

8:12 yet I know: Despite the many mysteries and uncertainties of life, Qoheleth is sure of one thing, that God will judge our lives and render to each as his works deserve (3:17; 11:9; 12:14). **those who fear God:** Destined to receive good from God, however long his rewards seem delayed in coming. See note on 5:7.

8:13 neither will he prolong: The wicked man may prosper for a time, but he cannot extend his days indefinitely. **shadow:** Here symbolizes a lengthening of life but elsewhere an image of the shortness of life (6:12; Job 8:9).

✠ **8:14 according to the deeds:** Evidence that God's justice is not fully administered in this life. Lacking fuller revelation concerning the afterlife, Qoheleth can only look upon the injustice that prevails in the world and declare it an inexplicable vanity. See note on 7:15. • In his mercy, God determines that scourges should afflict the righteous, lest they become elated by their works, and that the unrighteous should pass through this life without punishment, because they are hastening toward unending torments. That the righteous are sometimes scourged undeservedly is illustrated in the case of Job (St. Gregory the Great, *Moralia in Job* 23, 44).

✠ **8:15 eat and drink:** See note on 2:24. • The most plausible interpretation of this saying is in reference to the table of the Lord, a priest in the line of Melchizedek who furnishes it with his Body and Blood. This sacrifice has superseded all the Old Covenant sacrifices that foreshadowed it (St. Augustine, *City of God* 17, 20).

8:17 cannot find out: Qoheleth disputes reason's ability to make sense of God and his ways with the world. Traditional wisdom has some undeniable merits, but in the end even the wisest is left frustrated in his quest to solve the tantalizing riddles of life.

9:1 in the hand of God: Another way of saying "it will be well with those who fear God" (8:12). Later, when a clearer concept of life after death emerges in Israel's theology, God's favor and protection are said to extend beyond the grave, so that the souls of the righteous dead are likewise "in the hand of God" (Wis 3:1). **love or hate:** Ambiguous. In view of the observations made in 7:15 and 8:14, the point may be that man cannot identify those whom God favors (loves) or disfavors (hates) by observing the prosperity or adversity they experience in the world. On the other hand, love and hate are connected with human rather than divine actions in 9:6.

---

[m] Heb inserts an *I*.
[n] Syr Compare Gk: Heb *Everything before them is everything.*

wicked, to the good and the evil,° to the clean and the unclean, to him who sacrifices and him who does not sacrifice. As is the good man, so is the sinner; and he who swears is as he who shuns an oath. ³This is an evil in all that is done under the sun, that one fate comes to all; also the hearts of men are full of evil, and madness is in their hearts while they live, and after that they go to the dead. ⁴But he who is joined with all the living has hope, for a living dog is better than a dead lion. ⁵For the living know that they will die, but the dead know nothing, and they have no more reward; but the memory of them is lost. ⁶Their love and their hate and their envy have already perished, and they have no more for ever any share in all that is done under the sun.

7 Go, eat your bread with enjoyment, and drink your wine with a merry heart; for God has already approved what you do.

8 Let your garments be always white; let not oil be lacking on your head.

9 Enjoy life with the wife whom you love, all the days of your vain life which he has given you under the sun, because that is your portion in life and in your toil at which you toil under the sun. ¹⁰Whatever your hand finds to do, do it with your might; for there is no work or thought or knowledge or wisdom in Sheol, to which you are going.

11 Again I saw that under the sun the race is not to the swift, nor the battle to the strong, nor bread to the wise, nor riches to the intelligent, nor favor to the men of skill; but time and chance happen to them all. ¹²For man does not know his time. Like fish which are taken in an evil net, and like birds which are caught in a snare, so the sons of men are snared at an evil time, when it suddenly falls upon them.

Wisdom Superior to Folly

13 I have also seen this example of wisdom under the sun, and it seemed great to me. ¹⁴There was a little city with few men in it; and a great king came against it and besieged it, building great siegeworks against it. ¹⁵But there was found in it a poor wise man, and he by his wisdom delivered the city. Yet no one remembered that poor man. ¹⁶But I say that wisdom is better than might, though the poor man's wisdom is despised, and his words are not heeded.

17 The words of the wise heard in quiet are better than the shouting of a ruler among fools. ¹⁸Wisdom is better than weapons of war, but one sinner destroys much good.

Observations of Wisdom

10 Dead flies make the perfumer's ointment
  give off an evil odor;
 so a little folly outweighs wisdom and honor.
²A wise man's heart inclines him toward the right,
 but a fool's heart toward the left.
³Even when the fool walks on the road, he lacks
  sense,
 and he says to every one that he is a fool.

9:2 one fate: Death, which treats all men equally and exempts no living creature from its toll (3:19). The point here is that no merit or achievement gives one man an advantage over another in the face of his mortality. **clean ... unclean:** Ritual categories denoting persons fit to worship God and those unfit to participate in cultic liturgy because of some defilement.

9:3 full of evil: For the universal sinfulness of man, see note on 7:20.

9:4 living ... is better: From the perspective of man's potential for happiness, life with its difficulties is preferable to death in the numbing darkness of the netherworld.

9:5 the dead know nothing: A view of death in which the deceased are no longer capable of thinking, acting, or experiencing joys of any kind (9:6, 10). Moreover, they are quickly forgotten by the living (2:16). According to this view, the state of death barely qualifies as existence at all. • Qoheleth is either adopting the common view of his times or engaging in his own speculation about the state of death. Either way, his inspired words reveal the limits of reason rather than the actual circumstances attending the souls of the departed. It is only with the deposit of Christian revelation that we learn the full truth about what happens to man after death (particular and universal judgments, resurrection of the body, heaven, hell, etc.) (CCC 1006–41).

9:6 envy: Or, "jealous rivalry". See note on 4:4.

9:7–10 An appeal to take delight in the good things of life. Prompting these words is the grim finality of death that Qoheleth sees looming on the horizon. Some scholars consider these verses indebted to similar advice that appears in the *Epic of Gilgamesh* 10, 3 (Old Babylonian version).

9:7 your bread ... your wine: See note on 2:24. • Ecclesiastes alludes to the grace of the Eucharist, the mystical bread and the mystical wine. The Lord now approves what believers do, for before they came to this grace their deeds were "vanity of vanities" (St. Cyril of Jerusalem, *Mystagogical Catechesis* 4, 8). **approved:** Opportunities for happiness are gifts from the hand of God (2:24–25; 3:13).

9:8 garments ... oil: Associated with festive occasions (Gen 45:22; Jud 10:3; Esther 16:15).

9:9 wife whom you love: Compare with the touching words in Prov 5:18–19.

9:10 no work or thought: The basis of the statement is human speculation, not divine revelation. See note on 9:5. **Sheol:** Hebrew term for the netherworld of the dead. See word study: *Sheol* at Num 16:30.

9:11 is not: Means "is not always" or "is not necessarily". **time and chance:** The reasons for success and failure in life are sometimes elusive and even contrary to expectations. The instances noted in this verse show that wise action and thinking are not guarantees of a desired outcome because sometimes events are beyond human control. The ultimate factor to be reckoned with is God's Providence, which determines the time of everything (3:1–17; 7:14).

9:13–15 A parable on the value of wisdom and the vanity of disregarding it. Tragically, its counsels can triumph in difficult times and still be forgotten or despised.

9:16 better than might: Sayings on this theme also appear at 7:19 and 9:18.

10:1–11:6 Traditional wisdom sayings, many of which are similar to observations made in the Book of Proverbs, though a few are clearly expressions of the mind of Qoheleth (e.g., 10:5–7; 11:5–6). The author of Ecclesiastes was both a collector and a composer of proverbs according to 12:9–10.

10:1 little folly: Continuing the thought of 9:18, the proverb bemoans how easily wisdom and its benefits can be spoiled by foolishness.

10:2 right ... left: Symbolizes what is honorable and prosperous over against what is disreputable and ruinous (Mt 25:31–46). On the biblical theme of "the two ways", see note on Prov 1:15.

°Gk Syr Vg: Heb lacks *and the evil.*

⁴If the anger of the ruler rises against you, do not
leave your place,
for deference will make amends for great
offenses.

5 There is an evil which I have seen under the
sun, as it were an error proceeding from the ruler:
⁶folly is set in many high places, and the rich sit in a
low place. ⁷I have seen slaves on horses, and princes
walking on foot like slaves.

⁸He who digs a pit will fall into it;
and a serpent will bite him who breaks
through a wall.
⁹He who quarries stones is hurt by them;
and he who splits logs is endangered by them.
¹⁰If the iron is blunt, and one does not whet the edge,
he must put forth more strength;
but wisdom helps one to succeed.
¹¹If the serpent bites before it is charmed,
there is no advantage in a charmer.
¹²The words of a wise man's mouth win him favor,
but the lips of a fool consume him.
¹³The beginning of the words of his mouth is
foolishness,
and the end of his talk is wicked madness.
¹⁴A fool multiplies words,
though no man knows what is to be,
and who can tell him what will be after him?
¹⁵The toil of a fool wearies him,
so that he does not know the way to the city.

¹⁶Woe to you, O land, when your king is a child,
and your princes feast in the morning!
¹⁷Happy are you, O land, when your king is the son
of free men,

and your princes feast at the proper time,
for strength, and not for drunkenness!
¹⁸Through sloth the roof sinks in,
and through indolence the house leaks.
¹⁹Bread is made for laughter,
and wine gladdens life,
and money answers everything.
²⁰Even in your thought, do not curse the king,
nor in your bedchamber curse the rich;
for a bird of the air will carry your voice,
or some winged creature tell the matter.

The Value of Diligence

11 Cast your bread upon the waters,
for you will find it after many days.
²Give a portion to seven, or even to eight,
for you know not what evil may happen on
earth.
³If the clouds are full of rain,
they empty themselves on the earth;
and if a tree falls to the south or to the north,
in the place where the tree falls, there it
will lie.
⁴He who observes the wind will not sow;
and he who regards the clouds will not reap.

5 As you do not know how the spirit comes to the
bones in the womb ᴾ of a woman with child, so you
do not know the work of God who makes everything.

6 In the morning sow your seed, and at evening
withhold not your hand; for you do not know which
will prosper, this or that, or whether both alike will
be good.

Youth and Old Age

7 Light is sweet, and it is pleasant for the eyes to
behold the sun.

10:4 anger of the ruler: Discussed also in Prov 16:14;
19:12; 20:2.

10:5–7 Folly turns the world upside down (10:16) and
brings the "evil" of a disordered society and government
(10:5). In the words of Proverbs, it is "not fitting" to honor
fools and slaves with a promotion to the royal court in the
place of rightful princes (Prov 19:10; 26:1; 30:21–22).

10:8–11 Applying wisdom to everyday tasks in life can
lessen the chances of undesirable consequences. Similar imagery is used to teach other lessons in Ps 7:13–14; Prov 26:27;
Sir 27:26; Amos 5:19.

10:14 A fool multiplies words: Excessive speech is a mark
of foolishness (5:3), just as guarded speech is an exercise of
wisdom (Prov 10:19; 13:3; 21:23; Jas 1:19). **no man knows:**
Qoheleth again acknowledges the limitations of human intelligence, which is unable to see the future (6:12; 7:14; 8:7).

10:15 does not know: An absurd level of foolishness.

10:16 a child: A youth who lacks both maturity and com-
petency. **feasts in the morning:** Occasions for drunkenness
(10:17).

10:19 money answers everything: The meaning of this
remark is debated. It has been read as a sarcastic comment
(in view of 5:10), as a mere observation about the pleasures
money can buy (noted in 2:8–10), and as a recommendation
to earn one's living by hard work (in contrast to laziness, mentioned in 10:18).

10:20 do not curse: Recalls the similar sayings in 7:21–22
but looked at from the opposite perspective.

11:1–2 The subject of these verses is disputed: they are
either about charitable *giving* or commercial *trading*. If the
former, one is urged to be generous in almsgiving, assisting
as many people as possible, aware that blessings may eventually return to the giver (cf. Prov 11:24–25). If the latter, one
is advised to launch a business venture abroad, being careful
to diversify one's investments, so as to minimize losses and
increase the chances of making a profit (cf. Prov 31:14). Both
readings presuppose that life entails a certain amount of risk in
the face of an uncertain future.

11:3 falls: Falling rain and trees may be symbolic of the
"evil times" that befall people unawares (9:12). Just as one is
unpredictable, so is the other.

11:4 He who observes: The farmer who waits around for
the perfect weather symbolizes the person who misses opportunities in life because of his failure to act.

11:5 the spirit: The breath of life that comes from God
(12:7; Gen 2:7). The ways of God in the world are just
as mysterious and wondrous as the formation of a preborn
baby in the womb (Ps 139:13–14). ● Using similar language,
Jesus compares the supernatural work of the Spirit in Baptism
to the natural mystery of childbirth (Jn 3:5–8).

11:6 you do not know: The future is unpredictable, but
steps can be taken to promote a successful outcome.

11:7—12:8 Advice to young persons on enjoying life (11:7–
10) before the onset of old age (12:1–5) and death (12:6–8).

11:7 to behold the sun: To be alive in the world (Job 3:16;
Ps 58:8).

ᴾOr *As you do not know the way of the wind, or how the bones grow in
the womb.*

8 For if a man lives many years, let him rejoice in them all; but let him remember that the days of darkness will be many. All that comes is vanity.

9 Rejoice, O young man, in your youth, and let your heart cheer you in the days of your youth; walk in the ways of your heart and the sight of your eyes. But know that for all these things God will bring you into judgment.

10 Remove vexation from your mind, and put away pain from your body; for youth and the dawn of life are vanity.

Advice to the Young

12 Remember also your Creator in the days of your youth, before the evil days come, and the years draw nigh, when you will say, "I have no pleasure in them"; ²before the sun and the light and the moon and the stars are darkened and the clouds return after the rain; ³in the day when the keepers of the house tremble, and the strong men are bent, and the grinders cease because they are few, and those that look through the windows are dimmed, ⁴and the doors on the street are shut; when the sound of the grinding is low, and one rises up at the voice of a bird, and all the daughters of song are brought low; ⁵they are afraid also of what is high, and terrors are in the way; the almond tree blossoms, the grasshopper drags itself along^q and desire fails; because man goes to his eternal home, and the mourners go about the streets; ⁶before the silver cord is snapped,^r or the golden bowl is broken, or the pitcher is broken at the fountain, or the wheel broken at the cistern, ⁷and the dust returns to the earth as it was, and the spirit returns to God who gave it. ⁸Vanity of vanities, says the Preacher; all is vanity.

Epilogue

9 Besides being wise, the Preacher also taught the people knowledge, weighing and studying and arranging proverbs with great care. ¹⁰The Preacher sought to find pleasing words, and uprightly he wrote words of truth.

11:8 the days of darkness: Either death and the grave or possibly the "evil days" (12:1) ahead when health deteriorates and life becomes increasingly burdensome (5:17).

11:9 Rejoice ... in your youth: Encouragement to squeeze the most out of life while one is still in his prime. **judgment:** The reminder that God will hold each person accountable for his deeds (12:14) tempers the summons to youthful enjoyment, lest it be taken as a license for overindulgence. See note on 2:24.

11:10 vexation ... pain: Afflictions suffered by the elderly should not be allowed to plague one's younger years (Sir 30:23–24). **the dawn of life:** The Hebrew can also be read to mean "black hair", a sign of youth as distinct from white hair. **vanity:** In the sense of "fleeting" or "impermanent". See word study: *Vanity* at 1:2.

12:1 your Creator: To forget about God is to forget about the approach of death (12:7) and divine judgment (11:9; 12:14) (CCC 1007). **the evil days:** The days of suffering and decline that come with advanced age.

12:2–6 Images representing the end of life. These have been connected with such things as the onset of winter, a coming thunderstorm, a village funeral, a homestead in disrepair, and a day of apocalyptic judgment. Some interpret the passage as an allegory about the physical effects of growing old. Several lines in this section are difficult to interpret.

12:2 darkened: Cosmic darkness is a common theme in prophetic visions of God judging the world (Is 13:9–10; Ezek 32:7–8; Joel 2:31; Amos 5:18–20; Mt 24:29). • Remember the Creator by thanking and turning toward him before the sun is darkened, that is, before Christ, the Sun of justice, is darkened by a loss of faith and before the light is darkened, that is, before one loses love and thereby loses grace (St. Bonaventure, *Commentary on Ecclesiastes* 12, 9).

12:3 grinders ... are few: The scarcity of women left to work the grain mills symbolizes the cessation of normal daily activities (Jer 25:10; Mt 24:41; Lk 17:35). Those who read the passage allegorically envision a loss of teeth. **dimmed:** A reference to failing eyesight (Gen 27:1) or the blurred and teary vision that comes with extreme grief (Lam 5:17).

12:4 doors ... shut: Indicates the local marketplace is closed for business. **one rises up:** The Hebrew can also mean that the sound of birds "rises" or "grows louder". **the daugh-**

ters of song: Birds, whose squawking sounds may be likened to mourning (Mic 1:8). A similar Hebrew expression refers to birds (translated "ostriches" in the RSV) that make their homes in abandoned or devastated settlements (Is 13:21; 34:13; Jer 50:39).

12:5 blossoms: Or, "becomes repulsive". **desire:** Possibly a reference to the caper berry, known in antiquity as an appetite stimulant. **his eternal home:** The grave. **mourners go about:** Participants in a funeral procession.

12:6 silver cord: Part of a lampstand is meant, either a suspension chain or a solid support. **golden bowl:** An oil lamp (Zech 4:2). Death is indicated by the light of a lamp going out (Prov 13:9). **pitcher is broken:** Breaking clay jars was an ancient funeral rite symbolizing death (cf. Ps 31:12). **wheel:** A rounded vessel may be meant. **cistern:** Perhaps a water well no longer in use. However, the same term in Hebrew frequently refers to a grave, an image closely associated with the netherworld of Sheol (rendered "Pit" in the RSV: Ps 30:3; Prov 1:12; Is 14:19; Ezek 31:14).

12:7 dust: Biblical imagery for the substance of the mortal body (Sir 33:10) that dissolves into the ground after death (3:20). **the spirit:** The breath of life that animates the human body but departs at death (Job 34:14–15; Ps 104:29). God is the giver of life-breath (Job 33:4; Is 42:5) (CCC 362, 366). • Echoing the primeval stories in Genesis, Qoheleth envisions death as a reversal of the divine creation in Gen 2:7 and a fulfillment of the divine penalty in Gen 3:19.

12:8 Vanity of vanities: The theme of the entire book. See note on 1:2 and word study: *Vanity* at 1:2.

12:9–14 The epilogue. Many think these verses were added by a later editor who collected and compiled Qoheleth's sayings into their present form. This is uncertain, but notice (1) that the main body of the work ends in 12:8 just as it began in 1:2, and (2) that the perspective shifts from Qoheleth's own words (1st person) to someone speaking about Qoheleth (3rd person). Another view holds that Qoheleth has been engaging in a dialogue and disputing with contrary perspectives throughout the book, only to reveal his own perspective in the final verses.

12:9 wise: Qoheleth was a "sage" engaged in studying, teaching, and composing proverbs for his people (cf. Sir 37:23). His instruction was admired for its elegant expression and trusted as reliable advice (12:10). The statement evokes memories of Solomon, the wisest man of OT times (1 Kings 4:29–34).

---

^qOr *is a burden.*
^rSyr Vg Compare Gk: Heb *is removed.*

11 The sayings of the wise are like goads, and like nails firmly fixed are the collected sayings which are given by one Shepherd. [12]My son, beware of anything beyond these. Of making many books there is no end, and much study is a weariness of the flesh.

13 The end of the matter; all has been heard. Fear God, and keep his commandments; for this is the whole duty of man.[s] [14]For God will bring every deed into judgment, with[t] every secret thing, whether good or evil.

12:11 goads: Pointed tips attached to the ends of sticks that were used to prod cattle. Qoheleth's teachings were similarly meant to spur thoughtful reflection and move people to live wisely. **one Shepherd:** The image of a shepherd is used in the OT for God (Gen 49:24; Ps 23:1) and for the spiritual leaders of Israel (Jer 3:15; Ezek 34:2–23). Alternatively, the expression can be translated "a certain shepherd" and understood as a continuation of the herding metaphor.

12:12 My son: An address for someone learning wisdom, whether a child or a student. See note on Prov 1:8. **beyond these:** I.e., beyond the observations of Qoheleth. More books can be read and produced, and more learning can be acquired,

but the highest praise goes to Ecclesiastes (with some rhetorical exaggeration).

12:13 Fear God: Reverence for God is the primary religious virtue urged in the book (3:14; 5:7; 8:12) and is a classic teaching associated with Solomon (Prov 1:7; 3:7; 8:13; 9:10, etc.). It is a duty that includes faithful observance of the Torah, a link also made in the Book of Sirach (Sir 2:16; 10:19; 23:27). • With the statement "fear God" the Preacher ceases to be perplexed. This alone is profitable for your present life, to be taken through the confusion of things visible and unstable to things that are solid and immovable (St. Gregory Nazianzen, *Theological Orations* 7, 19).

12:14 judgment: The closing statement puts the entire book in perspective: what is of ultimate importance is not the vanity of the world but the verdict that God will render on our lives (11:9). See note on 3:17.

---

[s]Or *the duty of all men.*
[t]Or *into the judgment on.*

Study Questions
Ecclesiastes

Chapter 1

For understanding
1. **1:1.** What does the Hebrew term *Qoheleth* appear to mean? What is not certain about the term? To whom does the royal title "son of David" refer?
2. **Word Study: Vanity.** What does the term *hebel* or *habel* literally denote? What is it often used in the Bible to signify? What types of life experiences are pronounced vain?
3. **1:2.** What does the expression "vanity of vanities" mean? To what does the expression "all is vanity" apply? To what does it *not* apply?
4. **1:14.** To what does the saying "a striving after wind" refer? How do ancient Greek and Latin translations understand it?

For application
1. **1:3.** The note for this verse quotes the paraphrase of Ecclesiastes found in *The Imitation of Christ*: "Vanity of vanities and all is vanity except to love God and serve him alone." How would you evaluate your life as it stands right now from this perspective?
2. **1:4–7.** The expression "The more things change, the more they stay the same" is proverbial in our society. What does that expression mean to you? With what sorts of conditions, circumstances, or events do you tend to associate it (e.g., political developments)? What types of sins do you find yourself committing over and over again?
3. **1:10.** What do you think Qoheleth's opinion of the technological discoveries of the last century might be? Why might he dismiss them as vanity?
4. **1:11.** What have you learned from what has happened to you in the last year or so? Given what you have learned—or forgotten—how likely is it that you will retain the life lessons of the coming year?

Chapter 2

For understanding
1. **2:1–11.** In reporting on his experiment with pleasure, what did Qoheleth find? Why does he decide that overflowing riches are vain? According to St. Gregory of Nyssa, why is there no advantage for those who labor for what is vain?
2. **2:12–17.** Qoheleth partly endorses and partly disputes the traditional view that wisdom is better than folly. What does he dispute? While it is hard to refute Qoheleth's logic from a this-worldly standpoint, how else might one do it?
3. **2:24.** For what does the expression "eat and drink" stand? How do we know this is not an endorsement of hedonism and Epicureanism? What, then, is Qoheleth's point about eating and drinking?
4. **2:26.** How do the interpretations of the RSV translation and those of other commentators differ over how God distributes gifts? Of the two versions, which better coheres with the author's perspective?

For application
1. **2:4–9.** What have been some of the chief pursuits of your life? For example, if you have a business, military, or artistic career—or if you have been engaged simply in raising a family—what have you accomplished? How satisfied do you feel with what you have accomplished?
2. **2:9.** Qoheleth claims that he has engaged in every sort of luxury and self-indulgence and yet retained his wisdom. Do you agree that he has retained it? Why or why not?
3. **2:10.** Giving free rein to one's eyes by looking on whatever one wants (for example, looking at pornography) can be extremely dangerous for one's emotional and spiritual life. How would you describe some of these dangers to yourself? How have you dealt with temptations to look at what you should avoid?
4. **2:18–21.** As you reflect on these verses, what is your attitude to leaving everything you worked for to others when you die? Does it matter to you what they might do with your bequest?

Chapter 3

For understanding
1. **3:1–8.** What is the point in these verses of the litany of times and seasons that are ordained by God? What must man do about these times?
2. **3:5.** To what do the "casting away" and "gathering" of stones refer? What determines times to embrace or refrain from embracing?
3. **3:11.** What does the Hebrew term for *eternity* denote? What has Qoheleth's statement been taken to mean? What understanding does the divine gift *not* include? Why does St. Augustine believe that the Lord moves us to take pleasure in praise?
4. **3:17.** For what does Qoheleth say that God will hold men accountable? When? What was the early OT belief about when blessings and curses were meted out? What belief eventually emerged to replace it? What does Christian faith teach?

For application
1. **3:1–8.** Read the notes for these verses. How would you characterize the "times and seasons" in your life? Which "times and seasons" have already passed for you? Which may be still to come? With what satisfaction do you recall the past, and how do you anticipate the future?

2. **3:11.** The note for this verse gives two different understandings of what Qoheleth means by eternity. In your reading, with which do you agree? Why? How do you understand the concept of *eternity*?
3. **3:12–13.** What difference does it make whether you regard the good things in your life as God's gift to you or as a result of good luck? How *do* you regard the good things in your life?
4. **3:16–21.** Like Qoheleth, many people today believe that men and beasts suffer the same ultimate fate—they both have the same breath; both die and go down to the dust, and no one knows whether the human spirit is any different from that of an animal. What differences do you believe there are between men and animals? How does your belief influence your behavior toward animals?

Chapter 4

For understanding
1. **4:1–3.** What does Qoheleth lament in these verses? Why would he consider future generations more fortunate than the living and the dead?
2. **4:5.** Of what is the expression "folds his hands" an image? What does it mean that the fool "eats his own flesh"?
3. **4:9–12.** What practical advantage do these verses illustrate? What does Qoheleth have in mind, and how does the image of a rope illustrate it? How does St. Gregory the Great understand the image of the rope?
4. **4:13–16.** What illustration does the popularity of a king shifting to his successor provide? What biblical figure rose from poverty to royal power on the merit of his wisdom?

For application
1. **4:1–2.** These days, many people conclude with Qoheleth that conditions of oppression or disease make a person better off dead than alive. In your opinion, how can faith make life, even in the midst of terrible suffering, worth living?
2. **4:3.** Given the crime and other evils that occur in the world, what do you think is the value of begetting and raising children, especially if you will not be able to protect them from evil? How does your view compare to the Church's view that the begetting and raising of children is a great good?
3. **4:5–6.** These verses seem to talk about opposite extremes—of an extreme laziness, on the one hand, and workaholism, on the other. Toward which end of the spectrum of industry do you incline? What do you think is God's view of how hard you should be working and for what?
4. **4:9–10.** What resources are available through your church or community for the elderly who live alone and have no one to visit or aid them in trouble? If you are able, what can you do to assist such people?

Chapter 5

For understanding
1. **5:1.** How are readers advised to approach God? What does the Hebrew notion of *hearing* include? How could one's worship of God be unacceptable?
2. **5:4.** What does a vow to God impose? What must be done before such a pledge is made?
3. **5:6.** Who is the "messenger" in this verse? How does the Greek LXX interpret "the messenger"? If verse 6 is a continuation of verses 4–5, from whom does the excuse in this verse come, and why is he excusing himself?
4. **Word Study: Lot.** What does the Hebrew word *heleq* denote? For what things does the Bible use the term? In Ecclesiastes, what shades of meaning are evident? According to Qoheleth, why is it good to accept one's lot in life?

For application
1. **5:1.** How does your daily conduct reflect your religious beliefs? How can you ensure that the two coincide in practice?
2. **5:4–5.** What spiritual resolutions have you made to improve or enhance your spiritual life, such as through prayer, spiritual reading, or attendance at Mass? Have you kept them? How do you maintain your current level of spiritual activity when you feel depressed or dry? If you allow yourself to skip your spiritual disciplines at those times, how can you get back on track?
3. **5:6.** What system of spiritual accountability do you have in place, such as with a spouse, trusted friends, or a confessor? If you have none, what prevents you from establishing one? If you do, how often do you take advantage of it by being open about failures or weaknesses and listening to advice?
4. **5:12–15.** In terms of your material resources or investments, what are some chief areas of concern or anxiety? How pervasive (in Qoheleth's words) is darkness, grief, vexation, sickness, or resentment? What spiritual resources do you have for dealing with these things?

Chapter 6

For understanding
1. **6:3.** How did biblical Israel regard having a large family and a long life? Why is a stillborn baby better off, from Qoheleth's jaded perspective?
2. **6:7.** How is the never-ending quest for food emblematic of our desire for the goods of the world? How does St. Jerome understand the passage in the context of scriptural learning?
3. **6:12.** Of what is Qoheleth rightly skeptical in this verse? Of what is a shadow an image here?

For application
1. **6:1–2.** In terms of your overall outlook on life, would you consider yourself primarily optimistic or pessimistic? In other words, do you think that in the long run things will turn out well or badly for you? Considering the effort it takes to support yourself, how worthwhile is it to keep building an estate that others will inherit?

2.   **6:6.** How often do you find yourself thinking about your own death or the value of your life? To what conclusions have you come? To what extent are these thoughts influenced by Scripture and the teaching of the Church?
3.   **6:7.** Read the note for this verse. How satisfied are you with your current level of scriptural knowledge? What would you like to do to learn more? How might you pursue that desire?
4.   **6:12.** This chapter ends with a couple of questions. How would you answer them? How would you assess your strength in the Christian virtue of hope and the answers it provides? If hope is a weak area for you, how might you strengthen it?

Chapter 7

For understanding
1.   **7:1-14.** With what does this collection of wisdom sayings deal? How is the Hebrew term for "good" (*tob*) variously translated in this section? By using exaggerated language, what does Qoheleth contend?
2.   **7:15.** What is the conventional theory of rewards and punishments that Qoheleth is questioning? What does experience show about it? How does Christian faith regard the issue?
3.   **7:16.** What three interpretations are given for this verse? How can the third interpretation (that moral heroism can be personally disadvantageous) make sense to someone like Qoheleth?
4.   **7:29.** How was man created in the beginning? What responsibility does God bear for sin and evil? What does the Church teach about mankind before the Fall? What does the expression "sought out many devices" mean?

For application
1.   **7:1.** Christian spiritual tradition recommends that we reflect often on the four last things: death, judgment, heaven, and hell. From a Christian perspective, how can the day of death be better than the day of birth? Why is the date of a saint's death regarded as his birthday?
2.   **7:5.** Christianity praises fraternal correction (see Mt 18:15), though most people avoid either giving or receiving it. Why is fraternal correction necessary in the Christian life? How should you respond when someone corrects you? How might you correct someone with love, without giving offense?
3.   **7:16.** Read the note for this verse. Of the alternative interpretations given, which comes closest to your own? Since Jesus commands you to "be perfect as my heavenly Father is perfect" (Mt 5:48), how can you strive for holiness without becoming sanctimonious?
4.   **7:20-22.** What are some of the ways you have been offended by others' speech? What are some of the ways you have offended others by your speech; for example, by uncharitable criticism, verbal put-downs, gossip, barbed humor, and so on? What should you do to speak more charitably? How can prayer help?

Chapter 8

For understanding
1.   **8:1-17.** On what is Qoheleth insisting here? Of what is it a reminder?
2.   **8:8.** What does the expression "retain the spirit" mean? What is God's authority in this context? What does the expression "no discharge from war" have to do with matters of life and death?
3.   **8:14.** What evidence is this verse providing? Lacking fuller revelation concerning the afterlife, what is the only view Qoheleth can take? What does God's mercy determine for the righteous and the unrighteous, according to St. Gregory the Great?
4.   **8:17.** What does Qoheleth dispute about reason's ability? Although traditional wisdom has undeniable merits, with what is the wisest left?

For application
1.   **8:3.** How do you approach unpleasant tasks or assignments? Do you procrastinate, perform them first to get them out of the way, try to delegate the task to someone else, or avoid them as much as possible? What are some of the advantages of learning to do unpleasant tasks well?
2.   **8:5.** Is obeying the command of an authority always right? What is the responsibility of a citizen who is faced with an unjust exercise of authority, such as an immoral law (CCC 1900-1904)? What harm might come to you if you were to determine that your faith prevents you from obeying a law in good conscience?
3.   **8:10-13.** When you hear of a person who has lived a wild and profligate or perhaps truly evil life dying, being buried with honor, and being hailed as a cultural icon, what is your reaction? How does your Christian faith suggest you should respond? (Compare your answer with Mt 5:44-45 and Mt 7:1-2.)
4.   **8:16-17.** When you consider the direction your life has taken so far, how do you feel about it? How do you see the difference between resignation to God's will and acceptance of it? Have you thanked him, even though you do not understand why things have turned out this way?

Chapter 9

For understanding
1.   **9:1.** What does the expression "in the hand of God" mean for the wise and righteous? What will it mean later when a clearer concept of life after death emerges in Israel's theology? What might be the point of the ambiguous reference to love or hate?
2.   **9:5.** In this verse, of what are the dead no longer capable? Whether Qoheleth is citing a common view of his times or his own speculation, what do his inspired words reveal? What do we learn from Christian revelation about what happens after death?

3. **9:7–10.** To what do these verses appeal? What prompts these words? To what do some scholars consider these words indebted?
4. **9:11.** What does Qoheleth think of the reasons for success and failure in life? What is the ultimate factor to be reckoned with?

For application
1. **9:1.** What do you think of the common idea that God experiences emotions like love and hate? Assuming that God does not experience emotion, what does it mean to you that God loves you? How has he shown it?
2. **9:3.** How do you understand the Christian doctrine of Original Sin? Compare your answer with that of CCC 402–5. As you read paragraph 405, ask yourself how the weakness of Original Sin affects you personally—and, then, how the graces of Baptism have influenced your life. If you see no evidence of such graces, ask why not?
3. **9:7–10.** On the subject of the common priesthood of the faithful, the Vatican II Dogmatic Constitution on the Church *Lumen Gentium* (no. 34) regards relaxation and enjoyment as among the "spiritual sacrifices acceptable to God through Jesus Christ" (quoted in CCC 901). How can you make your enjoyment of life a personal sacrifice?
4. **9:13–16.** When you are called upon to give advice, how readily do you give it? How do you understand your role in dispensing advice? How do you respond when people ignore it, especially when you are confident that your advice is sound? What remedy does prayer provide?

Chapter 10

For understanding
1. **10:2.** What does the inclination of a person's heart to the right or left symbolize?
2. **10:5–7.** What does folly do to the world? In the words of Proverbs, what is it "not fitting" to do for fools?
3. **10:14.** Of what is excessive speech a mark? What about guarded speech? What is Qoheleth acknowledging here?
4. **10:19.** How do people interpret the meaning of the expression "money answers everything"?

For application
1. **10:1.** Which do you remember more—words of praise or of criticism? In the raising of children or the education of minors, which is more effective? How should one best use both of these?
2. **10:4.** What do Qoheleth's words indicate you should do if an employer or superior becomes angry with you? How does the virtue of meekness apply in a situation like this?
3. **10:12–14.** Have you ever betrayed a confidence or said something that should have been kept to yourself? What was the outcome? What should you do when you find that you have spoken imprudently, especially if your speech has harmed or endangered someone else? (Compare your answer with CCC 2487.)
4. **10:20.** Have you ever been the subject of someone else's gossip or acted on what "a little bird" told you about someone else? What was the effect on your relationships? When does careless speech become a sin? (Refer to CCC 2475–82.)

Chapter 11

For understanding
1. **11:1–2.** In what respect is the subject of these verses disputed? If the subject is charitable giving, what is one urged to do? If the subject is about commercial trading, how should the trader handle his affairs? What do both readings presuppose?
2. **11:5.** What does Qoheleth say about the ways of God in the formation of a preborn baby? Using similar language, what comparison does Jesus make?
3. **11:9.** What is Qoheleth encouraging youth to do? But of what is he reminding them to temper their enjoyment?
4. **11:10.** What is he reminding youth about the elderly? What other interpretation can the Hebrew translated as "the dawn of life" have? What does the word "vanity" mean in this context?

For application
1. **11:1–2.** Do you regularly engage in charitable donations? How do you determine how much to give and to whom or for what cause? If you give money to an organization, what do you know about where it actually goes?
2. **11:4.** How often has timidity or fear kept you from sharing your faith with others? Has prayer entered into your efforts to overcome timidity and fear? (See 2 Tim 1:7–8.)
3. **11:6.** How often has boldness in sharing your faith paid off? Even though you may not have seen the outcome in others, what has such boldness done for your own faith?

Chapter 12

For understanding
1. **12:2–6.** What do the images in these verses represent? With what are the images connected? Interpreted as an allegory, what may the meaning of these verses?
2. **12:6.** Regarding the images in this verse, to what do the silver cord, the golden bowl, the broken pitcher, the wheel, and the cistern refer?
3. **12:9–14.** What is the function of these verses? Who may have added these verses? Although this is uncertain, what two observations support that opinion? What is an alternative view of what Qoheleth has been doing?
4. **12:13.** What is the importance of reverence for God in the book, and what is its association with Solomon? What does this duty include? With the statement "fear God", what does the Preacher do? According to St. Gregory Nazianzen, what is profitable about the fear of God?

For application

1. **12:1.** Why is it important to train the young in practices of the spiritual life, such as prayer and reception of the sacraments? Of what benefit are these things as one grows older?

2. **12:5-8.** What are your thoughts about growing old? How confident or fearful of old age are you? What experiences of life lie behind these attitudes? How do you envision the nearness of God in your old age?

3. **12:11.** How often do you read Scripture? Which are your favorite passages? What is important for you about them? How do they build up your relationship with God?

4. **12:14.** Of the "four last things" referred to earlier, how often do you reflect on God's judgment? What are some of the "secret things, whether good or evil", in your behavior that God is likely to judge most strictly? How can reflection on his judgment help you improve your behavior?

INTRODUCTION TO THE SONG OF SOLOMON

Author and Date The mainstream of Jewish and Christian tradition identifies the author as King Solomon, who lived and reigned in the tenth century B.C. The ascription cannot be proven, but several features of the book are consistent with this classical position. (**1**) Solomon's name appears seven times in the work, most prominently in the opening verse, which most have read as an attribution of authorship (1:1, 5; 3:7, 9, 11; 8:11–12). (**2**) The content of the Song accords well with the tradition that Solomon was a prolific songwriter (1 Kings 4:32) whose love for women was legendary (1 Kings 11:3). (**3**) The bridegroom of the Song never identifies himself or his "bride" by name (4:9–12; 5:1); nevertheless, the only wedding mentioned in the book is that of "Solomon" (3:11). (**4**) The author evinces a broad knowledge of the natural world, being familiar with fifteen animal species and more than twenty varieties of plants and spices, some quite exotic. One would expect this of Solomon, who discoursed on the wonders of nature (1 Kings 4:33) and whose many commercial contacts, which extended throughout the Middle East and beyond, brought an influx of imported luxuries into Israel on an unprecedented scale (1 Kings 9:26–28; 10:11–12, 22–25). (**5**) The author's geographical outlook fits the conditions of the Solomonic age insofar as he speaks of localities in both northern (Carmel, Tirzah) and southern Palestine (Jerusalem, En-gedi) as though they were part of the same country. In other words, he shows no awareness that Israel split into rival kingdoms after the time of Solomon and remained divided for the rest of the preexilic period; nor do his words suggest that the northern sites mentioned in the book were no longer Jewish landholdings, which was the case for most of the postexilic period. (**6**) The author admires the loveliness of Tirzah and compares it to the beauty of Jerusalem (6:4), an assessment better accounted for in the reign of Solomon than afterward. Following Solomon's death, Tirzah became the rival capital of the breakaway Northern Kingdom (1 Kings 15:21, 33; 16:8), and eventually King Omri moved the royal administration to Samaria, leaving the city of Tirzah to decline sharply in importance (1 Kings 16:23–24). (**7**) Several parallels have been identified between the Song of Solomon and Egyptian love poems from the second millennium B.C. Likewise, the meaning of several terms in the Song has been illuminated by related words found in second-millennium Ugaritic texts. These resemblances do not prove that the Song of Solomon is a work of equal antiquity. However, they undermine claims that the book could not have been written as early as the tenth century B.C.

Much of modern scholarship considers the Song of Solomon an anonymous work of the postexilic period, written somewhere between 500 and 200 B.C. Among the reasons for this assessment are the following. (**1**) The superscription in 1:1 is technically ambiguous about Solomon's relation to the book. The critical Hebrew phrase, *lishlomoh*, can indicate that the Song was written "by Solomon" (the author of the work), "for Solomon" (the dedicatee of the work), or even "about Solomon" (the male protagonist of the work). Thus, while the expression can indicate authorship, as most have understood it, other options are also possible on grammatical grounds. (**2**) The statement in 8:12 seems to distinguish the bride and bridegroom of the Song from the historical figure of Solomon and his harem. This is especially so if, as many commentators hold, the words are attributed to the bridegroom. (**3**) Linguistic study has identified one Persian loanword ("orchard" in 4:13), possibly one Greek loanword ("palanquin" in 3:9), and several Aramaisms throughout the book. The implication, according to many, is that the Song must have been written either in the Persian period (5th–4th centuries B.C.) or in the early Hellenistic period (3rd century B.C.), when Aramaic, and to a lesser extent Persian and Greek, came to exert an appreciable influence on the language of the Jewish community. (**4**) Several commentators dispute the literary unity of the book and assert that the Song of Solomon is a collection of independent love poems having different authors and dates of origin. If true, this would effectively rule out the traditional view of the work having a single author and date of composition. (**5**) The references to northern and southern localities in the book (no. 5 above) suggest to some, not that the Song must be dated to the time of the United Monarchy, when Solomon ruled over north and south together, but that different poems within the Song hail from different regions, with some being written in Israel (Northern Kingdom) and others originating or being edited in Judah (Southern Kingdom).

In the end, one must admit that the Song of Solomon embodies a curious mixture of early and late features along with signs of northern and southern interests that make it difficult to settle questions concerning its authorship and date. The observations made by critical scholars should not be downplayed or ignored, but neither should those that favor the tradition of Solomonic authorship. In point of fact, arguments advanced to demonstrate that the Song is a postexilic work may tell us more about the date of its final form than about the date of its original composition. And because a uniformity of style and a punctuated use of refrains and recurrent images make the literary unity of the Song a defensible position, one could reasonably ascribe the substance of the book to Solomonic times, even to Solomon himself, and yet maintain that its language was modernized by a postexilic scribe for the benefit of later readers. Theorizing along these lines allows the traditional link between Solomon and the Song to be critically maintained without insisting that every detail of the book must be explained in the light of circumstances that obtained in the tenth century B.C. Still, the evidence is insufficient either to affirm or to deny the Solomonic authorship of the book with certainty. A majority of scholars today attribute the book to an unknown author writing after the Babylonian Exile in the fifth or sixth century B.C. or else to various anonymous authors writing at various times throughout the first millennium.

Title   The book takes its name from its introductory words, *Shir Hashshirim*, "The Song of Songs". Grammatically, this is a superlative expression in Hebrew meaning "the Greatest of Songs". The heading is translated literally by the Greek Septuagint as *Asma Asmatōn* and by the Latin Vulgate as *Canticum Canticorum*. Modern references to "Canticles" are indebted to the Vulgate tradition, whereas the RSV's title, "Song of Solomon", is based on the tradition of Solomonic authorship. Contemporary works often refer to the book with the abbreviated title, "The Song".

Structure   There is no consensus on the outline of the Song of Solomon. This is due mainly to the diversity of interpretations that are given to the book. Those who view it as an anthology of independent love songs have claimed to discover as many as thirty or more poems strung together. Those who maintain the substantial unity of the work tend to prefer far fewer divisions. One attractive possibility is a fivefold division, the first four of which are marked off by a similar concluding refrain (2:7; 3:5; 5:8; 8:4). Following the opening superscription (1:1), the poetry of the Song may be grouped into dialogue one (1:2—2:7), two (2:8—3:5), three (3:6—5:8), four (5:9—8:4), and five (8:5–14).

Place in the Canon   The Song of Solomon's inclusion in the canon of Scripture occasioned controversy in early Judaism. The most likely reason for this was its content, which is not explicitly religious. Nevertheless, most doubts about its inspiration were laid to rest when Rabbi Aqiba in the early second century A.D. declared the Song "the holy of holies" among the class of biblical books known as the Writings (Mishnah, *Yadaim* 3, 5). Thereafter,

the book went on to become one of the five scrolls, known as the *Megilloth*, that were read on major Jewish feast days (along with Ruth, Ecclesiastes, Esther, and Lamentations). The Song of Solomon was read on the eighth day of the spring festival of Passover, probably because the book mentions "Pharaoh's chariots" (1:9), calling to mind Israel's exodus from Egypt (Ex 14:6–9), and has its setting in the spring (2:11–13). In both the Greek Septuagint and Latin Vulgate, the Song is grouped with Proverbs and Ecclesiastes on the supposition that all three books were authored by Solomon. There is no evidence the ancient Church seriously disputed the canonicity of the Song.

Themes and Characteristics   The Song of Solomon is one of the most beautiful books of the Bible. On one level, it weaves together exquisite language and imagery to celebrate the experience of a bride and groom passionately in love. It is a dialogue of desire in which husband and wife express their deepest feelings of attraction for one another with startling boldness. On another level, the ecstasy of romantic love is a representation of the divine love that unites God and his people in a covenant of mutual affection and loyalty.

The Song of Solomon is also one of the most difficult books of the Bible to interpret. With the possible exception of 8:6, God is never mentioned by name in the Song, nor does the book convey an obviously spiritual or theological message. Beyond that, the poetry of the Song is overtly sexual at times; indeed, its expressions of longing for physical intimacy, while never indecent or obscene, are quite uninhibited. Additional challenges to interpretation are posed by uncertainties regarding the proper division of the book, the number of voices that contribute to the dialogue, the translation of several rare words, and the question of whether the book is a unified composition or an ensemble of originally independent songs.

A wide variety of interpretations, in ancient and modern times alike, have clustered around the Song of Solomon. These include both literal and nonliteral readings of the book. The following is a summary of the most popular approaches adopted over the centuries.

(1) *Religious Allegory*. By far the most common reading of the Song has been the allegorical. From this perspective, the sensual language of the book represents the language of spiritual experience. In Jewish tradition, the book is thought to depict Yahweh's spousal affection for Israel, his beloved people. In Christian tradition, the symbolism is transposed to Christ and his love for the Church, his spiritual bride. Variations on this theme made the application personal, either by interpreting the Song as Christ's passionate pursuit of the individual soul or by identifying the woman as the Blessed Virgin Mary. The allegorical approach, while focusing on

the overall presentation, also finds spiritual significance in the supporting details. It is sometimes unclear whether Jewish and Christian expositors of the Song considered the book to have its basis in actual historical events, each having an allegorical or prophetic meaning, or whether they deemed the book to be a pure literary allegory without underlying historical referents.

(2) *Literary Drama.* According to some ancient and modern scholars, the Song of Solomon tells a story that may have been sung or even acted out as a stage performance. In this case, the overall unity of the Song is assumed, and the dialogue between the lovers is believed to be organized around a developing plot. Modern versions of this approach fall into two basic categories. Some read the Song as a "love story" between King Solomon and a Shulammite maiden, who fall madly in love and seal their commitment in marriage ("the royal hypothesis"). Central to this interpretation is the notion that Solomon learns to rise above the passions of the flesh to a pure love and a newfound appreciation for monogamy. Others detect in the Song a "love triangle" in which Solomon intrudes upon a committed relationship between a beautiful maiden and her young fiancée, a rural boy and commoner ("the shepherd hypothesis"). On this interpretation, Solomon brings the girl to his palace and tries to win her over with the splendors of his court. Ultimately, however, the king fails to capture the heart of the maiden, who courageously resists his advances and remains true to her lover back home. Dividing these dramatic theories is the question of whether the dialogue of the Song alternates between one man and one woman or whether two male rivals (a "king" and a "shepherd") can be heard addressing the woman.

(3) *Collection of Love Poetry.* A considerable number of scholars today view the Song as an anthology of secular love poems that were never intended by their authors to have a religious significance. According to advocates of this thesis, the poems simply express the thrill of romantic love and sexual attraction. The extravagant symbolism of the book is neither ignored nor denied; it is merely appreciated as the language of passion. Some are open to the possibility that its content is based on one of Solomon's love affairs or foreign marriages, and others hold that it serves the didactic purpose of teaching the sanctity of married love, the value of spousal fidelity, and the essential goodness of human sexuality as a gift from God. Though mainly a modern perspective, the exclusively literal interpretation of the Song was already proposed in ancient Christian times by Theodore of Mopsuestia and judged erroneous by the Second Council of Constantinople in A.D. 553.

(4) *Wedding Song.* Several early Christian writers described the book as a bridal song that pronounces blessings and compliments on a newlywed couple (known in Greek as an *epithalamion*). More recent scholarship has hypothesized that the Song of Solomon preserves ancient wedding lyrics that were sung over the course of a several-day marriage celebration. This interpretation was suggested by similarities between the Song and modern marriage customs in Syria, where the bride and groom are praised by family and friends with songs that include a lyrical "description" of the couple's physical features (known in Arabic as a *waṣf*).

In the end, the most satisfying interpretation of the Song of Solomon is the most inclusive one. Several of the readings surveyed above, literal and nonliteral, may be said to touch in different ways on authentic facets of the book. For instance, it is difficult to escape the impression that the Song affirms the beauty of conjugal love. Far from being a subject unworthy of the Bible, marriage is seen by biblical texts to be a sacred covenant established by God (Gen 2:21–25; Mal 2:14). The Bible's wisdom literature even calls married persons to delight in their partner's love (Prov 5:18–19; Eccles 9:9) and declares the mystery of sexual attraction between man and woman a fitting subject for contemplation by the wise (Prov 30:19). Regardless of whether the book develops a single storyline or whether its poems are unified by nothing more than a common interest in romantic expression or even whether its lyrics were once recited in ancient wedding ceremonies, extoling the wonders of married love appears to be part of the total picture.

At the same time, inclusion of the Song of Solomon in the canon of Scripture justifies a theological reading of the book. The same Spirit who inspired the writing of the Song also inspired the prophets of Israel, as well as later the apostles of the Church, to speak of the Lord as the divine Husband of his people, who together constitute his bride (Is 54:5–6; 62:5; Jer 3:1, 20; Hos 1–3; 2 Cor 11:2; Eph 5:23–33; Rev 19:7–8). Insofar as the content and unity of the whole Bible form an authentic context for interpretation, and insofar as the marriage covenant between man and woman, the national covenant between Yahweh and Israel, and the new and everlasting covenant between Christ and the Church all have God for their Author, the book is legitimately read in reference to these analogous relationships. One need not deny an interest in human love in the Song to perceive something of the divine love that exceeds it in perfection. It is an authentically biblical perspective to view the former as a created image of the latter. Thus, to read the Song allegorically, as was traditionally done, or to call it a "parable" of the love uniting God and man, as modern scholars sometimes describe it, is to affirm a genuine religious message in the book that should neither be ignored as irrelevant nor denied as artificial.

Christian Perspective The New Testament never quotes the Song of Solomon directly, yet its portrayal of Jesus as the messianic Bridegroom is indebted in a general way to the OT theme of Yahweh's spiritual marriage to Israel (Mt 9:15; 25:1–13; Jn 3:29; 2 Cor 11:2; Eph 5:23–33; Rev 19:7–8). Still, a few NT passages do seem to evoke images from the book to convey a message about the believer's relationship with Christ (compare 5:2 with Rev 3:20) and the Spirit (compare 4:15 with Jn 4:10–14). It is by the Church Fathers, followed by a host of medieval theologians and spiritual writers, that the Song is given a detailed exposition in the light of Christian faith. These were allegorical readings that followed three distinct but interrelated trajectories: an *ecclesial* interpretation, in which the Song speaks of Christ lovingly wedded to the Church (St. Hippolytus, Origen of Alexandria, St. Bede), a *mystical* interpretation, in which Christ is the husband who pursues a bridal union with the individual soul (St. Gregory of Nyssa, St. Bernard of Clairvaux, St. John of the Cross), and a *mariological* interpretation, in which the bride of the Song is the Virgin Mother of God, who is the perfect realization of what the Lord desires for the Church as a whole and for each of her members (St. Ambrose, St. Peter Chrysologus, St. Francis de Sales). Many commentators developed two or even all three levels of the Song's allegorical meaning.

OUTLINE OF THE SONG OF SOLOMON

1. Dialogue One: Mutual Desire (1:1—2:7)
   A. Superscription (1:1)
   B. The Desire of the Bride for Intimacy with the Bridegroom (1:2–7)
   C. The Daughters of Jerusalem (1:8)
   D. The Exchange of Compliments by the Couple (1:9—2:6)
   E. Refrain (2:7)

2. Dialogue Two: The Overcoming of Separation (2:8—3:5)
   A. The Call of the Bridegroom and His Approach to the Bride (2:8–17)
   B. The Search of the Bride for the Bridegroom (3:1–4)
   C. Refrain (3:5)

3. Dialogue Three: The Admiration of the Bride, the Search for the Bridegroom (3:6—5:8)
   A. The Wedding Procession of Solomon (3:6–11)
   B. The Admiration of the Bridegroom for the Bride (4:1–15)
   C. The Union of the Bridegroom with the Bride (4:16—5:1)
   D. The Search of the Bride for the Bridegroom (5:2–7)
   E. Refrain (5:8)

4. Dialogue Four: Mutual Attraction and Belonging (5:9—8:4)
   A. The Daughters of Jerusalem (5:9)
   B. The Admiration of the Bride for the Bridegroom (5:10–16)
   C. The Daughters of Jerusalem (6:1)
   D. The Belonging of the Bride and Bridegroom to Each Other (6:2–3)
   E. The Admiration of the Bridegroom for the Bride (6:4–10)
   F. The Dialogue of the Bride with the Daughters of Jerusalem (6:11–13)
   G. The Admiration of the Bridegroom for the Bride (7:1–9)
   H. The Desire of the Bride for Intimacy with the Bridegroom (7:10—8:3)
   I. Refrain (8:4)

5. Dialogue Five: Strength and Worth of Love (8:5–14)
   A. The Daughters of Jerusalem (8:5)
   B. The Strength of Love (8:6–7)
   C. The Dispute of the Bride with Her Brothers (8:8–10)
   D. The Vineyard of Solomon and That of the Bridegroom (8:11–12)
   E. The Desire of the Bride and Bridegroom for Each Other (8:13–14)

THE
SONG OF SOLOMON

Song of the Bride and Her Companions

1 The Song of Songs, which is Solomon's.

[2] O that you[a] would kiss me with the kisses of
  your[b] mouth!
For your love is better than wine,
[3] your anointing oils are fragrant,
your name is oil poured out;
  therefore the maidens love you.
[4] Draw me after you, let us make haste.
  The king has brought me into his chambers.

We will exult and rejoice in you;
  we will extol your love more than
    wine;
  rightly do they love you.

[5] I am very dark, but comely,
  O daughters of Jerusalem,
like the tents of Ke′dar,
  like the curtains of Solomon.
[6] Do not gaze at me because I am swarthy,
  because the sun has scorched me.

1:1 Song of Songs: A superlative expression in Hebrew, analogous to "Lord of lords" (Deut 10:17) and "Vanity of vanities" (Eccles 1:2). The entire opening verse serves as a title for the book. **Solomon's:** Traditionally read as a statement of authorship. Other possible meanings include "for Solomon" or "about Solomon". Scripture relates that Solomon composed more than a thousand songs (1 Kings 4:32). His name appears six additional times in the book (1:5; 3:7, 9, 11; 8:11–12).

1:2–7 The voice of the bride, who desires intimacy with a man who is a king (1:4) and shepherd (1:7). The lovers are married for parts of the Song, but some poems seem to refer to their courtship or betrothal. • The metaphor of the Shepherd-King is used for Yahweh in the OT (Deut 33:5; Ps 23:1; 24:8; Ezek 34:1–15) and for Christ in the NT (Mt 25:31–34; Jn 10:11; 1 Pet 2:25; Rev 19:16).

1:2 kiss me: Introduces the theme of sensual love in the book. • The soul longs for the fountain of spiritual life, which is the mouth of Christ the Bridegroom. Since one who drinks must place his mouth to the fountain, the soul, being thirsty, desires to bring its mouth to that which pours forth life, saying: Let him kiss me with the kisses of his mouth (St. Gregory of Nyssa, *Homilies on Song of Songs* 1). • The mouth that kisses is the Word that takes on human nature, and the nature assumed receives the kiss. The kiss itself, constituted by the one giving and the other receiving, is a person, the one mediator between God and man, Christ Jesus. It is not simply the pressing of one mouth upon another; it is God uniting with man (St. Bernard of Clairvaux, *Sermons on Song of Songs* 2, 2). **your love:** Loving acts and gestures are meant. The Greek LXX and Latin Vulgate understood the Hebrew to mean "your breasts" (also in 1:4; 4:10; 7:12). **better than wine:** The king's affection is treasured above the luxuries of the royal palace.

1:3 anointing oils: Equivalent to ancient colognes and perfumes (4:10). God's anointing is the Spirit poured out on his chosen ones (1 Sam 16:13; Is 61:1; Acts 10:38) (CCC 91, 695). **the maidens:** Young women infatuated with the king—perhaps junior members of the royal harem or female servants connected to the royal court. In 6:8 "maidens" represent a third category alongside "queens" and "concubines".

1:4 king: Traditionally identified as Solomon, who reigned from ca. 970 to 930 B.C. Others claim that the royal imagery of the book is metaphorical, i.e., it is simply a way for the bride to idealize her groom as a man worthy of high honor.

1:5 dark: Her skin is tanned from tending vineyards in the summer (1:6). **comely:** Lovely to look upon despite her sunbaked complexion, which reveals her low social status as a field laborer. • The Church says in the Song of Solomon: I am dark but lovely. She is dark through sin, lovely through grace; dark by nature, lovely by redemption. She is dark while the struggle goes on but beautiful when crowned with victory (St. Ambrose, *On the Holy Spirit* 2, 10). **daughters of Jerusalem:** A female chorus that dialogues with the bride in the Song. Several times the bride addresses them (1:5; 2:7; 3:5; 5:8, 16; 8:4), and several times they affirm her love for the bridegroom (1:8; 5:1, 9; 6:1, 13; 8:5). The daughters of Jerusalem may be the same group as the "maidens" (1:3; 6:8) and the "daughters of Zion" (3:11). Whatever their historical identity, these girlfriends of the bride openly celebrate the couple's union. **tents of Kedar:** Made of black goat hair by a tribe in northern Arabia. **curtains of Solomon:** Otherwise unknown, unless the embroidered veils of the Temple are meant. Alternatively, the Hebrew letters *s-l-m-h* may be vocalized as "Salmah" (instead of "Solomon"), the name of a tent-dwelling tribe in southern Arabia.

1:6 angry with me: Perhaps the brothers, acting as guardians of their sister's chastity, disapproved of her romantic interest in the king and sought to keep her from him. Their words are quoted in 8:8–9. **my own vineyard:** Represents the maiden herself. Working outdoors, she has been unable to preserve a delicate, feminine appearance.

The full title is "The Song of Songs Which Is Solomon's." But, as in the case of other books, it is ascribed to him because of his fame. It is a love song or collection of love songs written probably in the fifth century B.C. The Jews had some doubts as to its canonical character but finally included it in their canon of Scripture, and it has always been accepted by the Christian Church as inspired and canonical.

The interpretations of the book have been of great variety. For our purpose we may summarize them thus: (1) It is purely allegorical. For the Jews it represented the relationship between God and his chosen people Israel, which is often in the Old Testament described under the figure of a marriage. The Christian Fathers, of course, saw it as an allegory of Christ and his Church, describing the mystic union between the two; cf. Eph 5:21–33. (2) Others hold it to be a poem describing human love between bride and groom without seeking to identify actual historical persons. The writer's purpose was to extol married love and the sanctity of the marriage bond as instituted and blessed by God. There is support in the Old Testament for this view, e.g., in Proverbs and Sirach. (3) Others again, while admitting the above literal sense of the book, say that it is to be taken in the typical sense of the union of God with Israel, and of the union of Christ with his Church.

Catholics tend to adopt the first or third of these positions. Either way, the interpretation can be developed to include the relations between God and the individual soul, as is done by mystical writers, e.g., St. John of the Cross. The Song of Solomon is extensively used in the liturgy, particularly on feasts of the Blessed Virgin Mary and of Holy Women.

Although this is the one book of the Bible where God is never mentioned by name, its presence in the Bible indicates the sanctity of human love.

[a]Heb *he.*
[b]Heb *his.*

My mother's sons were angry with me,
  they made me keeper of the vineyards;
  but, my own vineyard I have not
    kept!
[7]Tell me, you whom my soul loves,
  where you pasture your flock,
  where you make it lie down at
    noon;
for why should I be like one who wanders[c]
  beside the flocks of your companions?

[8]If you do not know,
  O fairest among women,
follow in the tracks of the flock,
  and pasture your kids
  beside the shepherds' tents.

[9]I compare you, my love,
  to a mare of Pharaoh's chariots.
[10]Your cheeks are comely with ornaments,
  your neck with strings of jewels.
[11]We will make you ornaments of gold,
  studded with silver.

[12]While the king was on his couch,
  my nard gave forth its fragrance.
[13]My beloved is to me a bag of myrrh,
  that lies between my breasts.

[14]My beloved is to me a cluster of henna blossoms
  in the vineyards of En-ge′di.
[15]Behold, you are beautiful, my love;
  behold, you are beautiful;
  your eyes are doves.
[16]Behold, you are beautiful, my beloved,
  truly lovely.
  Our couch is green;
[17] the beams of our house are cedar,
  our rafters[d] are pine.

A Springtime Canticle

2 I am a rose[e] of Sharon,
  a lily of the valleys.

[2]As a lily among brambles,
  so is my love among maidens.

[3]As an apple tree among the trees of the wood,
  so is my beloved among young men.
  With great delight I sat in his shadow,
  and his fruit was sweet to my taste.
[4]He brought me to the banqueting house,
  and his banner over me was love.
[5]Sustain me with raisins,
  refresh me with apples;
  for I am sick with love.
[6]O that his left hand were under my head,
  and that his right hand embraced me!

1:7 where . . . where: Love is expressed as a longing to be with the bridegroom (CCC 2709). **like one who wanders:** Literally, "like a covered woman". The maiden wants to be alone with her lover, but she would prefer not to sneak out after him wearing a veil to conceal her identity from others.

1:8 The voice of the daughters of Jerusalem. See note on 1:5.

1:8 O fairest among women: A supreme compliment paid to the bride also in 5:9 and 6:1. **pasture your kids:** The maiden is a shepherdess.

1:9-11 The voice of the bridegroom, who marvels at how his beloved's jewelry enhances her natural beauty (4:9).

1:9 my love: Means roughly "my darling" or "my sweetheart", an affectionate address used for the bride throughout the Song (1:15; 2:2; 4:1; etc.). **a mare:** Not just a decorated or stately horse, but a female that excites and distracts the stallions that typically served in the Egyptian chariot corps.

1:12-14 The voice of the bride, whose thoughts are stimulated by elegant fragrances.

1:12 the king: See note on 1:4. **nard:** Spikenard, a scented extract imported from India (4:13-14). • Jesus is anointed with costly nard by Mary of Bethany before his Passion (Mk 14:3; Jn 12:3). **myrrh:** The aromatic gum of a balsam tree that grows in parts of the Middle East. Among other things, it was used to make perfumes (Esther 2:12; Prov 7:17) and sacred anointing oils (Ex 30:23; Ps 45:8).

1:14 henna blossoms: The white flowers of a cypress shrub known for their pleasant aroma. **En-gedi:** A fertile oasis overlooking the western shore of the Dead Sea.

1:15 The voice of the bridegroom, who is captivated by his beloved's gaze (6:5; 7:4).

1:16—2:1 The voice of the bride.

1:16 beautiful: I.e., "handsome".

1:17 our house: Poetic language for a grove of shade trees (or a shepherd's hut) where the couple reclines together on the grass.

2:1 Sharon: The verdant coastal plain of central Palestine, stretching north to south from Mount Carmel to Joppa. **lily:** Possibly a crocus or lotus flower.

2:2 The voice of the bridegroom, in whose eyes the bride has no equal in loveliness (6:9).

2:3-7 The voice of the bride, who returns the compliments of the bridegroom (2:2).

2:3 apple tree: Symbolizes the bridegroom and the pleasures of being together with him. The species of the fruit tree is uncertain. **shadow:** A place of protection (Ps 17:8; 121:5). • Sitting in the shade is an image used elsewhere of Israel dwelling securely with the Lord (Hos 14:7). • What are we but wild and fruitless trees, useful merely for fire? What is Christ among us but an apple tree with beautiful fruit, the tree of life in the midst of a parched forest, whose wonderful fruit brings healing, whose shade is salvation, and whose leaves are medicine for the nations (St. Thomas of Villanova, *Commentary on the Song of Songs* 2, 3)?

2:4 the banqueting house: Literally, "the house of wine". It is not a tavern but either a royal hall where guests are entertained (Esther 7:8) or simply a metaphor for a vineyard (7:12). The setting symbolizes how the couple is intoxicated with love for each other. **banner:** The bridegroom's love is evident to all, much as a military standard is visible to vast numbers (Num 2:2; Ps 20:5).

2:5 raisins . . . apples: Symbolize the sweet gestures of love. **sick:** Lovesickness is a familiar theme in Near Eastern love poetry. The idea is that passion can be overwhelming to the point of making one feel weak or faint.

2:6 left hand . . . right hand: A yearning for physical closeness, as in 8:3. • The left hand is the present life, and the right hand the future life. It is said that the left hand supports the head, for the goods of this life must be ruled by the mind and used only as necessities. But the goods of our

---

[c]Gk Syr Vg: Heb *is veiled.*
[d]The meaning of the Hebrew word is uncertain.
[e]Heb *crocus.*

⁷I adjure you, O daughters of Jerusalem,
  by the gazelles or the deer of the field,
  that you stir not up nor awaken love until it please.

⁸The voice of my beloved!
  Behold, he comes,
  leaping upon the mountains,
  bounding over the hills.
⁹My beloved is like a gazelle,
  or a young stag.
  Behold, there he stands
  behind our wall,
  gazing in at the windows,
  looking through the lattice.
¹⁰My beloved speaks and says to me:
  "Arise, my love, my dove, my fair one,
  and come away;
¹¹for behold, the winter is past,
  the rain is over and gone.
¹²The flowers appear on the earth,
  the time of pruning has come,
  and the voice of the turtledove
  is heard in our land.
¹³The fig tree puts forth its figs,
  and the vines are in blossom;
  they give forth fragrance.

Arise, my love, my fair one,
  and come away.
¹⁴O my dove, in the clefts of the rock,
  in the covert of the cliff,
  let me see your face,
  let me hear your voice,
  for your voice is sweet,
  and your face is comely.
¹⁵Catch us the foxes,
  the little foxes,
  that spoil the vineyards,
  for our vineyards are in blossom."

¹⁶My beloved is mine and I am his,
  he pastures his flock among the
  lilies.
¹⁷Until the day breathes
  and the shadows flee,
  turn, my beloved, be like a gazelle,
  or a young stag upon rugged**ᶠ**
  mountains.

Love Seeking the Bridegroom

3 Upon my bed by night
  I sought him whom my soul loves;
I sought him, but found him not;
  I called him, but he gave no answer.**ᵍ**

---

future life, being divine, are an embrace that signifies what is supernatural (St. Cyril of Alexandria, *Commentary on Song of Songs* 2, 6).

2:7 I adjure you: Words for putting someone under oath (Mt 26:63). The expression is a refrain that appears four times in the Song (3:5; 5:8; 8:4). **daughters of Jerusalem:** See note on 1:5. **by the gazelles or the deer of the field:** Normally the name of God is invoked in an oath, in which case avoidance of the divine name seems intended here. Nevertheless, the expression in Hebrew sounds noticeably like "by the Lᴏʀᴅ of hosts or by God Almighty". **nor awaken love:** May mean that love should be spontaneous rather than stimulated or forced. But if the daughters of Jerusalem are young women, unmarried and inexperienced in love, the bride may also be cautioning them against an infatuation with romance that is immature and unprepared to deal with the emotional and psychological demands of a committed relationship. The admonition appears also in 3:5 and 8:4.

2:8–17 The voice of the bride, whose words include a quotation from the bridegroom (2:10b–14). The sights, sounds, and smells mentioned in her poem indicate the arrival of spring in full bloom. Note that "winter is past" in 2:11.

2:8 voice ... he comes: The man comes to fetch his beloved for a romantic rendezvous. • The Church recognizes Christ by his voice, which he sent ahead by the prophets, so that he was heard even when unseen. For ages the Bride only heard his voice, until the time when she saw the Bridegroom with her eyes, coming and leaping upon the mountains (Origen of Alexandria, *Commentary on Song of Songs* 3).

2:9 gazelle: Admired for its graceful appearance and movements. **leaping:** His swiftness bespeaks an eager excitement to be with the bride. **our wall:** Suggests the man approaches the home of the maiden and her family.

2:10 come away: I.e., into the flowering and fragrant countryside.

2:11 winter ... rain: The rainy season in Palestine runs from October to April.

2:12 turtledove: A migratory bird that reappears in Israel in the spring.

2:13 fig tree puts forth: A sign that summer is near (Mk 13:28). Likewise, the image of a budding **vine** points to a springtime setting (6:11). • Fig trees and vines are traditional images of the People of God in the Bible (Ps 80:8; Is 5:1–7; Jer 8:13; Hos 9:10; 10:1; Lk 13:6–9; Jn 15:1–11).

2:14 dove: Associated with such things as innocence and gentleness (Mt 10:16). In some Near Eastern religions, the dove is an icon of a love goddess. **clefts of the rock:** Suggests the maiden is hidden and inaccessible, frustrating the desires of her lover.

2:15 Catch us the foxes: The meaning of the saying is obscure, beyond the fact that foxes represent a threat to the couple's blossoming relationship. Some identify the pests as male suitors who could potentially claim the maiden in marriage. Recall that "my ... vineyard" in 1:6 and 8:12 stands for the young woman herself.

2:16 beloved is mine and I am his: The language of mutual belonging is the language of covenant commitment, where persons are bound together by reciprocal obligations of love and loyalty toward one another (Ezek 16:8). Marriage was considered a covenant in ancient Israel (Mal 2:14). Similar statements appear in 6:3 and 7:10. • The expression is much like the so-called "covenant formula" used elsewhere in Scripture to describe God and his people as belonging to each other (Lev 26:12; Jer 7:23; Ezek 34:30; 2 Cor 6:16; Rev 21:3).

2:17 the day breathes: Daybreak, with its morning breezes (4:6).

3:1–5 The voice of the bride, who pines for the bridegroom through a sleepless night and ventures out on a desperate search to find him. Her words are often thought to describe a dream. A similar experience is recounted in 5:2–8.

3:1 him whom my soul loves: The bridegroom is the object of the maiden's deepest affection. • Spiritual love, whether directed to God, an angel, or another soul, is properly and exclusively attributed to the soul. Thus, when the bride states that her soul loves the bridegroom, she uses an appropriate expression, for it indicates that the

---

ᶠThe meaning of the Hebrew word is unknown.
ᵍGk: Heb lacks this line.

²"I will rise now and go about the city,
 in the streets and in the squares;
I will seek him whom my soul loves."
 I sought him, but found him not.
³The watchmen found me,
 as they went about in the city.
"Have you seen him whom my soul loves?"
⁴Scarcely had I passed them,
 when I found him whom my soul loves.
I held him, and would not let him go
 until I had brought him into my mother's
 house,
 and into the chamber of her that conceived
 me.
⁵I adjure you, O daughters of Jerusalem,
 by the gazelles or the deer of the field,
that you stir not up nor awaken love until it
 please.
⁶What is that coming up from the wilderness,
 like a column of smoke,
perfumed with myrrh and frankincense,
 with all the fragrant powders of the merchant?
⁷Behold, it is the litter of Solomon!
 About it are sixty mighty men
 of the mighty men of Israel,

⁸all belted with swords
 and expert in war,
 each with his sword at his thigh,
 against alarms by night.
⁹King Solomon made himself a palanquin
 from the wood of Lebanon.
¹⁰He made its posts of silver,
 its back of gold, its seat of purple;
it was lovingly wrought withinʰ
 by the daughters of Jerusalem.
¹¹Go forth, O daughters of Zion,
 and behold King Solomon,
with the crown with which his mother crowned
 him
 on the day of his wedding,
 on the day of the gladness of his heart.

The Bride's Beauty Extolled

4 Behold, you are beautiful, my love,
 behold, you are beautiful!
Your eyes are doves
 behind your veil.
Your hair is like a flock of goats,
 moving down the slopes of Gilead.
²Your teeth are like a flock of shorn ewes
 that have come up from the washing,

---

bridegroom is spirit and, so, is loved with a spiritual rather than a physical love (St. Bernard of Clairvaux, *Sermons on Song of Songs* 75, 4) (CCC 2709).

3:2 the city: Unnamed but seemingly the hometown of the woman and her family (3:4). Some think Jerusalem is meant. **I will seek him:** Similar language is used by the prophets to encourage Israel's search for spiritual intimacy with the Lord (Jer 29:13; Hos 3:5; 5:15; Amos 5:5–6).

3:3 watchmen: Night guards on patrol in the city (5:7).

3:4 my mother's house: A place of privacy and family identity, as also in 8:2.

3:5 I adjure you: An oath formula. See note on 2:7. **daughters of Jerusalem:** See note on 1:5. **nor awaken love:** See note on 2:7.

3:6–11 Probably the voice of the female chorus, the daughters of Jerusalem. The scene depicts Solomon in ceremonial procession en route to the capital on his wedding day (3:11). For another marriage poem about Solomon, see Ps 45.

3:6 coming up: Suggests an ascent to Jerusalem (as in Ps 122:3–4). **column of smoke:** A dust cloud kicked up by the royal entourage. • Some relate this image to the pillar of cloud by which God guided the Israelites in the wilderness (Ex 13:21–22). **myrrh:** See note on 1:12. **frankincense:** An exotic resin powder imported from Sheba in southern Arabia (Is 60:6; Jer 6:20). • The bride clings to Christ and ascends with him from the wilderness of this world. The daughters of Jerusalem wonder how a soul can rise up like smoke that emits a pleasant fragrance. The aroma is that of reverent prayer, which asks not for earthly things but for eternal and invisible things. The scent of myrrh and frankincense indicates that the soul has died to sin and lives for God (St. Ambrose, *On Isaac* 5, 44).

3:7 litter: A portable bed or couch enclosed with curtains and carried with poles. The royal carriage is called a "palanquin" in 3:9. **sixty mighty men:** An elite unit of armed warriors provides a military escort. Solomon's personal protection force is twice the size of David's in 2 Sam 23:18–23.

3:8 alarms by night: Threats from bandits and thieves working under cover of darkness.

3:9 palanquin: Possibly a loanword from the Greek *phoreion*, but this remains uncertain. See note on 3:7. **wood of Lebanon:** Cedar wood, a superior quality of lumber used also in the construction of Solomon's Temple and palace (1 Kings 5:6–10; 6:9–10; 7:2).

3:10 its posts: Either its carrying poles, its support legs, or the framing rods of its fabric canopy. **purple:** The color most often associated with royal luxury in the Bible (Judg 8:26; Esther 8:15; Sir 40:4; Jn 19:2–3). **daughters of Jerusalem:** See note on 1:5.

3:11 daughters of Zion: The daughters of Jerusalem (3:10). For the name Zion, see note on 2 Sam 5:7. **the crown:** Possibly a royal diadem; others envision a garland of flowers placed on the head of the newlywed king (cf. Is 61:10). **his mother:** Bathsheba (2 Sam 12:24). For the nature of her office, see essay: *The Queen Mother* at 1 Kings 2. **day of his wedding:** Numerous attempts have been made to specify the occasion, such as Solomon's marriage to the Egyptian princess in 1 Kings 3:1, though none has won general acceptance.

4:1–15 The voice of the bridegroom, who gazes upon his beloved. He admires her physical features (4:1–7), urges her to come with him (4:8–9), and compares her to a garden of sensual delights (4:10–15). • The book speaks of kisses, breasts, cheeks, and limbs. By naming parts of the body, we are shown how marvelously God works with us, for he uses the language of sensual love to inflame our hearts with holy love. By lowering himself in this manner of speech, he lifts us up in understanding. From the words of this lower love, we are taught what should be the intensity of our love for God (St. Gregory the Great, *Exposition on Song of Songs* 3).

4:1 Behold ... doves: Repeats the words of 1:15. **behind your veil:** Presumably a bridal veil (Gen 24:65–67). **Your hair:** Long, black, and wavy like hillsides covered with **goats** in the fertile pasturelands of **Gilead**, east of the Jordan (Num 32:1).

4:2 Your teeth: Bright, clean, and nicely arranged. **not one ... bereaved:** None of her teeth is missing. The compliment is repeated in 6:6. • New members of the Church

---

ʰThe meaning of the Hebrew is uncertain.

all of which bear twins,
and not one among them is bereaved.
³Your lips are like a scarlet thread,
and your mouth is lovely.
Your cheeks are like halves of a pomegranate
behind your veil.
⁴Your neck is like the tower of David,
built for an arsenal,ⁱ
whereon hang a thousand bucklers,
all of them shields of warriors.
⁵Your two breasts are like two fawns,
twins of a gazelle,
that feed among the lilies.
⁶Until the day breathes
and the shadows flee,
I will hasten to the mountain of myrrh
and the hill of frankincense.
⁷You are all fair, my love;
there is no flaw in you.
⁸Come with me from Lebanon, my bride;
come with me from Lebanon.

Departʲ from the peak of Ama′na,
from the peak of Se′nir and Hermon,
from the dens of lions,
from the mountains of leopards.

⁹You have ravished my heart, my sister, my
bride,
you have ravished my heart with a glance
of your eyes,
with one jewel of your necklace.
¹⁰How sweet is your love, my sister, my bride!
how much better is your love than
wine,
and the fragrance of your oils than
any spice!
¹¹Your lips distil nectar, my bride;
honey and milk are under your tongue;
the scent of your garments is like the scent
of Lebanon.
¹²A garden locked is my sister, my bride,
a garden locked, a fountain sealed.

---

are teeth that resemble shorn sheep, for they have put aside the burden of worldly cares, they have been washed in baptism, and everyone bears twins because he fulfills the double commandment to love God and neighbor (St. Augustine, *Enarrations on the Psalms* 3, 7).

4:3 Your lips: Perhaps colored with lipstick, an ancient form of which was used by women in Egypt. **your mouth:** The Greek LXX and Latin Vulgate read "your speech". **Your cheeks:** Round and red like the cross-section of a **pomegranate**.

4:4 Your neck: Bedecked with gold jewelry (1:10; 4:9), much like an armory or defensive wall could be decorated with ceremonial shields (1 Kings 10:16–17; Ezek 27:11). **tower of David:** Only mentioned here in the Bible and otherwise unknown.

4:5 fawns: Symbolize elegance and youthfulness (7:3).

4:6 the day breathes: Daybreak, with its morning breezes (2:17). **mountain of myrrh ... hill of frankincense:** Meaning uncertain. Some think it a reference to the maiden and the scent of her perfumes (4:10–11). Others see a specific reference to the maiden's breasts, where a sachet of fragrant spices hung down (1:13). Still others detect a reference to the Temple Mount in Jerusalem, where myrrh and frankincense were used in the service of divine worship (Ex 30:23, 34; Sir 24:15). See notes on 1:12 and 3:6.

4:7 no flaw: Or, "no blemish". The Hebrew *mûm* refers to disfigurements of the body (Lev 21:18–21; 2 Sam 14:25) or defects of character (Deut 32:5; Job 11:15). • Paul uses this language to describe the Church as the Bride of Christ cleansed of imperfections and made "holy and without blemish" (Eph 5:26–27).

4:8 my bride: An endearing epithet used of the wife also in 4:9–12 and 5:1. It is possible the maiden is still a betrothed woman in this poem, i.e., she has the legal status of a wife, but she and the bridegroom have not yet begun their common life together. **Amana ... Senir:** Mountains north of Israel in the Anti-Lebanon Range. They represent barriers that separate the couple and keep them from being together. As in 2:14, the maiden appears to be hidden and inaccessible to the man for a time. **Hermon:** Another name for Mount Senir (Deut 3:9). **lions ... leopards:** Meaning obscure. Some view these wild animals as dangers that threaten the couple's relationship. Others consider them symbols of Israel's enemies, who typically invaded Palestine from the north.

4:10 better ... than wine: The same comparison is used in 1:4. **spice:** Listed among the gifts brought to Solomon by the queen of Sheba (1 Kings 10:2, 10).

4:11 nectar: Honey from the comb. It symbolizes the sweetness of the bride's loving words and kisses (7:9; Prov 5:3; 16:24). **honey and milk:** Often associated with the Promised Land (Ex 3:8; Num 13:27; Deut 6:3). **scent of Lebanon:** The pleasant aroma of its famous cedar trees.

4:12 garden: A metaphor depicting the bride as an exotic, natural paradise that delights the senses and awakens the romantic interests of the bridegroom (4:15–16; 5:1; 6:2). • Much of the imagery of the Song calls to mind the Garden of Eden story in Gen 2–3. In both, we visualize a

Word Study

My Sister (4:9)

'Aḥoti (Heb.): the noun "sister" with the possessive suffix "my". Typically the noun is used for a female relative of the same generation, a full sister (Num 26:59), a half-sister (Gen 20:12), or simply a kinswoman (Gen 24:59–60). Occasionally the prophets use the language of "sisters" to describe kingdoms or cities that act alike in their rebellion against the Lord (Jer 3:7–8; Ezek 16:46–52). Unusual is the fivefold description of the bride in the Song of Solomon as the "sister" of the bridegroom (Song 4:9–10, 12; 5:1–2). The Song does not envision a brother-and-sister marriage, as this is strictly forbidden by the incest laws of the Torah (Lev 18:9, 11; Deut 27:22). Rather, comparative studies have shown this to be conventional language in the ancient Near East, especially in love poetry from Egypt. Beyond this, the designation "sister" reflects the biblical vision of marriage as a covenant (Mal 2:14) that unites husband and wife in a flesh-and-bone relationship analogous to natural kinship (compare Gen 2:23 with Gen 29:14; Judg 9:2). References to one's wife as a "sister" (Gk., *adelphē*) also appear in the Book of Tobit (Tob 5:20; 7:16; 8:4, 7).

ⁱThe meaning of the Hebrew word is uncertain.
ʲOr *Look.*

¹³Your shoots are an orchard of pomegranates
    with all choicest fruits,
        henna with nard,
¹⁴nard and saffron, calamus and cinnamon,
    with all trees of frankincense,
        myrrh and aloes,
            with all chief spices—
¹⁵a garden fountain, a well of living water,
    and flowing streams from
        Lebanon.

¹⁶Awake, O north wind,
    and come, O south wind!
Blow upon my garden,
    let its fragrance be wafted abroad.
Let my beloved come to his garden,
    and eat its choicest fruits.

The Groom's Song of Love;
and the Torment of Separation

5 I come to my garden, my sister, my bride,
    I gather my myrrh with my spice,
    I eat my honeycomb with my honey,
    I drink my wine with my milk.

Eat, O friends, and drink:
    drink deeply, O lovers!
²I slept, but my heart was awake.
Hark! my beloved is knocking.
"Open to me, my sister, my love,
    my dove, my perfect one;
for my head is wet with dew,
    my locks with the drops of the night."
³I had put off my garment,
    how could I put it on?
I had bathed my feet,
    how could I soil them?
⁴My beloved put his hand to the latch,
    and my heart was thrilled within me.
⁵I arose to open to my beloved,
    and my hands dripped with myrrh,
my fingers with liquid myrrh,
    upon the handles of the bolt.
⁶I opened to my beloved,
    but my beloved had turned and gone.
My soul failed me when he spoke.
I sought him, but found him not;
    I called him, but he gave no answer.

---

garden of trees and fruit that is watered by a fountain spring. It is an idyllic setting where man and woman admire each other's bodies without shame and where they live in blissful harmony. Parallels such as these hint that married love offers a taste of paradise lost, a unique experience of the way things should have been had the first couple continued to live in the grace of God. **fountain:** Suggests the bride is refreshing and revitalizing to her husband. For the imagery, see note on Prov 5:15–18. **locked ... sealed:** Represents the exclusivity of marriage. The bride has entrusted herself to the bridegroom alone as a sexual partner and companion in life, i.e., she has made herself inaccessible to all others. • If the bride of Christ, the Church, is a garden enclosed, she cannot be accessed by outsiders. If she is a fountain sealed, the outsider cannot drink from the well of living water that lies within, that is, he can gain no life or sanctification from it (St. Cyprian, *Letters* 69, 2). Christ descended into the womb of the Virgin without injuring the enclosure of her body, and he left the womb without opening the door of her virginity. He thus fulfilled what is chanted in the Song of Songs: My sister, my spouse, is a garden enclosed, a fountain sealed (St. Peter Chrysologus, *Sermons* 145).

4:13 orchard: A Persian loanword meaning "park" or "forest enclosure" (Neh 2:8; Eccles 2:5). **henna:** See note on 1:14. **nard:** See note on 1:12.

4:14 saffron: Either spice granules or fragrant oil made from a crocus flower. **calamus:** An oil made from Arabian sweet cane (Jer 6:20). **cinnamon:** Its scent was thought to create a romantic atmosphere (Prov 7:17). **frankincense:** See note on 3:6. **myrrh:** See note on 1:12.

4:15 fountain ... of living water: An irrigation spring as distinct from a reservoir of stagnant water. • Using similar words, Jesus compared the gift of divine grace to a spring of living water that flows from the Spirit (Jn 4:10–14). **streams from Lebanon:** Melting snows that result from the spring thaw.

4:16 The voice of the bride. Alternatively, some limit the bride's words to 4:16c ("Let my beloved ... fruits."), assigning 4:16a-b to the bridegroom ("Awake ... abroad."). In any case, the **north** and **south** winds are summoned to carry the sweet fragrances of the bride to her distant bridegroom, so that his desire to possess her will be reawakened and increased.

5:1 The voice of the bridegroom is heard in 5:1a-b ("I come ... milk.") responding to the invitation to enjoy the bride's love

(4:16). The words in 5:1c ("Eat ... lovers!"), however, seem to be spoken by the daughters of Jerusalem (5:8).

5:1 my garden: See note on 4:12. **my sister:** See word study: *My Sister* at 4:9. **gather ... eat ... drink:** Symbolize gestures of intimacy. **wine ... milk:** Enjoyed by the palate, as in 4:10–11. The preposition **with** need not imply the two beverages were mixed together; hence, some translations render it "and". Sometimes the coupling of wine and milk constitute a sign of future prosperity (Gen 49:12; Joel 3:18).

5:2–8 The voice of the bride. She is awakened by the bridegroom knocking and calling for her, but before the bride can ready herself to open the door, he is gone. This sends her out into the streets on a dangerous nighttime search (3:1–5). Many interpret the account, which opens with the maiden sleeping, as a dream rather than a real-life experience. • The scenario resembles those times when Yahweh called to his people but they refused to heed his voice (Is 65:12; 66:4; Jer 7:27). As a result of their delayed response, the Lord and his favor were sought but not found (5:6; Prov 1:28; Is 1:15).

5:2 my beloved is knocking: An allusion to this passage appears in Rev 3:20, where Christ knocks and speaks at the door, waiting to be admitted to closer fellowship with the believer. **my dove, my perfect one:** Epithets repeated in 6:9. See notes on 2:14 and 4:7. • Rightly does the Lord name his Church "dove" and call her "perfect". She is not only constituted one community of the righteous, but she is perfect, having received every virtue and divine gift (St. Bede, *Exposition on Song of Songs* 4). **wet with dew:** Nights can be especially damp in Palestine.

5:3 garment: The bride is dressed for bed, not for visitors. **how could I ... how could I:** Not real objections to answering the door but the playful teases of love.

5:4 the latch: An opening into which a large wooden key would be inserted to unbolt the door.

5:5 myrrh: Perhaps the bridegroom smeared it on the lock to indicate that he had been there. See note on 1:12. • There is no resurrection unless a freely chosen death comes first. Such a death is indicated by the myrrh dripping from the hands of the bride, which signifies the soul's voluntary mortification of bodily pleasures (St. Gregory of Nyssa, *Homilies on Song of Songs* 12).

⁷The watchmen found me,
 as they went about in the city;
they beat me, they wounded me,
 they took away my mantle,
 those watchmen of the walls.
⁸I adjure you, O daughters of Jerusalem,
 if you find my beloved,
that you tell him
 I am sick with love.

⁹What is your beloved more than another beloved,
 O fairest among women?
What is your beloved more than another
 beloved,
 that you thus adjure us?

¹⁰My beloved is all radiant and ruddy,
 distinguished among ten thousand.
¹¹His head is the finest gold;
 his locks are wavy,
 black as a raven.
¹²His eyes are like doves
 beside springs of water,
 bathed in milk,
 fitly set.ᵏ
¹³His cheeks are like beds of spices,
 yielding fragrance.
His lips are lilies,
 distilling liquid myrrh.
¹⁴His arms are rounded gold,
 set with jewels.

His body is ivory work,¹
 encrusted with sapphires.ᵐ
¹⁵His legs are alabaster columns,
 set upon bases of gold.
His appearance is like Lebanon,
 choice as the cedars.
¹⁶His speech is most sweet,
 and he is altogether desirable.
This is my beloved and this is my friend,
 O daughters of Jerusalem.

Colloquy of the Friends and the Bride; the Bridegroom's Praise of the Bride

6 Where has your beloved gone,
 O fairest among women?
Where has your beloved turned,
 that we may seek him with you?

²My beloved has gone down to his garden,
 to the beds of spices,
to pasture his flock in the gardens,
 and to gather lilies.
³I am my beloved's and my beloved is mine;
 he pastures his flock among the lilies.

⁴You are beautiful as Tirzah, my love,
 comely as Jerusalem,
 terrible as an army with banners.
⁵Turn away your eyes from me,
 for they disturb me—
Your hair is like a flock of goats,
 moving down the slopes of Gilead.

5:7 watchmen: Night guards on patrol in the city (3:3). It is unclear why they treat the distraught woman so harshly; perhaps they mistake her for a prostitute (cf. Prov 7:6–13).

5:8 I adjure you: An oath formula. See note on 2:7. **daughters of Jerusalem:** See note on 1:5. **sick with love:** See note on 2:5.

5:9 The voice of the daughters of Jerusalem, addressed in 5:8. Their questions about the bridegroom are answered in the following verses.

5:10–16 The voice of the bride. She describes the bridegroom as physically impressive and romantically attractive. Her words evoke scenes from nature, scents from exotic plants, and features associated with statues made of precious materials.

5:10 ruddy: David, the father of Solomon, is so described in 1 Sam 16:12 and 17:42. • The beloved Bridegroom is radiant because he committed no sin and because no lie was found in his mouth when he came in the flesh. He is also ruddy because he cleansed us from sin by his blood (St. Bede, *Exposition on Song of Songs* 3).

5:11 wavy: Or thick like the fronds of a palm tree. **black:** Also the color of the bride's hair. See note on 4:1.

5:12 doves: Compare with 1:15. See note on 2:14. **springs:** Suggests that his eyes have a glassy shine, similar to the bride's in 7:4.

5:13 beds of spices: His beard may be scented with cologne. **lilies:** Thought to be crocus or lotus flowers (2:1). **distilling liquid myrrh:** Recalls how the woman's lips drip with honey in 4:11.

5:14 His body: A reference to his stomach or abdominal region (Dan 2:32). **sapphires:** Or, "lapus lazuli", a decorative blue stone used in Near Eastern art and architecture.

5:15 His legs: Some detect an allusion to Solomon's Temple, which also featured marble (1 Chron 29:2), twin pillars (1 Kings 7:15–22), and gold (1 Kings 6:21–22). **alabaster:** Or, "marble". **His appearance:** Majestic and sturdy like one of Lebanon's famous cedar trees. See note on 3:9.

5:16 His speech: The Hebrew refers to his mouth or palate, in which case the bridegroom's kisses and tender words may both be meant (1:2; 4:11).

6:1 The voice of the daughters of Jerusalem, who offer to join the bride in searching for the bridegroom. See note on 1:5.

6:2–3 The voice of the bride.

6:2 to pasture ... to gather: Probably a double reference to the bridegroom's activity in the royal gardens and to his intimacy with the bride, who is imaged as a "garden" in 4:12—5:1 and as a "lily" in 2:1-2.

6:3 I am my beloved's: Repeats the wording of 2:16 but in reverse order.

6:4–10 The voice of the bridegroom. As in 4:1-3, he praises the beauty of the bride's hair and face; as in 2:2 and 4:7, he pronounces her flawless and more attractive than any other woman. Some attribute 6:10, not to the man, but to the daughters of Jerusalem.

6:4 Tirzah: The original capital city of the Northern Kingdom of Israel (1 Kings 15:21). This was before King Omri moved government operations to Samaria around 879 B.C. (1 Kings 16:23-24). Nothing is known about the grandeur of ancient Tirzah, but ranking it alongside the holy city is a high compliment. **terrible:** In the sense of "awe inspiring".

6:5 they disturb me: The husband finds his wife's loving gazes overwhelming (4:9). **Your hair:** See note on 4:1.

ᵏThe meaning of the Hebrew is uncertain.
¹The meaning of the Hebrew word is uncertain.
ᵐHeb *lapis lazuli*.

⁶Your teeth are like a flock of ewes,
 that have come up from the washing,
all of them bear twins,
 not one among them is bereaved.
⁷Your cheeks are like halves of a pomegranate
 behind your veil.
⁸There are sixty queens and eighty concubines,
 and maidens without number.
⁹My dove, my perfect one, is only one,
 the darling of her mother,
 flawless to her that bore her.

The maidens saw her and called her happy;
 the queens and concubines also, and they
 praised her.
¹⁰"Who is this that looks forth like the dawn,
 fair as the moon, bright as the sun,
 terrible as an army with banners?"

¹¹I went down to the nut orchard,
 to look at the blossoms of the valley,
to see whether the vines had budded,
 whether the pomegranates were in bloom.

6:6 Your teeth: See note on 4:2.

6:7 Your cheeks: See note on 4:3.

6:8 queens ... concubines: The royal wives and female partners of the bridegroom. Many read the saying as an allusion to Solomon's harem, which grew to even larger numbers in the latter years of his reign (1 Kings 11:3). **maidens:** Identity uncertain, but see note on 1:3.

6:9 My dove, my perfect one: See note on 5:2. **only one:** The bride is unique, in a class by herself. • The holy Virgin is the daughter of incomparable love, the unique dove, the flawless spouse. All the saints and angels are compared to the stars, but she is as fair as the moon

and stands out from the saints as the sun does from the stars. The charity of this loving Mother is more perfect than that of all the saints in heaven (St. Francis de Sales, *Treatise on the Love of God* 3, 8). **maidens:** The Hebrew says "daughters", suggesting the daughters of Jerusalem are meant (1:5; 5:8, 16; 8:4).

6:10 terrible as an army: An awe-inspiring sight, not a frightening one.

6:11–12 The voice of the bride.

6:11 nut orchard: A grove of walnut trees. **the vines:** Presumably one of Solomon's royal vineyards (7:12; 8:11). **budded:** The season is spring (2:11; 7:12). **pomegranates:** A

The Song of Solomon and the Spiritual Life

Few books of Scripture have been as treasured down through the centuries as the Song of Solomon. The sheer number of writings devoted to preaching and expounding the work in patristic, medieval, and modern times is simply staggering. The reason, by and large, is the belief that it celebrates the mystical joys of falling in love with God. This is partly the result of allegorical interpretations that identify the bride of the Song as the soul that desires the embrace of the divine Bridegroom. Another factor is the tradition that the three books of Solomon—Proverbs, Ecclesiastes, and the Song of Solomon—relate to three stages of growth in the spiritual life.

At least one Jewish tradition connected these books with three stages in Solomon's own life. The Song of Solomon was thought to have been written in the king's youth, when the influence of the passions is strongest; Proverbs was said to have come from the king's mature years, once he had become wise in the ways of the world; and Ecclesiastes was considered the work of his old age, after a lifetime of experience had impressed upon him the vanity of this passing life (*Song of Songs Rabbah* 1, 1, 10).

Christian tradition took a different approach, based on the canonical order of the books in the Greek and Latin translations of the Old Testament. The sequence, going from Proverbs to Ecclesiastes to the Song of Solomon, embodied lessons for those moving from beginning to intermediate to advanced stages of Christian maturity. For instance, in the third century, Origen of Alexandria held that Solomon teaches rules for upright living in Proverbs, especially habits that will lead us onward in virtue; he teaches on the subject of nature in Ecclesiastes, distinguishing what is profitable in this world from what is not, so that we will forsake vain things and cling to what is useful; and he teaches love for divine things in the Song of Solomon, stressing that communion with God is attained principally by love (Prologue to *Commentary on Song of Songs* 3). Likewise, in the sixth century, St. Gregory the Great envisioned these three books as a ladder leading upward to God. Thus, the moral life is put forward in Proverbs; the natural or reflective life, by which all things are examined closely and the vanities here below are despised, is dealt with in Ecclesiastes; and the contemplative life, which entails fixing our hearts on things above, is promoted in the Song of Solomon (*Exposition on Song of Songs* 9). Again, in the thirteenth century, St. Bonaventure stated that Solomon composed three wisdom books in order to instruct us on how to reach beatitude. In Proverbs, Solomon teaches us how to live wisely in the world; in Ecclesiastes, he teaches contempt for this present world; and in the Song of Solomon, he teaches us to love heavenly things, especially the divine Bridegroom (introduction to *Commentary on Ecclesiastes* 15).

Given this line of interpretation, the Song of Solomon has always been a favorite book of Christian men and women seeking spiritual perfection. Only its language of sexual attraction was strong enough to capture the thrill of experiencing deep intimacy with God. Of course, this level of spiritual maturity is not possible unless one's moral life is in good order and one's vision of reality penetrates beyond the glitter and tinsel of the world to see the vanity and brevity of it all. So it is that Proverbs comes first, Ecclesiastes comes second, and together they lead the way to the mystical paradise of the Song of Solomon.

[12]Before I was aware, my fancy set me
  in a chariot beside my prince.[n]

[13o]Return, return, O Shu'lammite,
  return, return, that we may look upon
  you.

Why should you look upon the Shulammite,
  as upon a dance before two armies? [p]

Colloquy of the Bride and the Groom

7 How graceful are your feet in sandals,
  O queenly maiden!
Your rounded thighs are like jewels,
  the work of a master hand.
[2]Your navel is a rounded bowl
  that never lacks mixed wine.
Your belly is a heap of wheat,
  encircled with lilies.
[3]Your two breasts are like two fawns,
  twins of a gazelle.
[4]Your neck is like an ivory tower.
Your eyes are pools in Hesh'bon,
  by the gate of Bath-rab'bim.

Your nose is like a tower of Lebanon,
  overlooking Damascus.
[5]Your head crowns you like Car'mel,
  and your flowing locks are like purple;
  a king is held captive in the tresses.[q]

[6]How fair and pleasant you are,
  O loved one, delectable maiden![r]
[7]You are stately[s] as a palm tree,
  and your breasts are like its clusters.
[8]I say I will climb the palm tree
  and lay hold of its branches.
Oh, may your breasts be like clusters of the vine,
  and the scent of your breath like apples,
[9]and your kisses[t] like the best wine
  that goes down[u] smoothly,
  gliding over lips and teeth.[v]

[10]I am my beloved 's,
  and his desire is for me.
[11]Come, my beloved,
  let us go forth into the fields,
  and lodge in the villages;

---

staple fruit in Palestine having a thick rind and a red interior with many seeds (4:3; 7:12).

6:12 a chariot beside my prince: The Hebrew is notoriously obscure. The Greek LXX and Latin Vulgate both read "the chariots of Aminadab".

6:13 The voice of the daughters of Jerusalem is heard in the first half of this verse ("Return ... upon you."); the voice of the bride is heard in the second ("Why ... two armies?"). See note on 1:5.

6:13 Return, return: The prophets use this language in their appeals for repentance, which entails turning back from sin and renewing one's commitment to the Lord (Is 55:7; Jer 3:12-14; Hos 6:1; Joel 2:12-13; Zech 1:3-4). **Shulammite:** Various interpretations of this term have been offered. (**1**) The RSV takes it to mean "woman from Shulam", although no town of this name is known to have existed in ancient Palestine. (**2**) Others consider it a variant spelling of "Shunammite" (1 Kings 1:3), although evidence for this is minimal. (**3**) Perhaps best, it has been identified as a feminine form of the name Solomon, which means roughly "man of peace" (1 Chron 22:9). The address might thus be rendered "O woman of peace" or even "O Solomonness". **dance:** Women traditionally performed a victory dance following a military triumph (Ex 15:20; Judg 11:34; 1 Sam 18:6). **two armies:** The Hebrew *mahanaim* means "two camps" and was also the name of a town near the Jabbok River, east of the Jordan (Gen 32:2; 2 Sam 17:24). The meaning of the bride's question is notoriously obscure, beyond the fact that she does not wish to make a spectacle of herself.

7:1-9 The voice of the bridegroom, who again remarks on the stunning beauty of the bride. This time his gaze scans upward from her feet to her head (7:1-5) rather than downward from the top as previously (4:1-5; 6:5-7).

7:1 sandals: Enhance her feminine appeal (Jud 16:9). **queenly maiden:** Or, better, "noble daughter", an indicator of her regal or stately appearance. It is not a comment about her social rank. **like jewels:** The comparison is with a ring or earring (Prov 25:12; Hos 2:13).

7:2 mixed wine: Apparently flavored with spices (8:2). **heap of wheat:** It is uncertain whether the image connotes beauty (in reference to her stomach) or fertility (in reference to her womb). **encircled with lilies:** Some picture a floral garland around her waist.

7:3 fawns: Symbolize elegance and youthfulness (4:5).

7:4 ivory tower: Something smooth and graceful. Perhaps the bride is wearing an ivory necklace as well (cf. 4:4). **pools:** Suggests that her eyes have a glassy shine, similar to the bridegroom's in 5:12. **Heshbon:** A city northeast of the Dead Sea. **Bath-rabbim:** Otherwise unknown. **tower of Lebanon:** One of the peaks of the Anti-Lebanon Range, possibly Mount Hermon (4:8). Comparing this to the bride's nose is doubtless intended as a compliment, though it may seem unflattering to modern sensibilities.

7:5 Carmel: A forested range of peaks and cliffs overlooking the Mediterranean Sea in northwest Israel (1 Kings 18:42-43). **purple:** The color of royalty. See note on 3:10. **a king:** Here the bridegroom refers to himself in kingly terms, just as the bride has done in 1:4, 12. Solomon is the only named personality given the royal title elsewhere in the Song (3:9, 11). **captive in the tresses:** I.e., captivated or enchanted by her flowing ringlets of hair.

7:7 palm tree: The fruit-bearing date palm.

7:8 climb ... lay hold: Euphemistic language to say the man is resolved to embrace and kiss his bride passionately and thus experience the sensuous delights of her love. **apples:** Emit the smell of sweetness (cf. 2:3, 5).

7:9 the best wine: Her kisses give more pleasure than the finest fermented juices.

7:10—8:4 The voice of the bride. As in 2:10-13, she invites the bridegroom to join her for a romantic getaway in the blossoming countryside.

7:10 I am my beloved's: Repeats the sentiments of 2:16 and 6:3.

---

[n]Cn: The meaning of the Hebrew is uncertain.
[o]Ch 7:1 in Heb.
[p]Or *dance of Mahanaim.*
[q]The meaning of the Hebrew word is uncertain.
[r]Syr: Heb *in delights.*
[s]Heb *This your stature is.*
[t]Heb *palate.*
[u]Heb *down for my lover.*
[v]Gk Syr Vg: Heb *lips of sleepers.*

¹²let us go out early to the vineyards,
and see whether the vines have budded,
whether the grape blossoms have opened
and the pomegranates are in bloom.
There I will give you my love.
¹³The mandrakes give forth fragrance,
and over our doors are all choice fruits,
new as well as old,
which I have laid up for you, O my beloved.

Metaphors of Love

8 O that you were like a brother to me,
that nursed at my mother 's breast!
If I met you outside, I would kiss you,
and none would despise me.
²I would lead you and bring you
into the house of my mother,
and into the chamber of her that conceived me.ʷ

I would give you spiced wine to drink,
the juice of my pomegranates.
³O that his left hand were under my head,
and that his right hand embraced me!
⁴I adjure you, O daughters of Jerusalem,
that you stir not up nor awaken love
until it please.

⁵Who is that coming up from the wilderness,
leaning upon her beloved?

Under the apple tree I awakened you.
There your mother was in travail with you,
there she who bore you was in travail.

⁶Set me as a seal upon your heart,
as a seal upon your arm;

7:12 the vineyards: Perhaps one of Solomon's royal vineyards (8:11). The woman herself is symbolized by a vineyard in 1:6. **budded:** The season is spring (2:11; 6:11). **I will give you my love:** I.e., I will give you myself entirely and uninhibitedly.

7:13 mandrakes: Herbs thought to be a natural aphrodisiac that promoted fertility (Gen 30:14–16). **our doors:** The entryway of the couple's home. **fruits, new ... old:** Unless one is to think of fresh and dried fruits, the expression is likely a merism meaning "fruits of every kind".

8:1 like a brother: The bride wishes she could be affectionate with her beloved in public without criticism from others. • Many prayed for the coming of our Lord and Savior, even the spouse in the Song of Solomon, saying, "O that you were like a brother to me." The meaning of the prayer is, "O

that you were like man and would assume human nature for our sake" (St. Athanasius, *Festal Letters* 1, 1).

8:2 house of my mother: Mentioned earlier in 3:4. **the chamber:** The bride wants to consummate her love for the bridegroom in the very place where he was begotten by his parents. • The Mother of God is the treasure of spiritual praise, the beautiful Bride of the Song who reverently receives the immortal Bridegroom into the nuptial chamber of her soul (St. Germanus of Constantinople, *Homily on the Annunciation*). **wine ... juice:** Symbolic of intimate pleasures. **pomegranates:** See note on 6:11.

8:3 left hand ... right hand: A yearning for physical closeness, as in 2:6.

8:4 I adjure you: An oath formula. See note on 2:7. **daughters of Jerusalem:** See note on 1:5. **nor awaken love:** See note on 2:7.

8:5–7 The first half of 8:5 ("Who ... her beloved?") is probably spoken by the daughters of Jerusalem; the second half of 8:5 ("Under ... in travail."), along with 8:6–7, are spoken by the bride. Some of the most profound expressions of love are vocalized in these few verses.

8:5 Who is that: Harkens back to the royal wedding procession in 3:6–11. **your mother:** The bridegroom's. **was in travail:** Or, "conceived" (as in Ps 7:14).

8:6 seal: A signet ring or carved cylinder bearing the marks of one's personal identity, almost like a signature stamp, except that it was pressed into clay or wax (Gen 38:18; Jer 22:24). • Christ is a seal on the heart that we may always love him and a sign on the arm that we may always do his work (St. Ambrose, *On Isaac* 8, 75) (CCC 1295). **love is strong as death:** The climactic statement of the Song. Though death has a relentless appetite for human life (Ps 89:48), love is more persistent still, for it bears every burden and overcomes obstacles in pursuit of the beloved (1 Cor 13:7). • Christian faith teaches that love outlasts all other things in this world; it "never ends" (1 Cor 13:8) because "God is love, and he who loves abides in God, and God abides in him" (1 Jn 4:16). Neither death nor any other force in the cosmos can separate us from the love of God in Christ (Rom 8:38–39) (CCC 1040, 1611). • Love is strong as death either because no one can conquer it, as no one conquers death, or because the full measure of love is shown in death, for the Lord said there is no greater love than to lay down one's life for his friends (St. Augustine, *Letters* 167, 11). **jealousy:** I.e., ardent desire. **cruel:** Or "hard" in the sense of "enduring". **the grave:** Literally, "Sheol", the realm of the dead. **a most vehement flame:** Can also be translated "flames of Yah(weh)", hinting that love has its origin and intensity from the Lord, who is himself a "devouring fire" of jealous love for his people (Deut 4:24)

ʷGk Syr: Heb *mother; she* (or *you*) *will teach me.*

Word Study

Desire (7:10)

Teshuqah (Heb.): A strong attraction toward someone or something, i.e., a "longing" or "craving". The word appears three times in the OT, twice in Genesis and once in the Song of Solomon. **(1)** In Gen 3:16, amid the penitential curses pronounced upon the disobedience of Adam and Eve, God tells the woman that her "desire" will be for her husband, even though he will want to dominate her. Emotionally and otherwise, she will attach herself to a spouse who may or may not reciprocate her affection. **(2)** In Gen 4:7, God warns Cain that sin is like a predator whose "desire" is to devour fallen man. Unless this interior impulse is mastered, he will be a victim rather than a victor in the struggle against temptation. **(3)** In Song 7:10, the bride rejoices that the bridegroom's "desire" is for her alone. According to some, this signals a healing of the spousal relationship depicted in Gen 3:16. It hints that where true conjugal love is found, a mutuality of love and respect between husband and wife can be restored. The bridegroom of the Song is not domineering and controlling over his bride; rather, his "desire" is to possess her and to return her tender affections in kind.

for love is strong as death,
>jealousy is cruel as the grave.
>
>Its flashes are flashes of fire,
>a most vehement flame.

[7]Many waters cannot quench love,
>neither can floods drown it.
>
>If a man offered for love
>all the wealth of his house,
>it would be utterly scorned.

[8]We have a little sister,
>and she has no breasts.
>
>What shall we do for our sister,
>on the day when she is spoken for?

[9]If she is a wall,
>we will build upon her a battlement of silver;
>
>but if she is a door,
>we will enclose her with boards of cedar.

[10]I was a wall,
>and my breasts were like towers;

then I was in his eyes
>as one who brings[*] peace.

[11]Solomon had a vineyard at Ba'al-ha'mon;
>he let out the vineyard to keepers;
>
>each one was to bring for its fruit a thousand
>pieces of silver.

[12]My vineyard, my very own, is for myself;
>you, O Solomon, may have the thousand,
>and the keepers of the fruit two hundred.

[13]O you who dwell in the gardens,
>my companions are listening for your voice;
>let me hear it.

[14]Make haste, my beloved,
>and be like a gazelle
>
>or a young stag
>upon the mountains of spices.

(CCC 218-21). **Many waters:** Often considered a reference to the primeval waters of chaos that engulfed the earth in the beginning and that God alone has the power to control (Gen 1:9-10; Ps 104:5-7).

8:7 all the wealth: Love has a value that exceeds any price paid in created goods.

8:8-10 The voice of the bride. She quotes the words of her brothers in 8:8-9 ("We ... boards of cedar.") and disputes their claim that she is too young for marriage in 8:10 ("I ... brings peace."). The brothers, mentioned earlier in 1:6, decided that her virginal innocence must be carefully guarded.

8:8 when she is spoken for: I.e., when a man asks for her hand in marriage.

8:10 I was a wall: The young woman claims to have guarded her chastity responsibly, quite apart from her brother's efforts. **like towers:** She now has the physical maturity for marriage. **one who brings peace:** A possible allusion to the epithet "Shulammite". See note on 6:13.

8:11-12 Commentators are divided over whether the voice of the bridegroom or the voice of the bride is heard in these verses.

8:11 vineyard: One of Solomon's royal garden estates, which he either planted (Eccles 2:4) or inherited from his father David (1 Chron 27:27). Some think the vineyard represents Solomon's harem of one thousand women (1 Kings 11:3); hence, its produce is worth one **thousand** silver coins. **Baal-hamon:** Means "master of a multitude", but its location is unknown. Perhaps it is the "Balamon" near Dothan (Jud 8:3). **keepers:** Tenant farmers.

8:12 My vineyard: Refers to the bride herself (1:6). The statement seems to contrast the bride and bridegroom's monogamous love with Solomon's polygamous excess. Likewise, the couple's relationship is more precious than anything the king's fabulous wealth could ever buy (8:7).

8:13 The voice of the bridegroom, who desires to hear the **voice** of the bride (as in 2:14).

8:14 The voice of the bride, echoing the words of 2:17. See note on 2:9.

---

[*]Or *finds*.

Study Questions
The Song of Solomon

Chapter 1

For understanding
1. **1:1.** What does the expression "song of songs" mean? What does Scripture relate about Solomon?
2. **1:2–7.** Who is speaking in these verses? Are the lovers married or betrothed? For what is the metaphor of the Shepherd King used in the OT? in the NT?
3. **1:2.** What theme does the bride's desire for a kiss introduce? According to St. Gregory of Nyssa, for what does the soul long? According to St. Bernard of Clairvaux, what do the mouth that kisses and the kiss itself stand for? How highly is the king's affection treasured?
4. **1:5.** Why is the speaker's skin dark? What does her sunbaked complexion reveal about her social status? According to St. Ambrose, what does "I am dark but lovely" mean? Who are the daughters of Jerusalem? What alternative meanings are provided for the phrase "curtains of Solomon"?

For application
1. **1:2.** What does the name of Jesus mean to you? What ideas come to mind as you meditate on it?
2. **1:5.** How confident are you that God loves you regardless of your sinfulness? How willing are you to believe that, despite sinfulness, you are beautiful to him?
3. **1:11.** Just as the bridegroom provides jewelry to enhance the bride's natural beauty, so God provides grace to beautify the soul. What opportunities for grace is he providing for you today?
4. **1:15–16.** Read the notes for these verses, where the bridegroom and the bride admire each other's beauty. How do you respond when someone compliments you for your appearance? Do you compliment others for theirs? Do you ever express admiration for the beauty of God? What effect would such an expression have on your affection for him?

Chapter 2

For understanding
1. **2:3.** What does the apple tree symbolize? What does the beloved's shadow represent? According to St. Thomas of Villanova, what does Christ represent for us?
2. **2:6.** For what does the bride yearn by referring to the beloved's left and right hands? According to St. Cyril of Alexandria, what does each hand represent?
3. **2:7.** To what do the words "I adjure you" refer? What does the reference to gazelles or deer in this verse sound like in Hebrew? What two things might the caution against awakening love mean?
4. **2:16.** To what might this verse's language of mutual belonging refer? To what is the expression similar elsewhere in Scripture?

For application
1. **2:3.** The note for this verse describes the image of the Bridegroom's shadow as a place of protection or security. Describe what that security means to you—for example, whether prayer gives you a sense of security and delight, and, if so, in what way. Where do you like to go for your personal prayer?
2. **2:5–6.** What was your first experience of falling in love like? Have you wished to have that feeling in relation to God? If lovesickness is not part of your spiritual experience or expectation, what shape does love for God take for you? What might God's "embrace" mean for you?
3. **2:7.** Assuming that there are appropriate times for physical expressions of marital love, is the same ever true of one's love for God? How "moderate" should one's love of God be? If love should not be forced, what might help to awaken if freely?
4. **2:15.** What are some of the "little foxes" that pester your own religious life? What have you done to deal with them?

Chapter 3

For understanding
1. **3:1–5.** What is the bride doing in these verses? What are her words often thought to describe?
2. **3:1.** What does the maiden's reference to "him whom my soul loves" indicate? What does St. Bernard of Clairvaux attribute to the soul? What does it indicate about the Bridegroom and the type of love involved?
3. **3:6.** What do the words "coming up" and "column of smoke" suggest? How does St. Ambrose interpret the ascent, the smoke, and the aroma of incense?
4. **3:7.** What does the litter look like? What is the royal carriage called? Who are the "sixty mighty men"? How does Solomon's personal protection force compare with David's?

For application
1. **3:1.** What are some of the difficulties you have in prayer, such as dryness or distraction? What does "seeking" God mean to you? How do you go about it?
2. **3:2.** How difficult is it for you to profess love for God? How determined are you to continue seeking intimacy with God even if it seems that he does not answer?

3. **3:4.** Recall a conversion experience or a moment when you felt that God was especially near. How strong was the desire to "hang on" to the experience? How long did it last? How ready were you for the moment when the experience faded or ended?

4. **3:9–10.** These verses describe a richly ornamented litter used to carry the king, emblematic of an elaborately decorated monstrance used in eucharistic adoration. Do you find that such a vessel attracts your gaze to the Host in the center, or is it a distraction? How often do you take part in eucharistic adoration at Benediction, 40 Hours Devotion, or in a chapel? What is your prayer like at such times?

Chapter 4

For understanding
1. **4:1–15.** Who is speaking in these verses? What is he doing? How does St. Gregory the Great interpret these references to body parts?
2. **4:8.** Although the beloved refers to the maiden as his bride, how else might his reference to her bridal status possibly be understood? What are Amana and Senir, and what do they represent? What does the reference to lions and leopards mean?
3. **Word Study: My Sister.** For what is the Hebrew noun *ahoti* typically used? What do the prophets occasionally use the language of "sisters" to describe? Though referring to the bride as the bridegroom's sister is unusual, what do comparative studies show it to be? Beyond that, what does the designation "sister" reflect?
4. **4:12.** What does the metaphor of the bride as a garden depict? What does much of the imagery of the Song call to mind, particularly about married love? What does the figure of her as a *locked* and *sealed* garden represent? How does St. Cyprian apply this imagery to the Church? How does St. Peter Chrysologus apply it to Mary?

For application
1. **4:1–15.** Read the note for these verses. What does such erotic language suggest that God is trying to accomplish in us? How do you respond to such language?
2. **4:8.** God's mercy often leads us away from environments that are sinful, full of temptations, or merely spiritually counterproductive. Has he ever done that for you? How can you recognize situations, circumstances, or relationships that do you no spiritual good? What can you do to come away from them?
3. **4:9.** Read the word study on the word "sister" in this verse. How might it be beneficial to a marital relationship for the spouses to regard each other as brother and sister? Why might God use such a term of you, or you of him? (Compare your answer with Mt 12:48–50.)
4. **4:12.** The image of an enclosed (or locked) garden is often treated by spiritual writers as representing a chaste soul open only to God. What does the image suggest about yourself—about your spiritual chastity and your availability to the Holy Spirit?

Chapter 5

For understanding
1. **5:2–8.** What is the bride doing in these verses? How do many interpret the account that opens with the maiden sleeping? What does the scenario resemble?
2. **5:2.** What does the allusion to this passage in Rev 3:20 say about Christ? How does St. Bede apply this passage to the Church? Why is the bridegroom's head wet with dew?
3. **5:10–16.** How does the bride describe the bridegroom? What do her words evoke?
4. **5:10.** How is David, the father of Solomon, described in 1 Samuel? According to St. Bede, why is the beloved Bridegroom radiant?

For application
1. **5:2–3.** In your own spiritual life, have you ever missed spiritual opportunities when they were presented to you? Have you ever made excuses for not responding to the invitation of God to come deeper? If so, what were they?
2. **5:6.** Have you ever realized that you missed an opportunity to draw closer to God? What did you do when you realized it?
3. **5:9.** Have friends or family members questioned your devotion or your faith? What were some of their questions?
4. **5:10–16.** Following on the previous question, what answers did you give to those who questioned or took issue with your devotion or your faith? If you avoided giving an answer, what motivated you to do so?

Chapter 6

For understanding
1. **6:4.** What is Tirzah? What did King Omri have to do with it? What does the word "terrible" mean in this context?
2. **Topical Essay: The Song of Solomon and the Spiritual Life.** What reason, by and large, is given for the staggering number of books written about the Song of Solomon, and what two factors play into it? How does one Jewish tradition connect Proverbs, Ecclesiastes, and the Song of Solomon to the three stages of Solomon's life? How does the different approach taken by Christian tradition explain the order of these three books? What level of spiritual maturity is needed to read these three books profitably?
3. **6:9.** How do the descriptions of the bride in this verse apply to the holy Virgin, according to St. Francis de Sales? To whom does the Hebrew word for "maidens" appear to refer?
4. **6:13.** How do the prophets use the language of "return"? What various interpretations of the term "Shulammite" have been offered? What does the Hebrew word *mahanaim* mean? What is the meaning of the bride's question?

For application
1. **6:3.** Whether you are a professed religious or not, can you honestly take the bride's statement as your own? If so, what does it mean to you? If not, what prevents you?
2. **6:9–10.** These verses are often applied to the Blessed Virgin Mary, who is uniquely flawless among human beings. What is your relationship with Mary? What (if any) Marian devotional practices do you have?
3. **6:10.** Do you have access to any sort of spiritual direction? If so, how fruitful has it been? If not, what prevents you from finding a spiritual director or spiritual mentor?

Chapter 7

For understanding
1. **7:1–9.** Who is speaking in these verses? In which direction is his gaze moving?
2. **7:5.** What and where is Carmel? What does the color purple denote? Who is the only personality given a royal title in the Song?
3. **Word Study: Desire.** What does the Hebrew word *teshuqah* mean? How often does it appear in the OT? How is the word used in Gen 3:16 of Eve? About what does God warn Cain in Gen 4:7? About what does the Bride rejoice in the Song of Solomon, and how is that different from the references to desire in Genesis?
4. **7:13.** What are mandrakes thought to symbolize? What is the likely meaning of the reference to fruits?

For application
1. **7:1–5.** Contemplation is described as a "mental gaze", a way of simply looking at and appreciating something or someone without analytical thought. Describe a time when you contemplated someone by letting your gaze roam over interesting features. How hard would it be to put into words your response to the object of your gaze? How does one contemplate God?
2. **7:10.** What is your response to the realization that someone you love loves you? What effect does that realization have on your love for that person? How do you respond when reminded that God loves you?
3. **7:11–12.** What kinds of enjoyment do you get from going on outings with your spouse or a close friend? How do such outings enhance relationships?

Chapter 8

For understanding
1. **8:1.** Why does the bride wish the bridegroom were like a brother? How does St. Athanasius apply her wish to Jesus Christ?
2. **8:2.** Where does the bride want to consummate her love for the bridegroom? According to St. Germanus of Constantinople, where does the Mother of God reverently receive her immortal Bridegroom?
3. **8:6.** What is the seal mentioned here? How is Christ a seal? Though death has a relentless appetite for human life, in what way is love more persistent? In what ways, according to St. Augustine, is love as strong as death? How else can the expression "most vehement flame" be translated, and at what does it hint? What are the "many waters" often considered to mean?
4. **8:8–10.** Who is speaking in these verses? What is the bride disputing with reference to her brothers' decision regarding her?

For application
1. **8:1.** How hesitant are you to display elements of your faith in public; for example, by making the sign of the cross in a restaurant or reading a Bible on a bus? What embarrasses you about your faith or causes you to want to hide or disguise it?
2. **8:3.** What kinds of spiritual experiences have you dreamed of enjoying? What are the realities of spiritual life for you? Why do you think certain mystics like John of the Cross (who did enjoy such things as ecstasies) would teach that such experiences are not important? On the other hand, what should you do if God grants them? (Compare your answer with CCC 800.)
3. **8:6.** Read the note for this verse. If the practice of the Christian faith were curtailed or outlawed, how far would you be willing to go to continue in it? For what would you be willing to die?
4. **8:7–10.** We live in an era when physical virginity and sexual chastity are utterly scorned. What are some *religious* reasons why virginity is so highly prized in the Catholic Church? If physical virginity is lost through sexual sin, what can repair the loss?

BOOKS OF THE BIBLE

THE OLD TESTAMENT (OT)

Gen	Genesis
Ex	Exodus
Lev	Leviticus
Num	Numbers
Deut	Deuteronomy
Josh	Joshua
Judg	Judges
Ruth	Ruth
1 Sam	1 Samuel
2 Sam	2 Samuel
1 Kings	1 Kings
2 Kings	2 Kings
1 Chron	1 Chronicles
2 Chron	2 Chronicles
Ezra	Ezra
Neh	Nehemiah
Tob	Tobit
Jud	Judith
Esther	Esther
Job	Job
Ps	Psalms
Prov	Proverbs
Eccles	Ecclesiastes
Song	Song of Solomon
Wis	Wisdom
Sir	Sirach (Ecclesiasticus)
Is	Isaiah
Jer	Jeremiah
Lam	Lamentations
Bar	Baruch
Ezek	Ezekiel
Dan	Daniel
Hos	Hosea
Joel	Joel
Amos	Amos
Obad	Obadiah
Jon	Jonah
Mic	Micah
Nahum	Nahum
Hab	Habakkuk
Zeph	Zephaniah
Hag	Haggai
Zech	Zechariah
Mal	Malachi
1 Mac	1 Maccabees
2 Mac	2 Maccabees

THE NEW TESTAMENT (NT)

Mt	Matthew
Mk	Mark
Lk	Luke
Jn	John
Acts	Acts of the Apostles
Rom	Romans
1 Cor	1 Corinthians
2 Cor	2 Corinthians
Gal	Galatians
Eph	Ephesians
Phil	Philippians
Col	Colossians
1 Thess	1 Thessalonians
2 Thess	2 Thessalonians
1 Tim	1 Timothy
2 Tim	2 Timothy
Tit	Titus
Philem	Philemon
Heb	Hebrews
Jas	James
1 Pet	1 Peter
2 Pet	2 Peter
1 Jn	1 John
2 Jn	2 John
3 Jn	3 John
Jude	Jude
Rev	Revelation (Apocalypse)